J. MAYER H.

J. MAYER H.

EDITED BY HENRY URBACH AND CRISTINA STEINGRÄBER

ESSAYS BY STEPHEN HARTMAN, JOHN PAUL RICCO, ILKA & ANDREAS RUBY, FELICITY D. SCOTT, HENRY URBACH, AND PHILIP URSPRUNG

SELECTED PROJECT TEXTS BY ANDRES LEPIK

INTERVIEW BY ROLF FEHLBAUM IN CONVERSATION WITH JÜRGEN MAYER H.

HATJE CANTZ

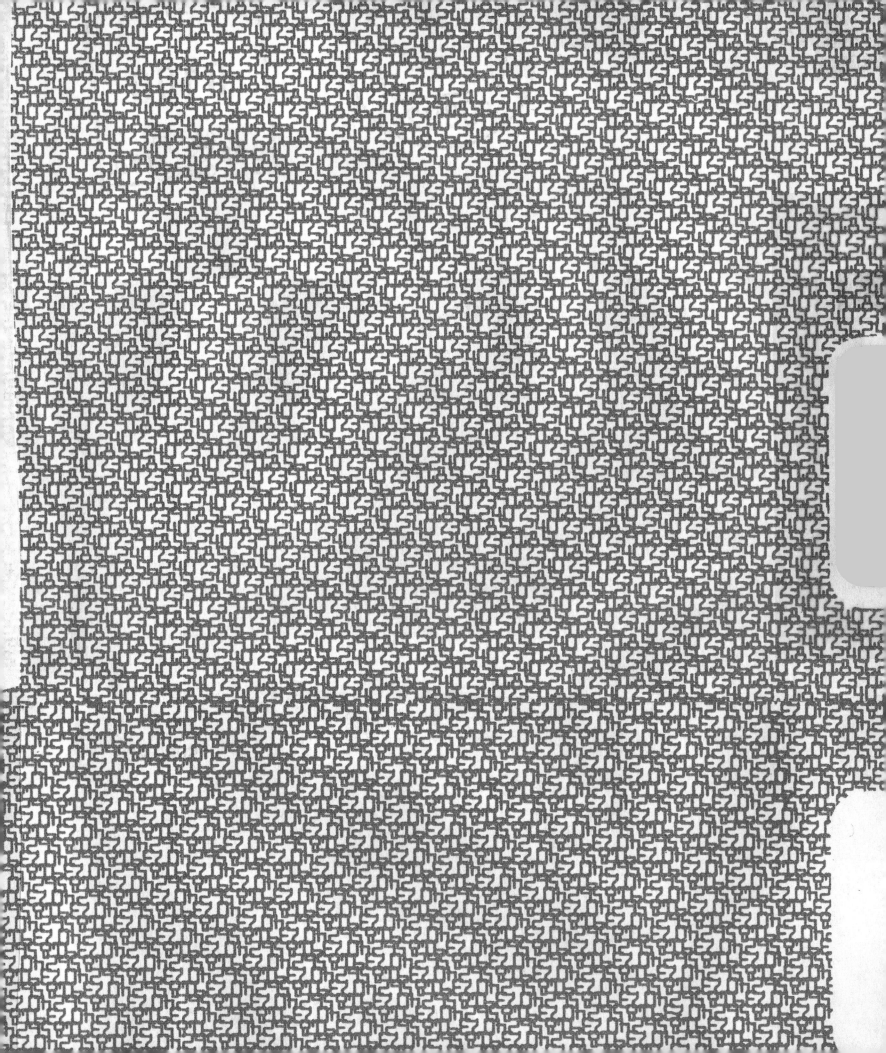

Bitte haben Sie Verständnis dafür, daß wir we
gen der elektronischen Datenverarbeitung nich
immer verhindern können, daß Sie mehrer
Briefsendungen an einem Tag von uns erhalter
Das Zusammensortieren aller Sendungen fü
denselben Empfänger wäre aus Zeit- und Ko
stengründen nicht zu vertreten.

Dieser Umschlag wurde aus chlorfreiem Papier hergestellt

J. MAYER H., ETC.

HENRY URBACH

More than a year after moving from New York to San Francisco, I still found myself unsure about the signage at the Bay Bridge toll. "VALID ETC." the light blinked, as the exact toll was deducted from my Fast Track device. For my whole life I'd understood "etc." as the abbreviation for etcetera, so it took some time to realize it was an acronym here, not an abbreviation—even despite the final period—and that it belonged, as an acronym, to an exploding subset of the English language. DIY, LOL, PDA, ETA, KIT (my acquaintance quipped: "Obviously you don't have kids!"), SPF, STMP, TTYL: every day new acronyms are coined as people race to express things more efficiently, more generically through SMS messaging, email, and rapid-fire speech. An acronym, then, ETC., but for what exactly? Eventually, in order to relax and enjoy the scenery while crossing the Bay, I made my decision: "Exact Toll Collected," a fitting finale to the sequence of passing through the gate, being scanned, and then authorized to proceed.

In Tokyo for the first time, however, it didn't take more than a day to rediscover my doubt. The double-decker expressway offered a lane marked with a sign, otherwise incomprehensible, that flashed ETC. Electronic toll collection, I decided, designating the type of lane rather than what happens at the toll gate. And still I don't know, I'm only guessing, and probably going too far as I speculate that Japan and the West Coast share some sort of dialogue about this that the East Coast doesn't yet participate in, with its more forthright toll booths that say "Paid $6.00" or whatever as you zoom past. I don't know, and probably won't ever know for sure.

⁂ ⁂ ⁂

It was in the early nineties that Jürgen Mayer added an H. to his name and, with that, launched his professional practice. His first, foundational act was to create a kind of a mask, a persona that would become the Jürgen Mayer H., then the J. MAYER H. whose work you see elaborated in the pages of this volume. I remember when he told me that Mayer was too common a name in Germany, like Smith in the US, and that there was a famous artist with whom he didn't want to be confused. Already Jürgen knew that fame lay ahead and his response, as it would be with so many subsequent projects, was to produce a coded interface, asserting and veiling his own presence and that of his built work. Jürgen Mayer went to work for Jürgen Mayer H., who in turn went to work for J. MAYER H. Change your name before someone says, "Hey, you! I know you!" Then J. MAYER H. went to work: coding and recoding the surfaces of everyday life; indicating and providing a meaningful reflection on the indeterminacy of cultural forms, the slippage one encounters between the "ETC" of here and there, of us and them; and demonstrating the ways in which architecture can either mask or embrace this indeterminacy, or maybe try to do both at the same time by hiding buildings in plain sight.

⁂ ⁂ ⁂

Alphabet soup was introduced by Campbell's in the first few years of the twentieth century. It offered the possibility of creating, then ingesting words by combining letters in a fluid medium. Concurrently, "alphabet soup" became a term, now obscure, that signified linguistic abuse, the articulation of random, free-floating concepts instead of sound, deductive reasoning; an excess of creative license. Curiously enough, around the same time, "alphabet soup" also came to describe a way of relying on acronyms instead of elaborating things more fully. It was not long afterward, especially in the US, that acronyms took hold as, for example, the CIA, FBI, and WPA gained increasing prominence under FDR's New Deal administration. All the while, children were learning to finish their soup by eating their words, their interpellation into language and society reinforced by the fun of moving letters around and then gobbling them up.

❋ ❋ ❋

We are thrust into the world as into language and socio-spatial norms, and the creativity afforded us involves the appropriation and manipulation of these givens.

❋ ❋ ❋

From the start J. MAYER H. was concerned with readymade patterns found in the world as a source of conceptual, and then formal, inspiration. Data-protection patterns evolved from technical processes of printing, capturing errors of doubled and blurred type to become systematic forms of anti-information. Outcasts become guardians. A textual counterpart to other forms of camouflage, data-protection patterns serve to make something invisible through an oversaturation of surface. Masquerading as pattern or ornament, they serve a tactical role, strengthening portions of semitransparent surfaces like a coat of armor, to ensure that language reaches its proper destination.

As J. MAYER H. appropriated these patterns and began to explore their logic, the studio hit upon an important aspect of the architectural envelope and found its way toward a critical architecture. Words, and the access they yield, are offered, but unequally: to you, but not to you—and never to you. It may be a matter of communication and comprehension; it may be a matter of power and class. Either way, in the work of J. MAYER H., architectural surfaces register inequities of access, and the failed promise of transparency and the Modernist striving after an even, universal distribution of space. With patterns, then with thermosensitive surfaces, and finally with an expanded panoply of formal maneuvers—including buildings that evoke the forms of hills and clouds—the work of J. MAYER H. would evolve according to principles of coded, rather than given, meaning, reproducing the architectural envelope as a site of masquerade.

Again and again, the surfaces of J. MAYER H. assume an agonistic role. As they articulate a vision of the social order through built form, they register an order of difference—differences playing off one another—and the possibility of establishing a significant intervention by registering this dissonance. Though built and, in this sense, final, they aim towards a kind of incompletion, a tentative assertion of presence that offers the possibility of making, unmaking, and remaking itself in a different way.

❋ ❋ ❋

Around the same time that alphabet soup came into the world, under a different set of social and technical pressures, military camouflage was invented. Studying the surfaces of animals, military minds imagined covering bodies in strong, arbitrary patterns of color that would conceal the wearer by appearing to distort the body's contours. By 1914 the French army deployed *zébrage* across soldiers' bodies to confuse or dazzle snipers. Soon ships would be covered in what became known as "dazzle camouflage": erratic patterns painted on the surfaces of vessels, which, through visual excess, would confuse the submarine gunner.

❋ ❋ ❋

Jürgen Mayer H. is fascinated by the translation of *Vorwand* into English as Pretext. Before, perhaps against, the wall, stands something that both lies (as in a false pretext) and precedes (or comes before). The trajectory of his studio's work to date may be seen as an effort to create the condition of *Vorwand* through building. And why? It is, to no small degree, a political gesture, a recognition of and reaction to the long-standing participation (to say the least) of architecture in establishing the dominance of the ruling order; an effort to make architecture—influential architecture, architecture that is not marginalized—which posits an other order, or at least holds open the possibility of other orders.

And this is done with patterns. Patterns as codes. Patterns as acronyms. Patterns as camouflage. Patterns as pretext. Patterns that pretend to be ornament, only to become structure. The patterns of J. MAYER H. refuse, however solid they may appear, to be fully *there;* instead, they stand up to perform their part. They offer a provisional gathering, an appearance, fully theatrical, ready at any moment to transform into something else, something other.

❋ ❋ ❋

I eat my alphabet soup and I make this word, shift the vegetables and noodle letters around a bit and make another. If only architecture were so responsive! The pleasure of making "cat," then "can," then "candy," then "dandy," then "rat a tat tat." With language it is so easy—cheap, really. You say something, make it go away, then you say something else, or something else again. It depends who you are talking to. And who you are in that moment, which includes the situation and what you are trying to achieve.

❊ ❊ ❊

This is my point: there is a productive hesitation in the work of J. MAYER H., a hesitation born from a kind of politics, and perhaps a biography but, in any case, a trajectory pursued with conviction. An architecture of hesitation, which is by no means a critique of its accomplishment on so many levels. On the contrary. I know no one practicing today who so sensitively perceives the double bind of asserting presence in an architecture that aspires to critical engagement. Me? I work on this through para-architectural practices: writing and making exhibitions, mostly. Words and temporary constructions. J. MAYER H. takes it on at the field's core, making buildings that, on some level—do you agree with me?—seek to undo themselves. They want to appear, they want to recede, they want to try something else on for size, for color, for show. They want to be there, but maybe not entirely and certainly not forever. Inspired by patterns, animated by codes, the architecture of J. MAYER H. holds open the possibility of other elaborations, putting into the world an architecture fully committed to the manifold possibilities of etc., ETC, and ETC.

Nur vom Empfänger zu öffnen

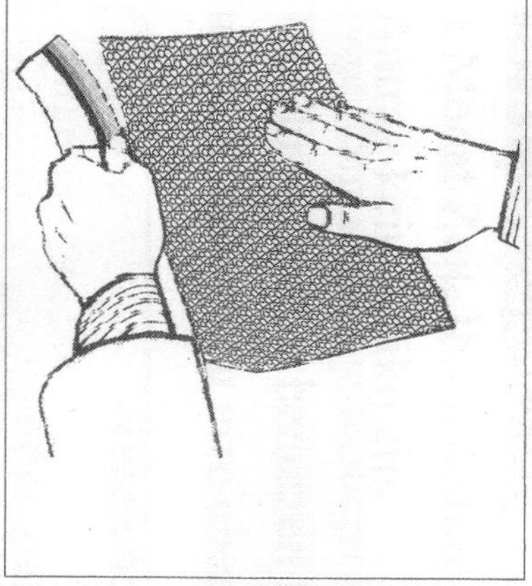

Bitte den gesamten oberen Teil am Perforations-Rand (unter dem schwarz-rot-goldenen Streifen) abtrennen!

MENSA MOLTKE

STUDENT CANTEEN, KARLSRUHE, GERMANY

CLIENT: VERMOEGEN UND BAU, BADEN-WUERTTEMBERG, AMT KARLSRUHE

USER: STUDENTENWERK KARLSRUHE

INTERNATIONAL COMPETITION: 2004, 1ST PRIZE
PROJECT DATE: 2005–07

J. MAYER H.
PROJECT TEAM: JÜRGEN MAYER H., ANDRE SANTER, JULIA NEITZEL, SEBASTIAN FINCKH, WILKO HOFFMANN, MARCUS BLUM
COMPETITION TEAM: JÜRGEN MAYER H., DOMINIK SCHWARZER, WILKO HOFFMANN, INGMAR SCHMIDT, DARIA TROVATO, SEBASTIAN FINCKH
CONCEPT GUM.GRAM: JAN-CHRISTOPH STOCKEBRAND

ARCHITECT ON SITE: ULRICH WIESLER, STUTTGART
MULTIDISCIPLINARY ENGINEERS: ARUP GMBH, BERLIN
MULTIDISCIPLINARY ENGINEERS CONSTRUCTION MANAGER: H. M. JICHA, NEIDENSTEIN
KITCHEN ENGINEERS: MARTIN SCHERER, DARMSTADT
BUILDING PHYSICS: DR. SCHAECKE UND BAYER, WAIBLINGEN
LANDSCAPE ARCHITECTS: BAUER UND PARTNER, KARLSRUHE

PERMANENT COLLECTION OF THE MUSEUM OF MODERN ART, NEW YORK

The competition assignment was to build a joint canteen for the Technical College, the Teaching Academy, and the Academy of Fine Arts in Karlsruhe. These institutions were to acquire a common building that would provide an attractive environment in which to spend time beyond the usual lunchtime meal, while also serving as a place of communication between diverse disciplines. The design of the building as realized uses the largest possible construction surface: a skewed rectangle topped by a roof with identical dimensions. In the design process, ground plane and roof were pulled away from one another, figuratively speaking. Through this process, it is as if a viscous mass generated vectors of force joining these two levels. The structure realized on the basis of this concept thereby translates an image of movement and immobility, visualizing nonlinear fields of energy. Originally envisioned in reinforced concrete, timber was substituted when construction of the slanting supports in concrete proved too expensive. As an organic and replenishable material, wood also proved far more sustainable. Polyurethane coating provides the timber with long-term protection against the impact of weathering. The structure's dynamic character is emphasized by flowing transitions between supports and walls, and by the rounded windows which protrude from the plane of the wall.

The plan of the canteen is simply and clearly structured. Opening directly behind a two-story entry loggia, the large dining hall is also two stories in height toward the front. The interior reflects the concept of the three-dimensional façade skeleton, so that the homogeneous surface design generates a total impression that indivisibly unites exterior and interior. A cafeteria—which can remain open outside of canteen operating hours—expands the building's use potential. An exposed staircase within the space, aligned on its transverse axis, offers access to a gallery story with additional seating. Set into the sloping, green roof is a terrace on which students can dine in summer. The pale-green coloration of its surfaces emphasizes the canteen's character as a nontraditional, individually shaped building—demonstrating that even with limited public funds, it is possible to realize an incisive and conceptually sophisticated type of architecture.

—Andres Lepik

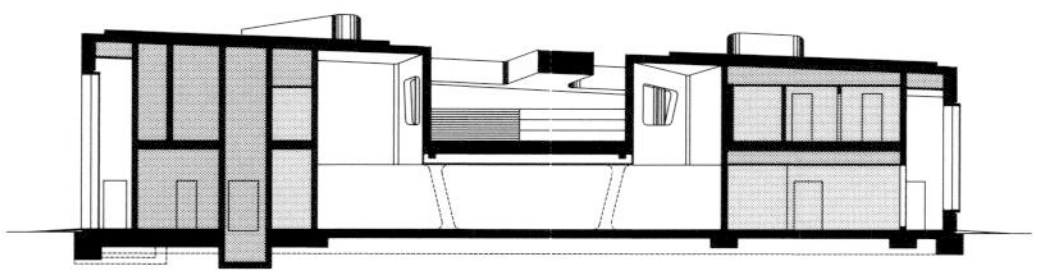

CROSS SECTION

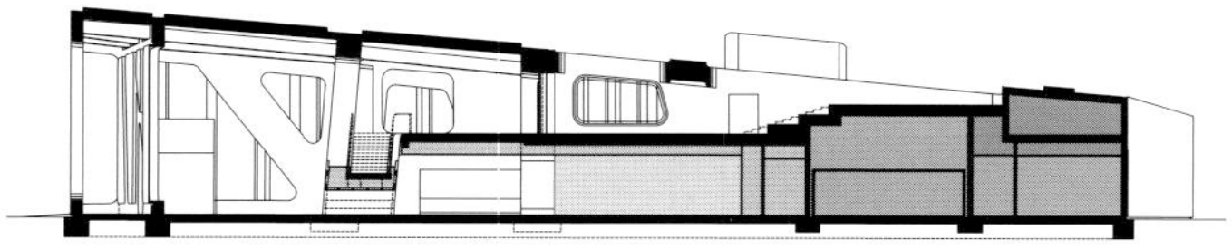

LONGITUDINAL SECTION

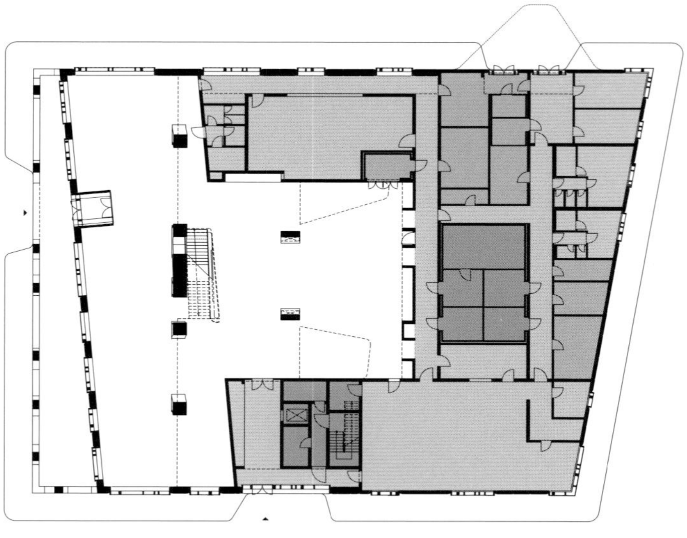

GROUND FLOOR

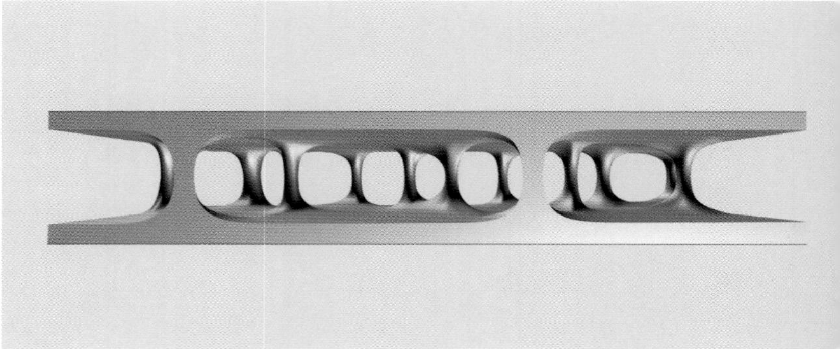

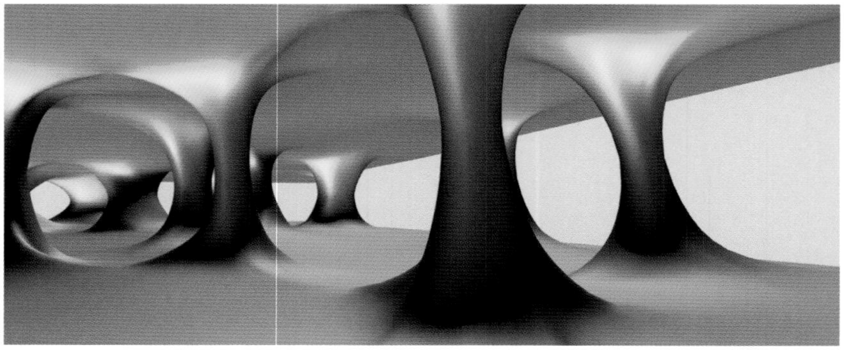

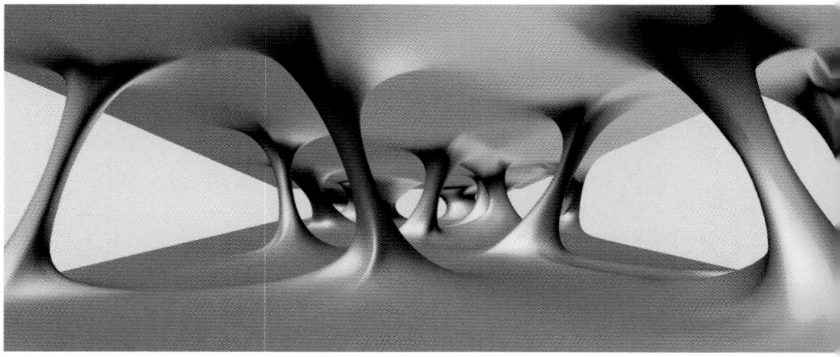

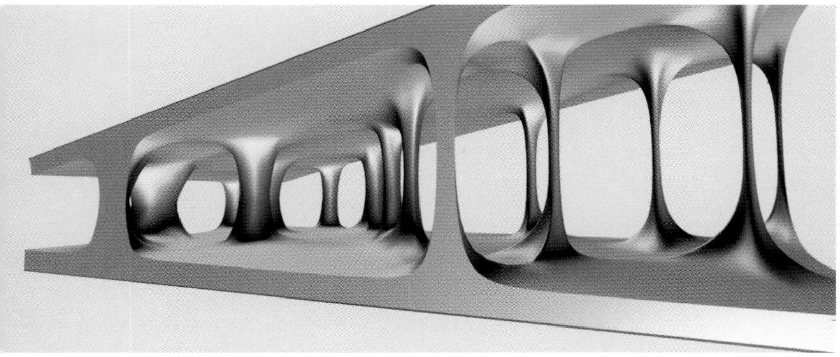
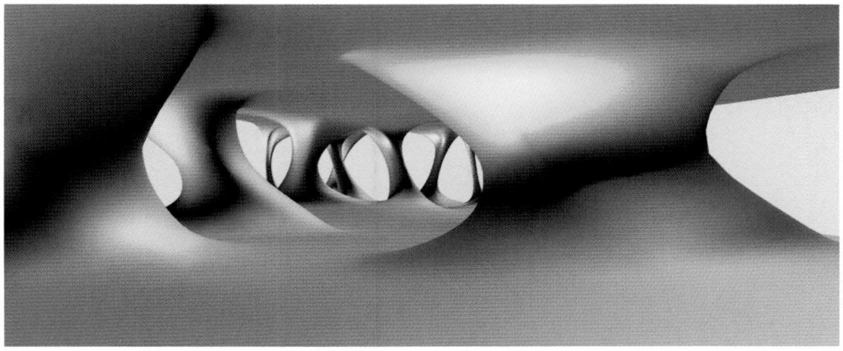
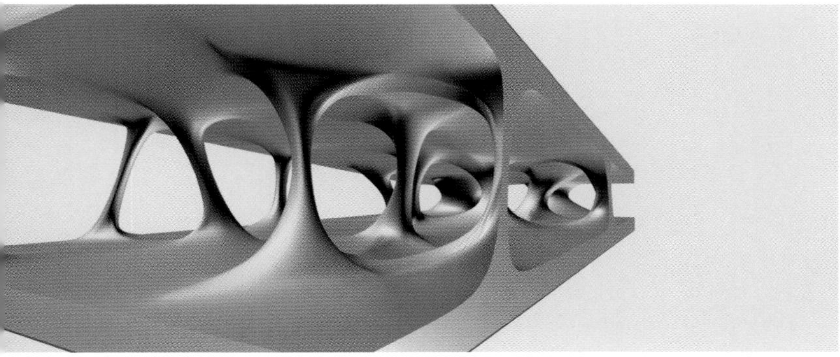
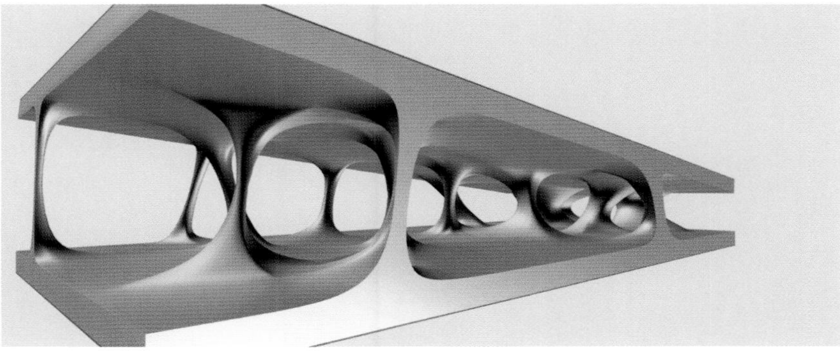

ADA1

OFFICE BUILDING, HAMBURG, GERMANY

CLIENT: COGITON PROJEKT ALSTER GMBH, HAMBURG

INVITED COMPETITION: 2005, 1ST PRIZE
PROJECT DATE: 2005–07

J. MAYER H.
PROJECT TEAM: JÜRGEN MAYER H., HANS SCHNEIDER, WILKO HOFFMANN, ANDRE SANTER, SEBASTIAN FINCKH, MARTA RAMÍREZ IGLESIAS, GEORG SCHMIDTHALS, MARCUS BLUM
COMPETITION TEAM: JÜRGEN MAYER H., JAN-CHRISTOPH STOCKEBRAND, MARCUS BLUM, KLAUS KÜPPERS, HANS SCHNEIDER

ARCHITECT ON SITE: IMHOTEP, DONACHIE UND BLOMEYER, BERLIN; ARCHITEKTURBÜRO FRANKE, HAMBURG
STRUCTURAL ENGINEERS: CBP, HAMBURG
BUILDING SERVICES: ENERGIEHAUS, HAMBURG; SINEPLAN, HAMBURG
LIGHTING ENGINEERS: ANDRES—LICHTPLANUNG, HAMBURG
LANDSCAPE ARCHITECTS: BREIMANN & BRUUN, HAMBURG
MODEL: WERK5, BERLIN

The AdA1 office building is sited in an interesting city-center location in Hamburg, directly on the boundary between dense inner-city development and a public park that lies along the Alster lake. Its conspicuous situation, between two main traffic axes and the northern tip of a block development, means that the building is highly visible from three sides. In order to achieve optimal utilization of the site, its predecessor—a building from the nineteen-sixties—was demolished. Given its position within the adjacent block configuration, the new building was subject to strict design criteria. Nevertheless, its double façade—necessary as a climate-control device and a noise buffer—was designed in such a way that it endows the building with a striking visual identity that is visible from afar. The elongated horizontal strip windows of the exterior façade—some of which continue around corners—are interrupted at irregular intervals by rounded termini. Set between these as additional accents are "eyes." This alternating between glazed strips and stucco panels set flush with them produces an impression of flowing movement that glides across surfaces and around the building—a metaphor for both the nearby river and the surrounding traffic streams.

The main entrance is set at the center of the principal façade, and emphasized by a two-story lobby. From here, access to the interior is provided by a staircase whose glass rear wall offers open views onto the landscaped zone within. The interior is laid out on a flexible grid structure that can be reconfigured by various users as needed. The rear ventilation of the double façade, and the use of the concrete core for storing both thermal energy and cold, renders an air-conditioning system unnecessary. In the interior, the "eyes" of the façade—which offer spectacular views of the Alster—can be used as particularly prominent conference rooms or executive offices. All these factors make the AdA1 a prime example of a new generation of office architecture which offers high flexibility and optimal working conditions within, while at the same time providing a strong external visual identity in the surrounding cityscape. —Andres Lepik

1ST FLOOR

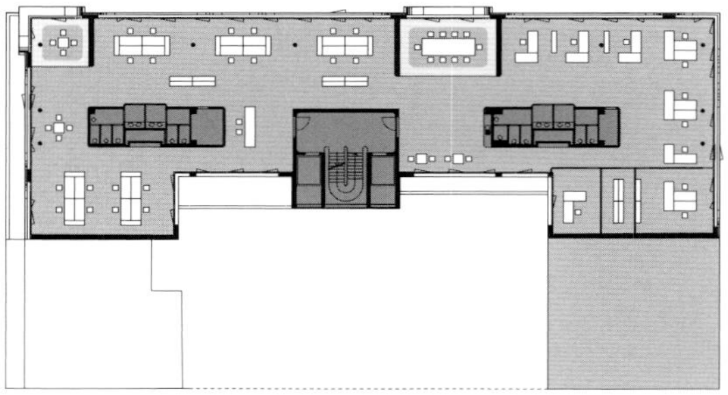

5TH FLOOR

GROUND FLOOR

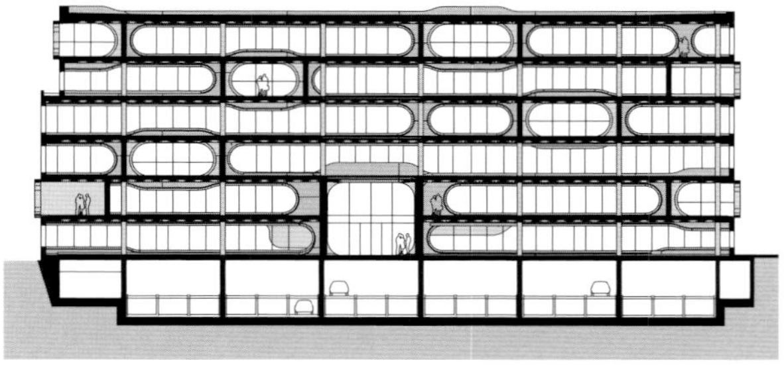

SECTION

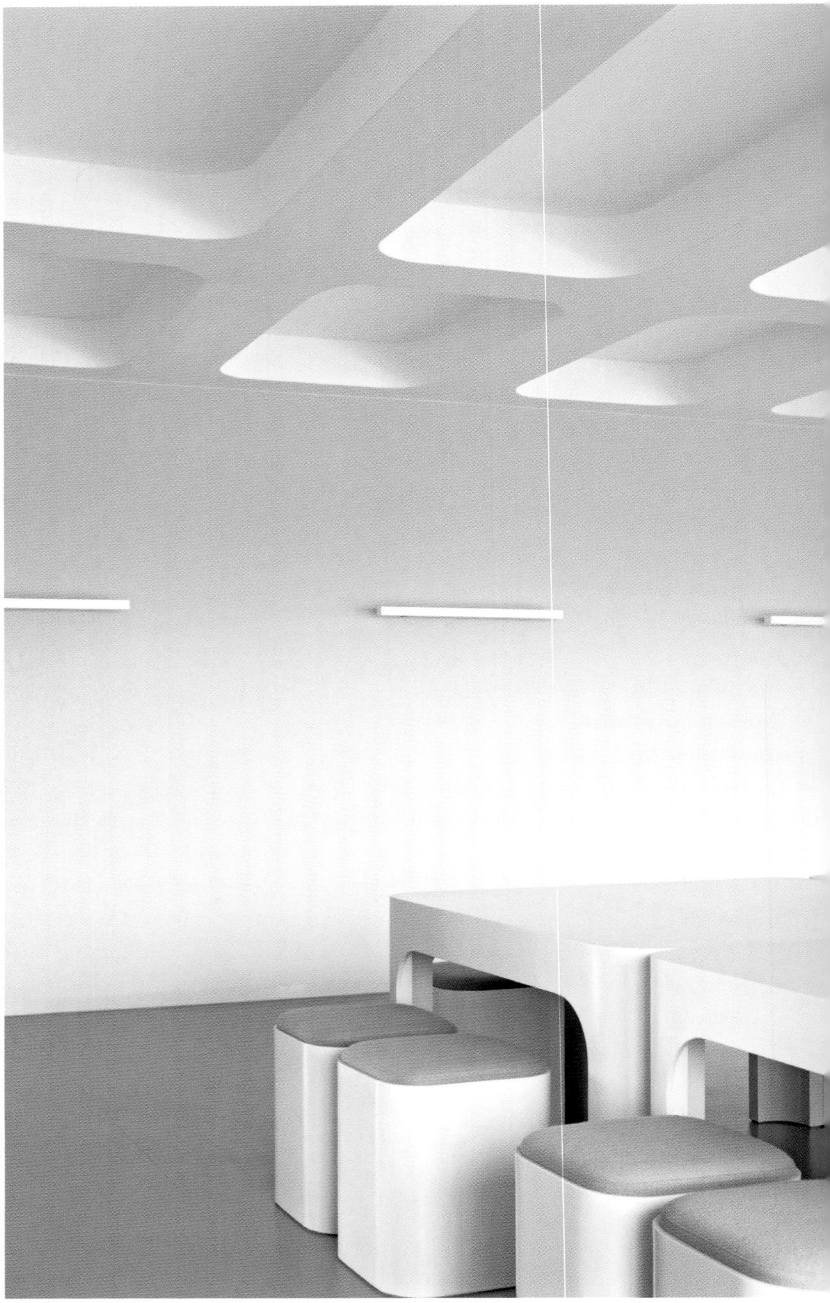

HASSELT COURT OF JUSTICE

CLIENT: STATIONSOMGEVING NV HASSELT, HASSELT, BELGIUM

INTERNATIONAL COMPETITION: 2005, 1ST PRIZE
PROJECT DATE: 2005–11

J. MAYER H.
A2O-ARCHITECTEN, HASSELT
LENS°ASS ARCHITECTEN, HASSELT
PROJECT TEAM: JÜRGEN MAYER H., GEORG SCHMIDTHALS, MARCUS BLUM, GÜVENC ÖZEL, JAN-CHRISTOPH STOCKEBRAND

COLLABORATION: A2O-ARCHITECTEN, HASSELT: LUC VANMUYSEN, JO BERBEN, TIM VEKEMANS, MANNFRED BENDITZ
LENS°ASS ARCHITECTEN, HASSELT: BART LENS, MASSIMO PIGNANELLI, PHILIPPE DIRIX, JAN ACHTEN

PHASE 1: REDEVELOPMENT OF THE RAILWAY-STATION AREA IN HASSELT BASED ON THE WEST 8 MASTERPLAN, INCLUDING TWO ICONIC BUILDINGS AND LOW-RISE BLOCKS FOR HOTELS, OFFICES, AND HOUSING

PHASE 2: HASSELT COURT OF JUSTICE

The Court of Justice is one of two iconic projects within the new urban development around the main rail station. The logistics and siting of a courthouse with multiple security barriers results in a massing composed of three interconnected volumes. References include the old industrial steel structures that formerly occupied and definined the site, their organic Belgian Art Nouveau forms constituting part of the cultural heritage of Hasselt. There are also echoes of a tree, which, in addition to being the Hasselt town emblem also harks back to the pre-medieval European tradition of holding a special "place of speaking justice" underneath a large tree in the center of a dwelling.

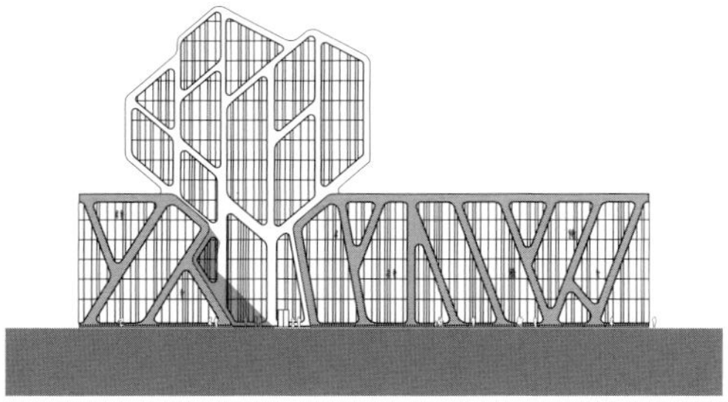

SOUTH-EAST

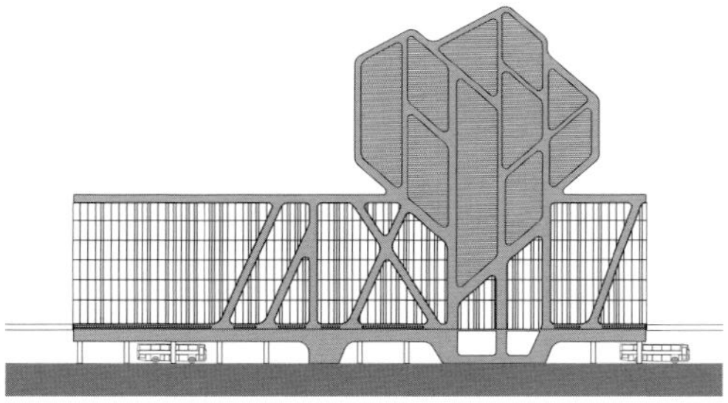

NORTH-WEST

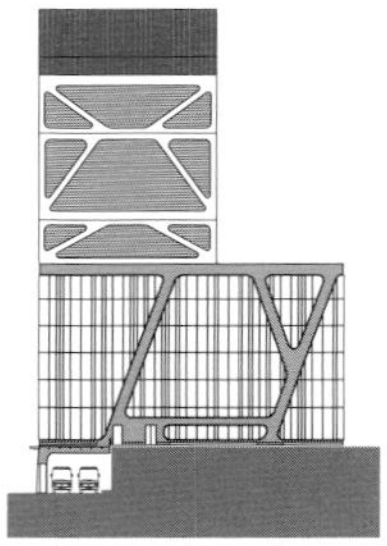

NORTH-EAST

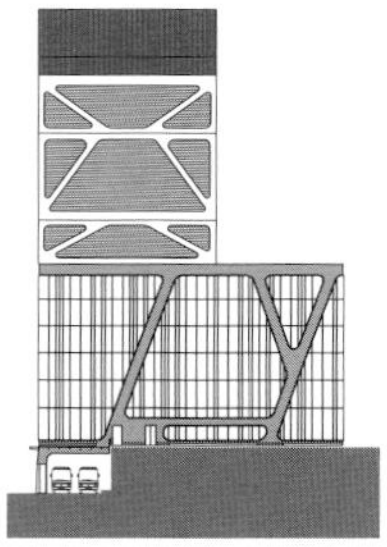

SOUTH-WEST

NOAH'S ARK

SPATIAL ANALYSIS OF STRATEGIC SYSTEMS
THE COOPER UNION, NEW YORK, US

PROJECT DATE: 1990

J. MAYER H.

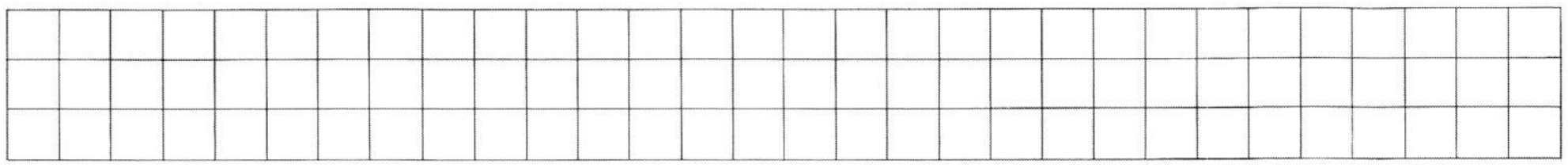

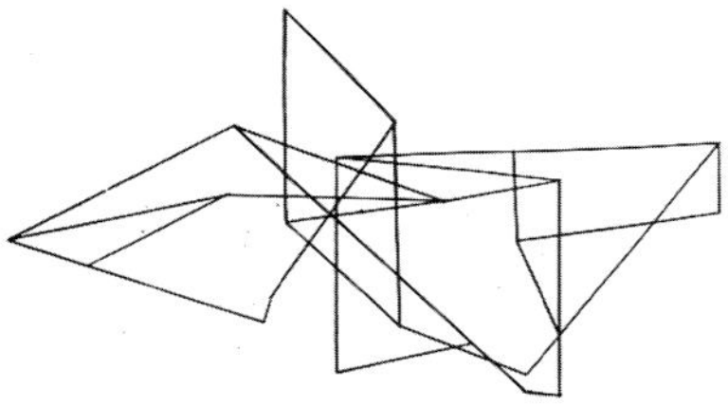

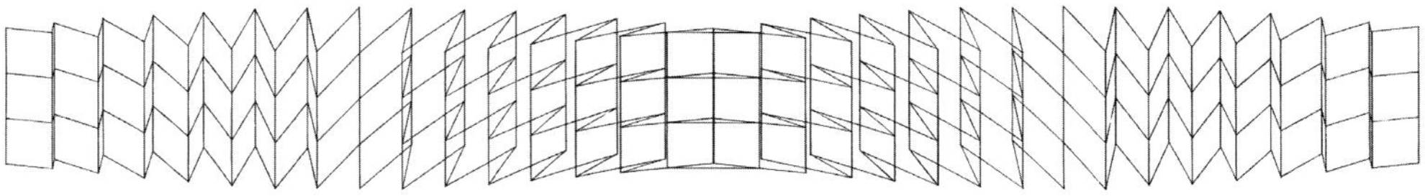

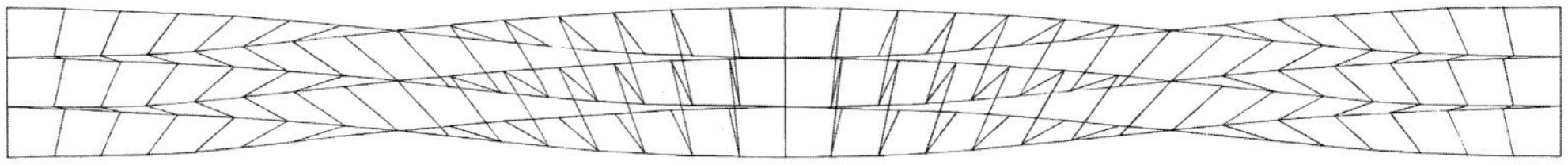

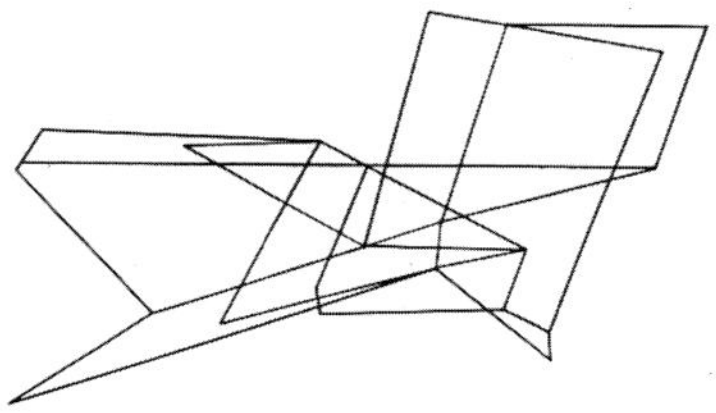

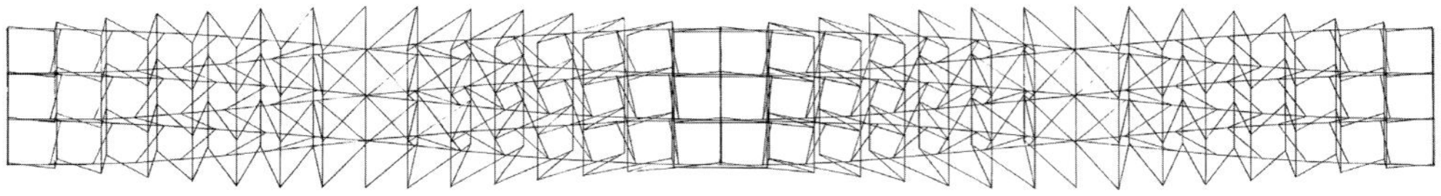

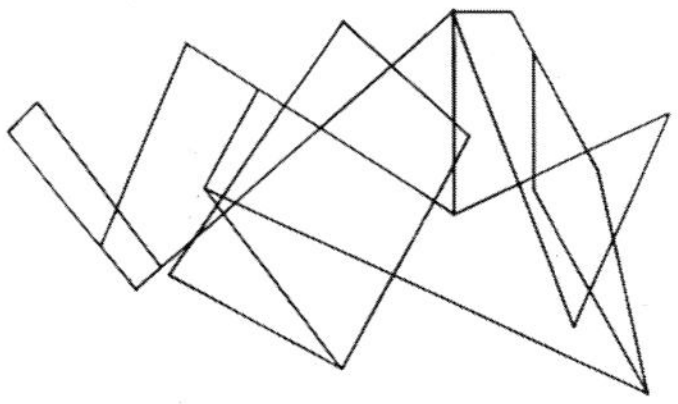

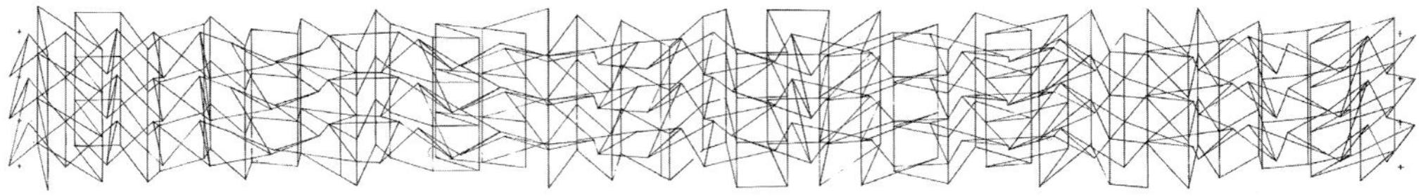

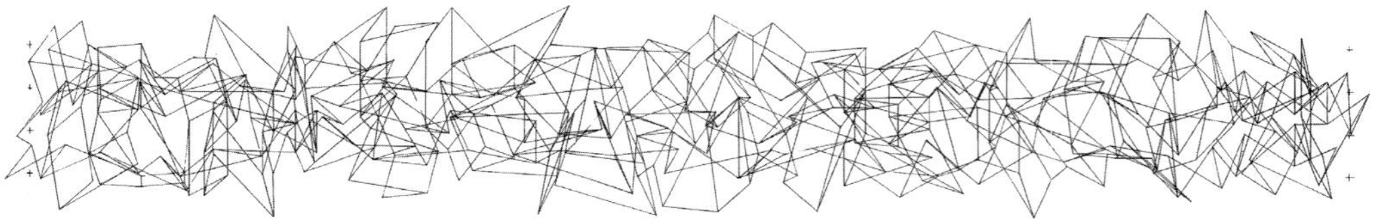

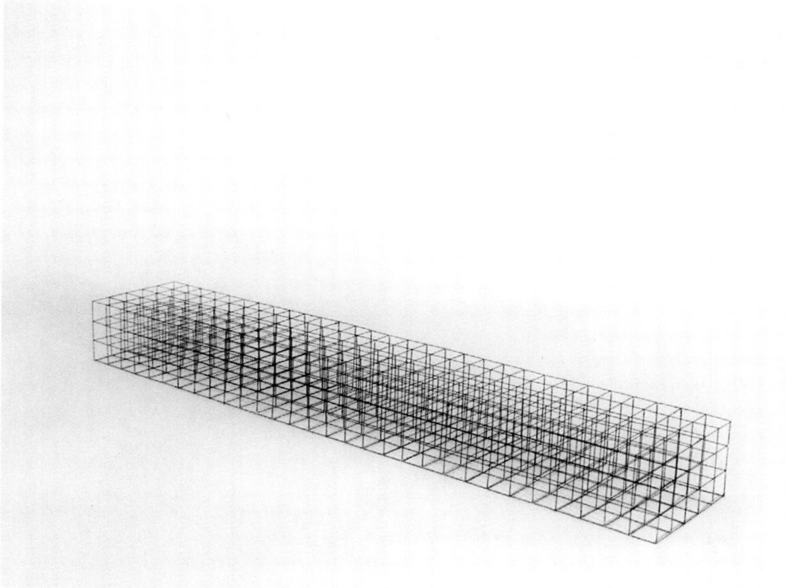

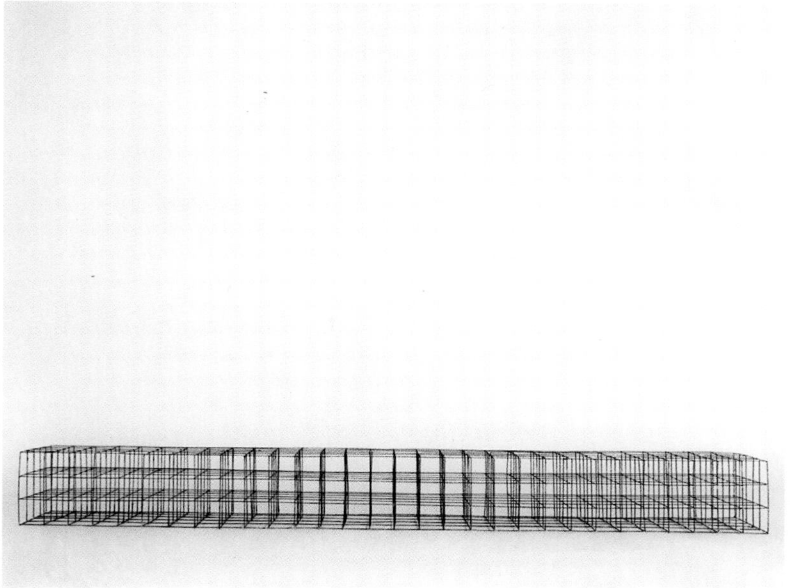

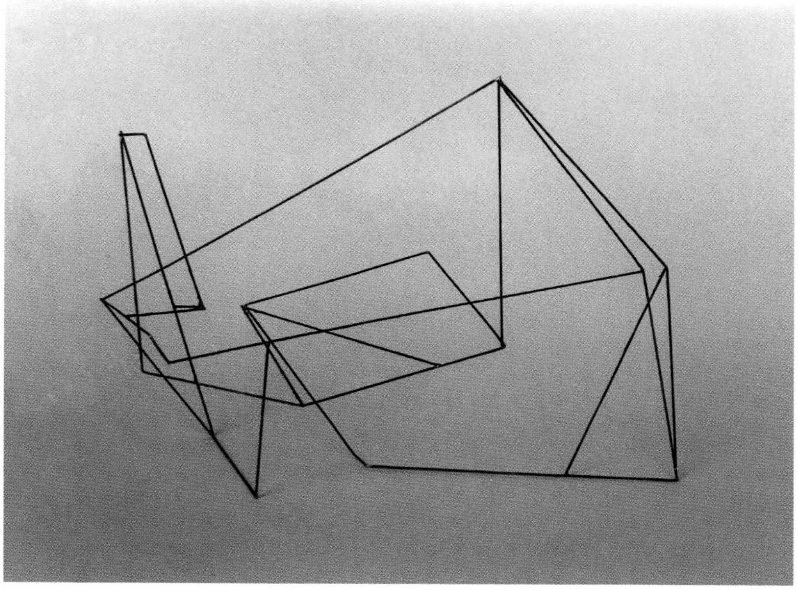

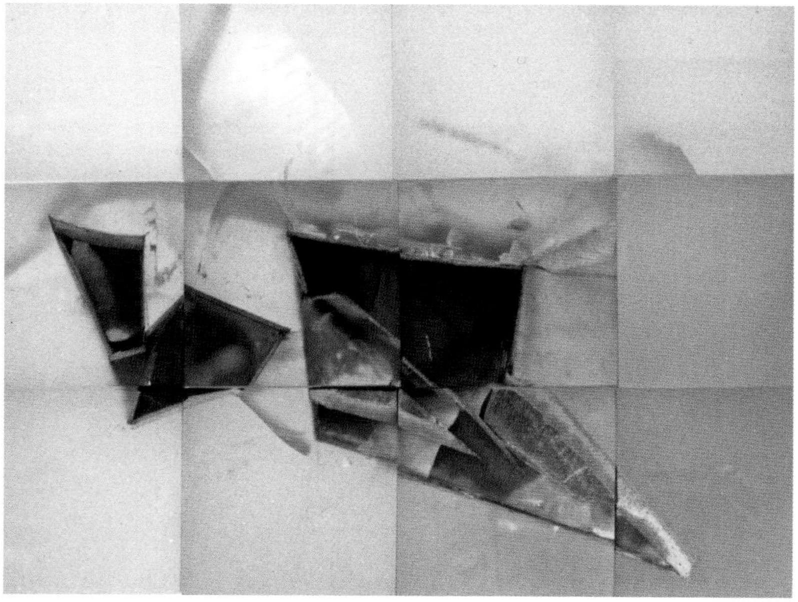

TOWER OF BABEL

CANON STRUCTURES
THE COOPER UNION, NEW YORK, US

PROJECT DATE: 1991

J. MAYER H.

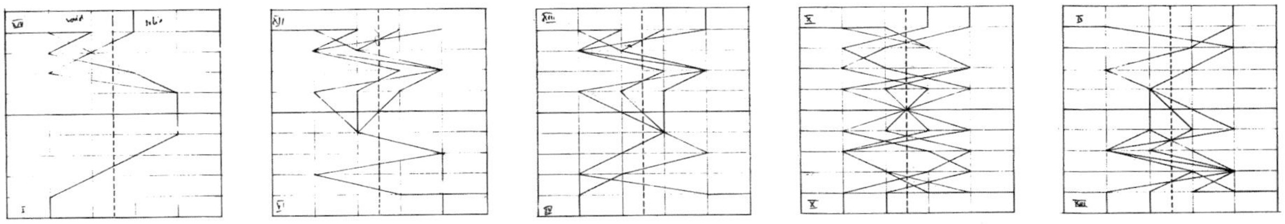

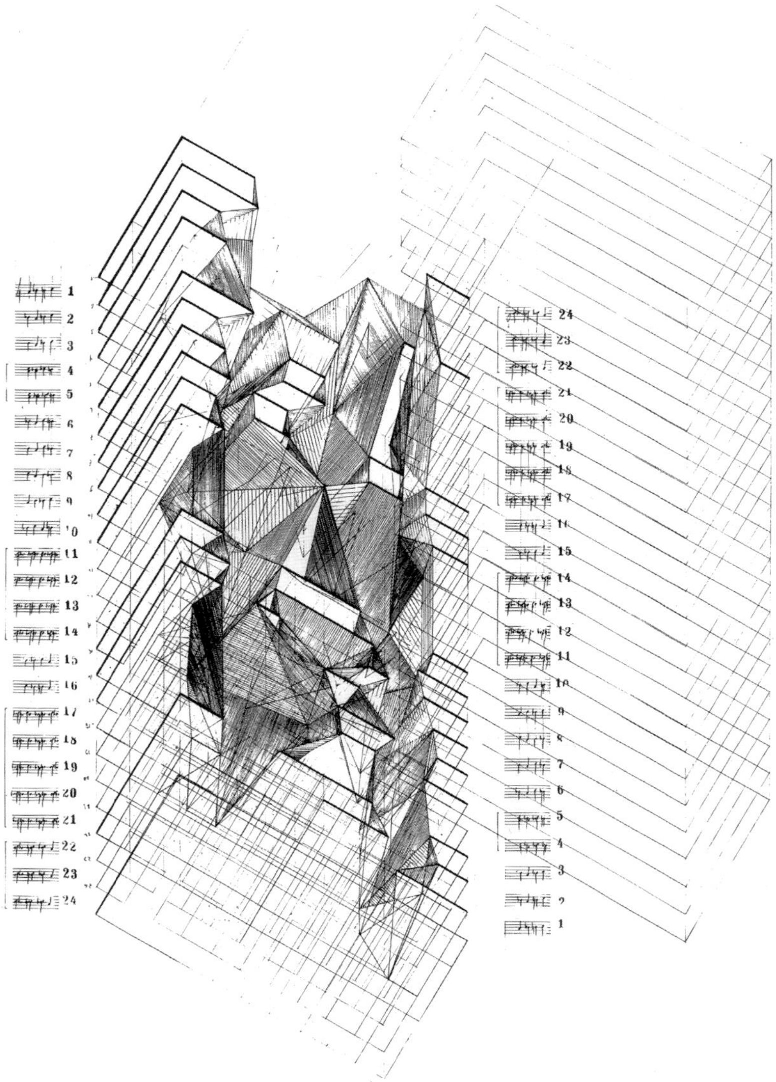

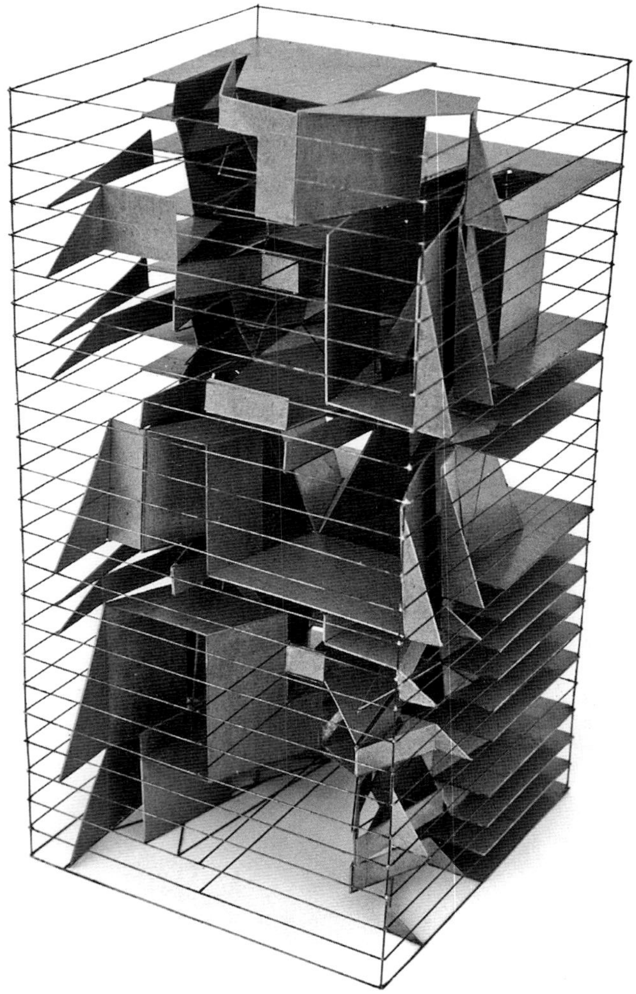

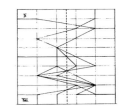

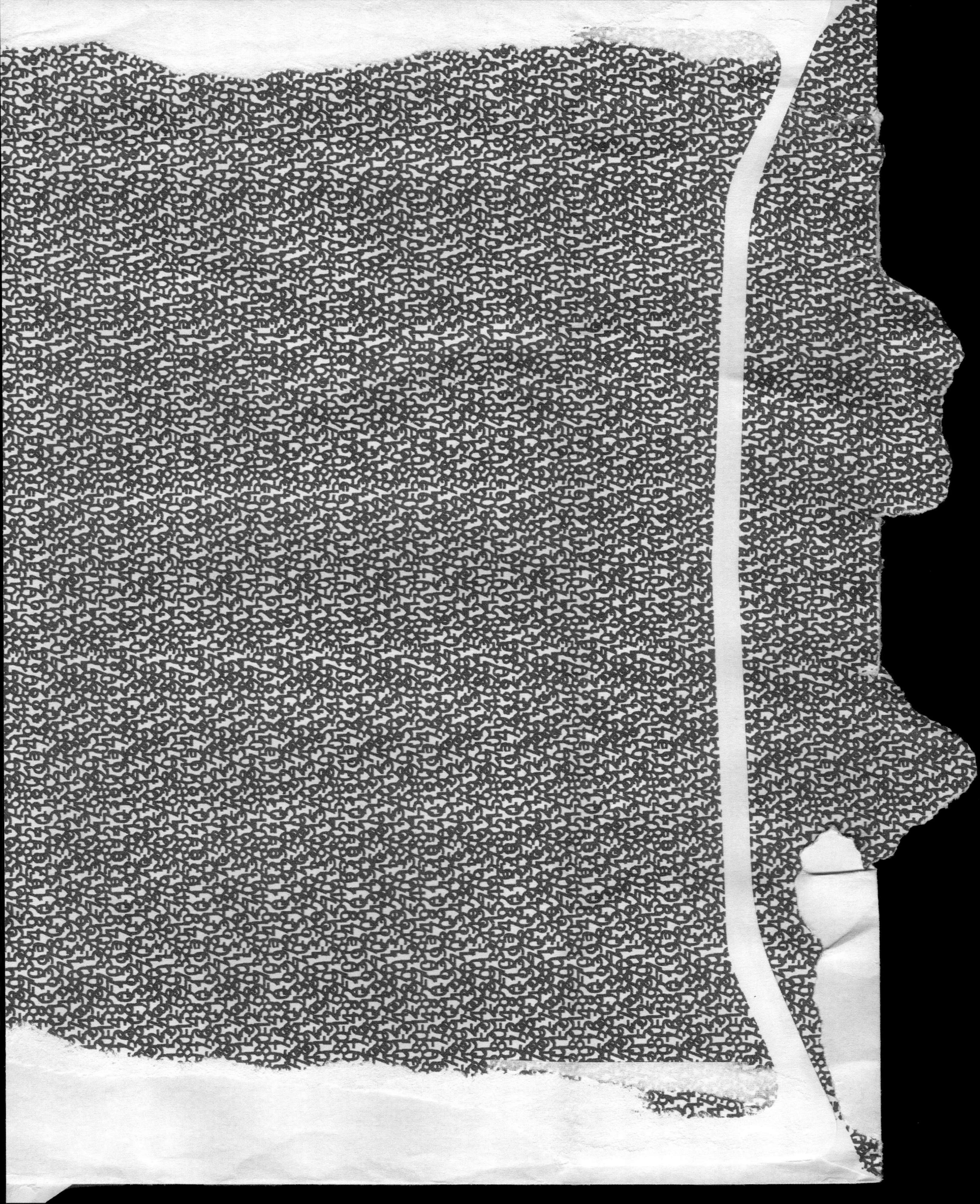

INVITATION TO PLAY

ILKA & ANDREAS RUBY

BUILDING HONESTY

Something in the work of J. MAYER H. catches our eye immediately, a strange beauty born out of an uncanny fusion of elegance and heaviness, iconicity and disfiguration. Layers of (dis)information wrap around the objects and prevent us from getting to the heart of things too easily. As if embarrassed by its own discipline, the architecture of J. MAYER H. often seems to come in disguise, cross-dressing as the "other" of itself. There is a sense of self-detachment vaguely reminiscent of René Magritte, as if wanting to suggest that "ceci n'est pas une architecture."

This intense urge to remove architecture from its recognizable representation and displace it into more ambiguous territories surely does not come out of nowhere, but has a lot to do with the architectural culture that Jürgen Mayer H., born near Stuttgart in 1965, happened to grow up with. Stuttgart lies in the southwest of Germany, which, in economic terms, is one of the country's most thriving regions and the headquarters to some of its most powerful and technologically advanced corporations (Mercedes-Benz, Porsche, Bosch, etc.). Its population is reputed for a rigorous work ethic, which has been molded over centuries by its Protestant religion. A predilection for technology, combined with Protestant fervor, produces a local species of architecture that gives an almost moral precedence to the virtues of functionalism—particularly that of honesty.

There is an honesty of materials (to show the materials of which a building is made), an honesty of structure (to show what holds the building upright), and an honesty of program (to express the functional purpose to which the building is dedicated)—after all, "seeing is believing." Finally, perhaps to exorcise even the faintest residue of insecurity that may be lurking somewhere in the hidden depths of this architecture, there is an honesty of space as well: a cult of transparency, which has become one of the trademarks of German architecture. But in the homeland of religious reformation, transparency is more than just a visual phenomenon. It is part of a controlling regime of the everyday, which can be traced back to the Calvinist idea of public privacy. Not to draw curtains behind your windows is, according to Calvinism, the best way to show the world that you lead a life free of sins. Along the same lines, transparency became the technological tool of modernist architecture in order to ensure the moral integrity of the life within by displaying it to the outside. In postwar German architecture transparency became a metaphor for democracy, a symbolic merger of the optical and the ethical most notoriously promoted by a Stuttgart-based circle of practitioners centered around the architect Günter Behnisch. His Bundestag, the new Parliament Building in Bonn (1973–92) with its plenary hall set in a transparent glass box, became the built manifesto of this movement. The power of this alignment between transparency and democracy in Germany even appears in Sir Norman Foster's Reichstag Building in Berlin, which replaced Behnisch's Bundestag. In Foster's Reichstag the ceiling of the plenary hall is partially glazed to grant the visitors to the transparent cupola on top a view to their lawmakers at work down below.

If we take this excess of honesty, legibility, and integrity as a common denominator of German architecture from the prosperous postwar years until today, then the work of J. MAYER H. appears like one continuous effort to break away. If the mainstream of German architecture after World War II was interested in making a case for the rational nature of architecture, the work of Jürgen Mayer H. is directed toward the contrary view. His radar is scanning the real for the incoherent, irrational, and unexplainable in order to blur the over-transparency of the world produced by a reason that ceaselessly tries to predict the course of things. Yet what drives Jürgen Mayer H.'s research is not an attraction to obscure things for the sake of obscuring. Rather, he wishes to "inscribe" elements of the real in a sequence of experience that allows us to be surprised once again by what had come to feel so overtly familiar. What makes this "deconstruction of the obvious" so effective is the fact that it does not simply unroll as a stage act in front of our eyes. Ultimately we realize that we are standing on the stage as well: cast as actors by the event itself, in order to make it happen.

WHAT YOU SEE IS NOT WHAT YOU GET

To launch this deconstruction of the obvious, Jürgen Mayer H. strategically chose to bypass architecture and to use art as an operative platform at the beginning of his career. Instead of designing buildings he designed responsive interfaces, which would disclose their information only upon interference by the viewer. As if in a late meditation on the overdose of transparency referred to earlier, he started to work with data-protection patterns, which are normally used in banking-correspondence envelopes in order to obscure confidential information. Thus, the pages of his Guest Book (1996) were covered with data-protection patterns, which seemed to leave no place to inscribe anything. However, the patterns were printed in a heat-sensitive color. When writing in the book, one would touch the paper and therefore "heat" it, making the data-protection pattern invisible and revealing one's own writing in the process. As soon as one lifted one's hand from the book again, the paper's temperature would sink below the critical visibility threshold and the data-protection patterns started to fill the page once more.

With Face (1998), the tactile element passed from the hand to the face. This was a painting whose canvas had been upholstered to form a cushion and painted a heat-sensitive red color. Pressing one's face into the cushion (painting) would cause the red color to disappear, leaving a thermo-print of one's profile. A Polaroid photograph was taken in order to conserve this portrait, which, on the canvas, would disappear again as soon as the heat impulse from one's facial contact faded away. Subsequently, the Heat.Seats took the entire body on a tour of self-discovery, again spurred by the use of heat-sensitive color. Oblivious to the "plot" into which one is being lured, one gratefully accepts the invitation to rest one's body on the *chaise longue*-cum-bench, only to discover when one rises again that a part of one remains seated on the bench (the X-ray image of our intimate flesh).

While the works using heat-sensitive color and data-protection patterns come to an end with the rising number of architectural projects in the office, some of the issues explored in that research clearly reappear later under different circumstances. Thus the Heat.Seats are given a new lease of life as furniture with Pixy.Pieces. These strange objects confuse their users with contradictory signals. At first glance they seem to evoke childhood memories of one's teddy bear, but, just when we are about to happily cuddle our body into its lap, we realize that its entire surface is covered with glass mosaic tiles. Mostly used to clad wet environments like bathrooms, this material is not only harder but also colder than we have assumed. Perplexed, we take a seat with a slightly stiff backbone, only to discover the next deception: holding our breath we feel our bottom sinking into the bathroom floor as if into a stuffed armchair—so the soft-looking shape carries a soft core under its hard skin after all. Yet, unlike a car seat, these chairs do not ergonomically fit the body—rather, we have to mold our body over their "Haribo-geometry." They stage comfort without actually being comfortable, but as our culture holds that a chair has to be comfortable we start to doubt whether these are chairs at all. Awkwardly probing its curvy surface, we wonder how to properly sit on this thing.

Our miscomprehension leaves us in the clouds, much like Monsieur Hulot in Jacques Tati's movie *Mon Oncle* (1958). Looking for a place to sleep, Hulot ends up abusing a seating bench (rotating it laterally by ninety degrees) as a *chaise longue*, which looks like a do-it-yourself version of Le Corbusier's masterpiece. Suddenly we realize that a lack of knowledge or even a blunt misunderstanding can create a space of freedom. Herein lies, ultimately, Jürgen Mayer H.'s interest: creating objects that a) appear to be something which they are not (i.e., hard rather than soft), b) attract us to use them, which c) makes us realize their true nature. It is a play of false promise, disappointment, and finally the pleasure of discovering something truly unexpected instead.

TRUE ILLUSIONS

Interestingly enough, it is predominantly thanks to our tactile perception that we can unearth the true nature of these objects. It is by touching, sitting, or lying on these objects that we are able to deconstruct the impression we received from first looking at them. This crucial importance of the bodily experience is exactly the reason we no longer find this approach in the works of Jürgen Mayer H. Because of the scale difference between architecture and humans, we can no longer embrace a building in the same immediate way as we can a piece of furniture. Architecture ultimately transgresses the human scale no matter how hard it feigns not to. If a chair, bed, or table can always be complementary to the body, by offering points of contact or surfaces for interaction, a building is, by default, something "other than me." I do not sit on a building, I sit on one of its elements at best. Therefore, Jürgen Mayer H. cannot rely on a primarily tactile strategy if he wants to continue his project of delaying truth for the sake of experience (and, by extension, the experience of "presence").

What appears instead is a constant estrangement of the functional and typological codes of architecture, which violates yet another commandment of functionalism: the honesty of program (complementing the honesty of materials and honesty of structure mentioned before). Jürgen Mayer H. consciously undermines the recognizability of a building's program by estranging the very codes that would give away its programmatic identity—which in turn loops back to his long-standing interest in data-protection patterns.

Already in his first building, the Stadthaus Scharnhauser Park (Stuttgart-Ostfildern), he made a point of disappointing all expectations of how a (German) city hall should look, wrapping the building in a mostly opaque metal envelope when local common sense would have insisted on a transparent building that unequivocally broadcasts its program to the city's public realm. In his later projects, Jürgen Mayer H. has further pursued this approach while using different formal repertoires, which include more explicit instrumentalizations of data-protection patterns such as his Mensa Moltke (Karlsruhe). Clearly, this structure makes no effort to communicate the fact that it houses a student canteen.

Like Jürgen Mayer H.'s design objects, the building is actively engaged in concealing its identity—the true condition of its materials, structure, and program being illegible. However, in contrast to his design objects, it does so not by covering the real thing with a deceptive cover which one then takes away to get to the truth, but by creating an intrinsically erratic configuration that one cannot compare to (and therefore test against) any other familiar experience. As such, the true structural and material properties of the building are consciously not made clear. Thus, we cannot see that the structure of the building actually consists of wood because it is seamlessly coated in a homogenizing skin of polyurethane. Yet at the same time, the building does not give one any clues to help one identify its actual materials. In a similar way, Jürgen Mayer H. blurs the boundaries between structure and sculpture. For the most part, the sculptural shape of the building is identical with that of its load-bearing structure, but some beams below the ceiling appear to be structural, while in reality they only serve a sculptural purpose. The difference between the two is no longer articulated, and it is impossible to discover it if one bases one's judgment purely on direct experience—knowledge has to come into play as well.

The point, therefore, is no longer about being able to tell truth from fiction but is about the *verisimilitude* of fiction, a concept which is beautifully addressed in the German notion of *Wahrscheinlichkeit,* which combines the seemingly opposite notions of "truth" (*Wahrheit*) and "appearance" (*Schein*) in order to indicate something that *appears to be true,* without actually being verifiable through a rational mode of thought. We are ultimately forced to accept the impossibility of finding absolute truth—a situation which could lead us to the theories of Karl Popper, who argued that a theory can be regarded as valid only until it is falsified (which turns truth into a temporary good); or, alternatively, could make us adopt the "gay science" of Friedrich Nietzsche, who left behind philosophy's century-long ontological hunt for truth when declaring, in his seminal essay *On Truth and Lies in a Nonmoral Sense* (1872) that "truths are illusions which we have forgotten are illusions." And *illusion,* as the late Jean Baudrillard pointed out, can be etymologically traced back to the Latin *illudere,* which literally means "to put something in the mode of playing."

This is a kind of playing, of course, which is not to be misunderstood as light entertainment, but as a commitment to the very essence of humanity. As Friedrich Schiller put it in his letters *On the Aesthetic Education of Man* (1795) "Man only plays when he is in the fullest sense of the word a human being, and he is only fully a human being when he plays." This is ultimately what we could take the work of Jürgen Mayer H. for: an invitation to play.

Wir können leider nicht immer verhindern, dass Sie mehrere Briefsendungen an einem Tag von uns erhalten. Das manuelle Aussortieren der Sendungen wäre teurer als das übliche Porto. Bitte haben Sie dafür Verständnis.

DANFOSS UNIVERSE

FOOD FACTORY AND CURIOSITY CENTER, NORDBORG, DENMARK

CLIENT: DANFOSS UNIVERSE, NORDBORG

PROJECT DATE: 2005–07

J. MAYER H.
PROJECT TEAM: JÜRGEN MAYER H., MARCUS BLUM, THORSTEN BLATTER, ANDRE SANTER, ALESSANDRA RAPONI

ARCHITECT ON SITE: HALLEN & NORDBY, ESBJERG, KOLDING
TECHNICAL CONSULTANTS: CARL BRO, ESBJERG
MODEL: WERK5, BERLIN

PERMANENT COLLECTION OF NAI NETHERLANDS ARCHITECTURE INSTITUTE, ROTTERDAM, THE NETHERLANDS

Danfoss is a leading international company, which produces and develops mechanical components for heating and climate-control technology. "Danfoss Universe", a foundation conceived as a public-experience park to be sited on the premises of the firm's headquarters—a place where visitors of all ages can interact in an entertaining way with the topics and phenomena of technology and science. The masterplan for the Danfoss Universe envisioned an ensemble of structures—with an exhibition building (the Curiosity Center) and, later, a restaurant (the Food Factory) to be realized in a second phase by J. Mayer H. Architects. This architectural ensemble—erected in the absence of any built context, and responsible for endowing it's essentially characterless surroundings with a new face—succeeds in generating a new and distinctive environment.

The two buildings are playful, visually striking, and, hence, highly memorable. Seen from their narrow sides, they rise from the site in swooping concavities, while, from the long sides, their profiles take on the form of a complex series of curves. The remarkable and conspicuous look of these abrupt contours within an otherwise gentle landscape generates curiosity about their interiors. The spacious exhibition building functions like a black box: an open space, within which the visitors' attention can be turned toward exhibition objects, experiments, and projections. A raised platform offers views of current exhibitions. The development of additional portions of the masterplan will convert the Danfoss premises into a highly unusual park, whose bizarre forms are seemingly drawn from science-fiction comic books. The convergence of "edutainment" and "architainment," reality and fantasy, free play and experiment, sets the stage for a new comprehension of science. Each building will be a component of an educational landscape—and, hence, of knowledge culture. —Andres Lepik

CURIOSITY CENTER

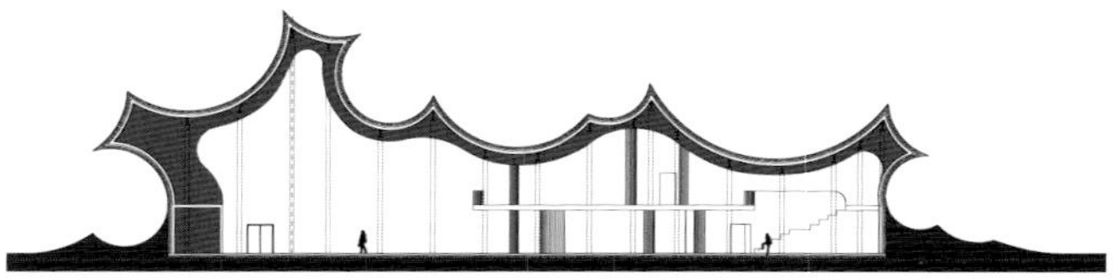

SECTION CURIOSITY CENTER

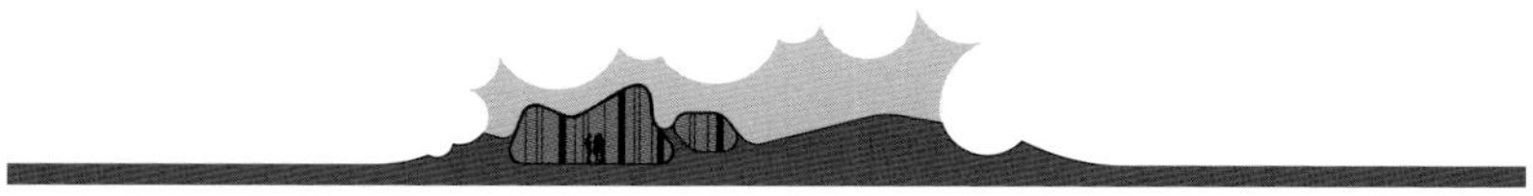

FOOD FACTORY

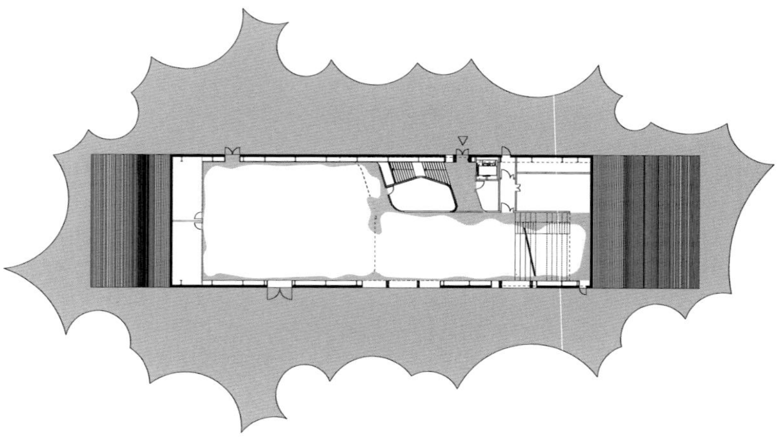

FLOORPLAN CURIOSITY CENTER

SEASONSCAPE

LAKESHORE, ASCONA, SWITZERLAND

CLIENT: MUNICIPALITY OF LIGNANO SABBIADORO, IN COLLABORATION WITH THE CHAMBER OF COMMERCE, INDUSTRY, HANDICRAFTS, AND AGRICULTURE OF THE PROVINCE OF UDINE (CCIAA), SWITZERLAND

INTERNATIONAL COMPETITION: 1999–2000, 3RD PRIZE

J. MAYER H.
COMPETITION TEAM: JÜRGEN MAYER H., MARCO ZÜRN, CHRISTOF ZELLER, SEBASTIAN FINCKH

STRUCTURAL ENGINEERS: LYDIA THIESEMANN, HAMBURG

Seasonscape comprises a proposed floating pier in front of the town of Ascona, doubling the surface of its lakeside promenade as well as creating new infrastructure for tourism. This new surface oscillates at water level and houses a ferry terminal offering various tourist programs. The structural concept resembles a human spine. All its pontoons are connected by compressible rubber points and anchored to the bottom of the lake. Surface treatments can be modified for different seasons as well as temporary functional needs.

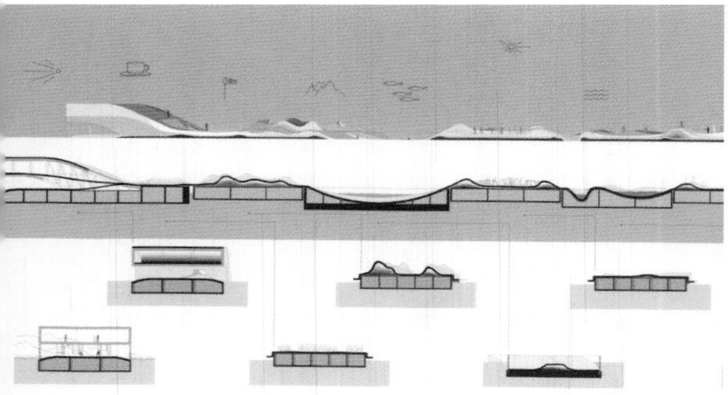

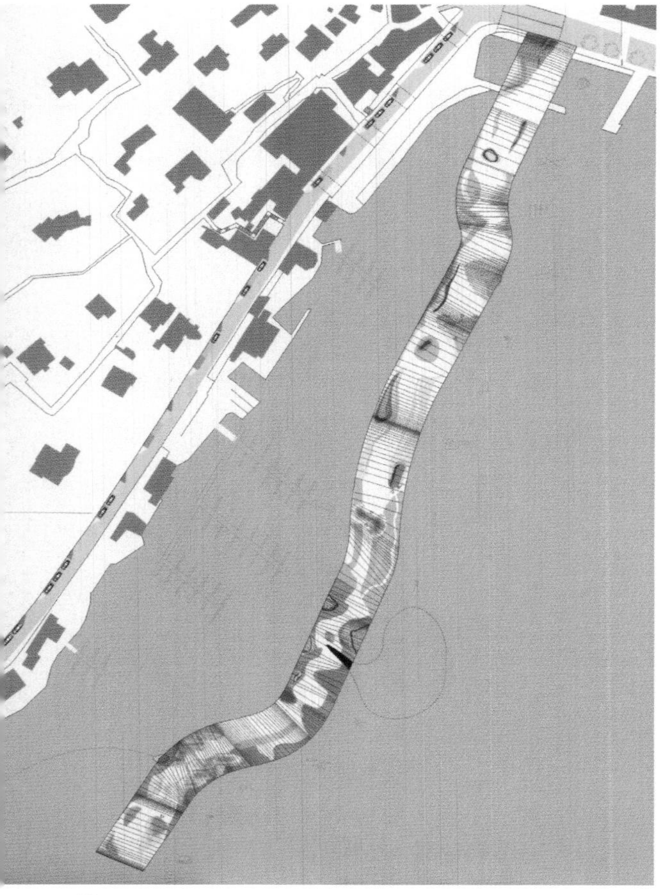

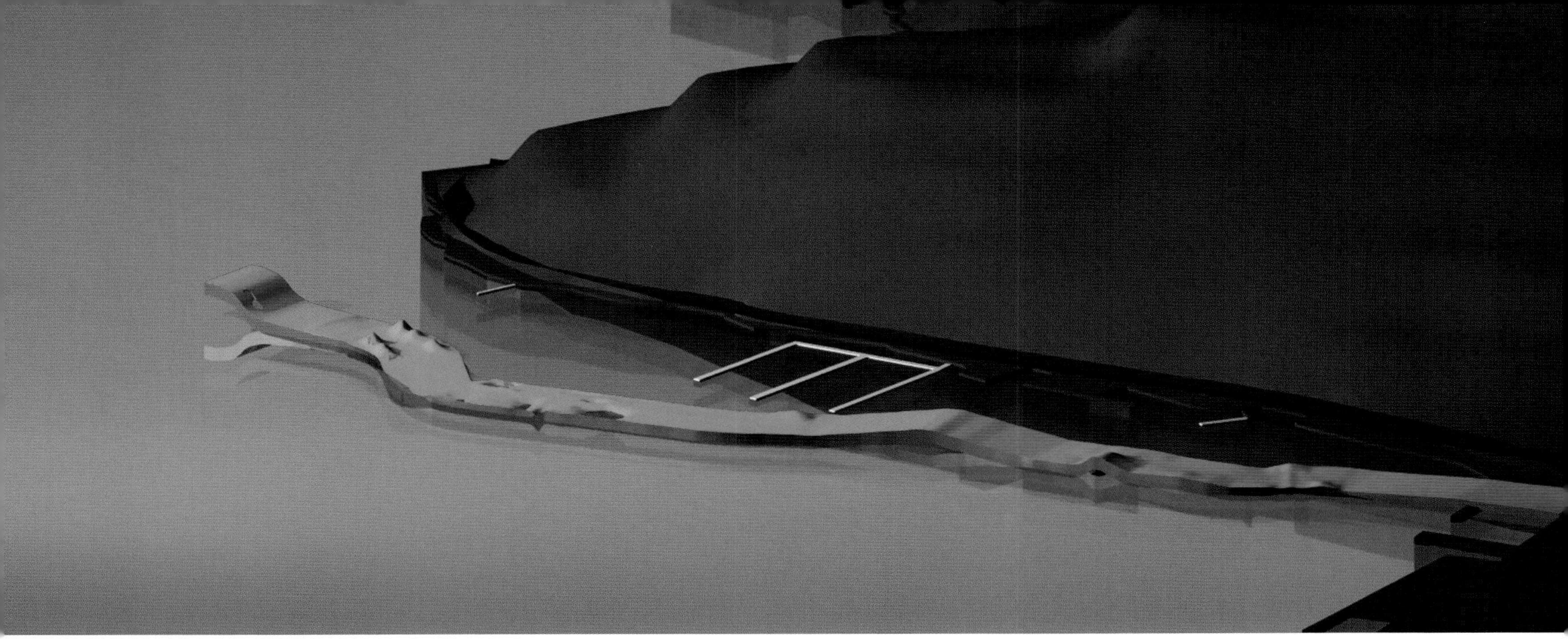

CULTURE AND CONGRESS CENTER WÜRTH

CLIENT: ADOLF WÜRTH GMBH & CO. KG, KÜNZELSAU, GERMANY

INTERNATIONAL COMPETITION: 2006

J. MAYER H.
COMPETITION TEAM: JÜRGEN MAYER H., JAN-CHRISTOPH STOCKEBRAND, SIMON TAKASAKI, PAUL ANGELIER, MARCUS BLUM, ALESSANDRA RAPONI, CHRISTOPH EMENLAUER

LANDSCAPE ARCHITECT: KLAUS WIEDERKEHR, NÜRTINGEN
STRUCTURAL ENGINEERS: KREBS UND KIEFER, KARLSRUHE
BUILDING PHYSICS: NEK INGENIEUR GRUPPE GMBH, BERLIN
KITCHEN ENGINEERS: MARTIN SCHERER, DARMSTADT
MUSEUM CONSULTANT: ANDRES LEPIK, BERLIN

PERMANENT COLLECTION OF THE WÜRTH ART COLLECTION, KÜNZELSAU

The aim of this project is to transform an existing, dynamic cultural location into a lively, pivotal center with charisma and destination-appeal. The stand-alone building, comprising four separate wings joined at the center, is situated on the highest point of the site, growing out of the landscape and commanding unparalleled views over the surrounding countryside. Its vibrant composition of year-round, mixed-use performance spaces; museum; conference facilities; library; and hospitality spaces creates a new venue, in which landscape and architecture can unite.

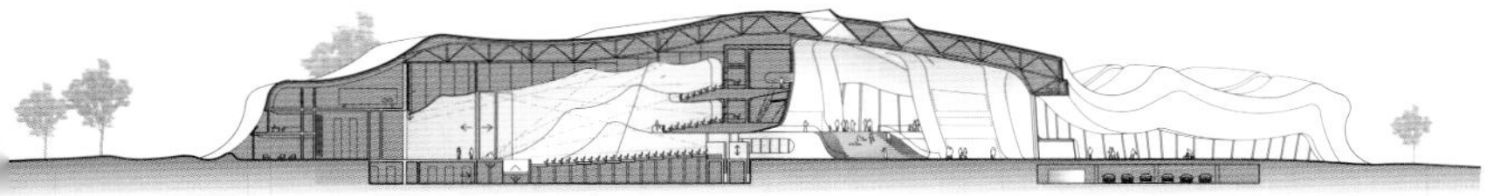
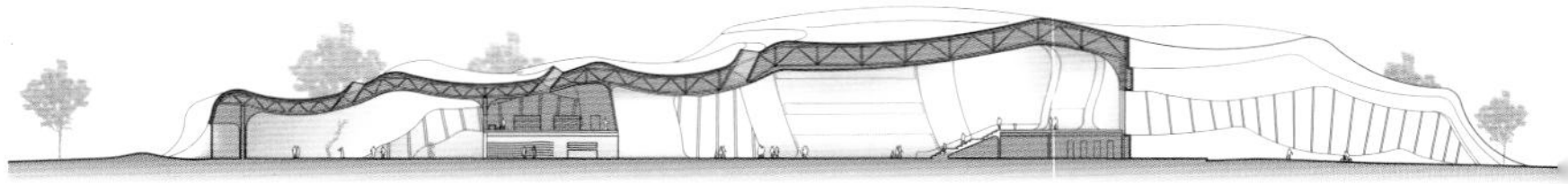

CROSS SECTIONS

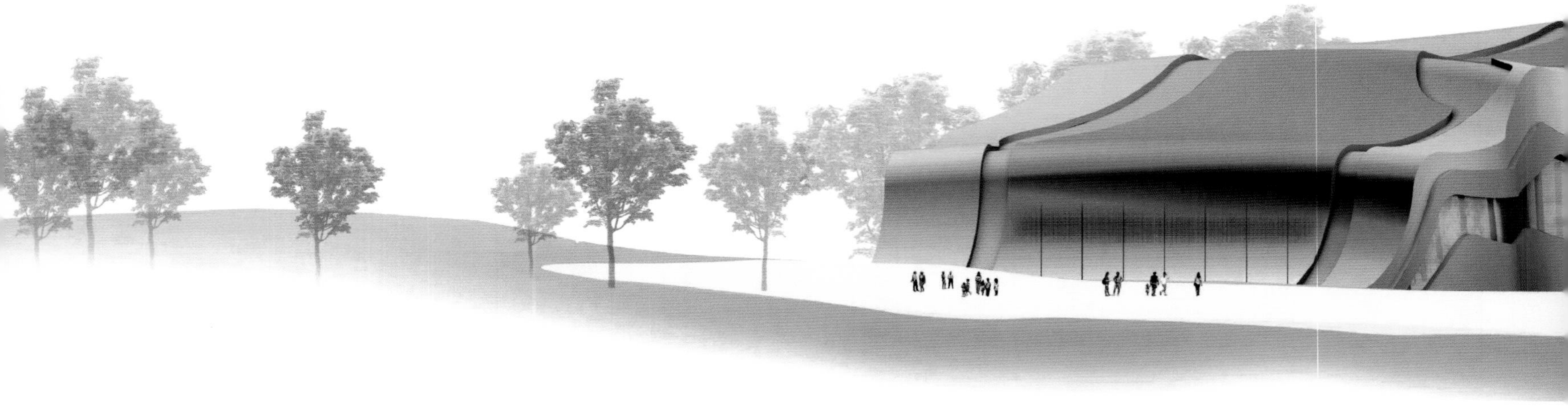

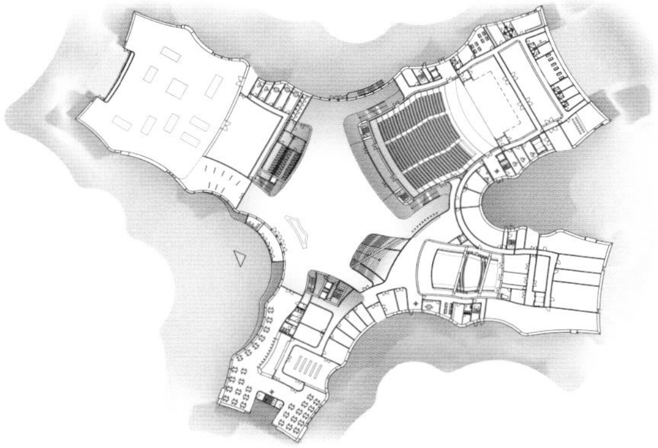

GROUND FLOOR

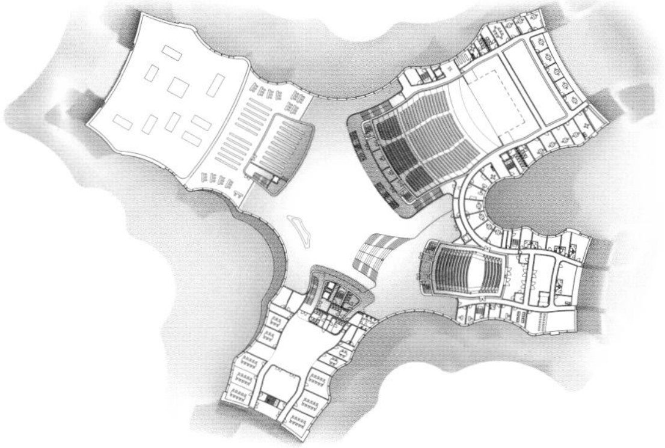

FIRST FLOOR

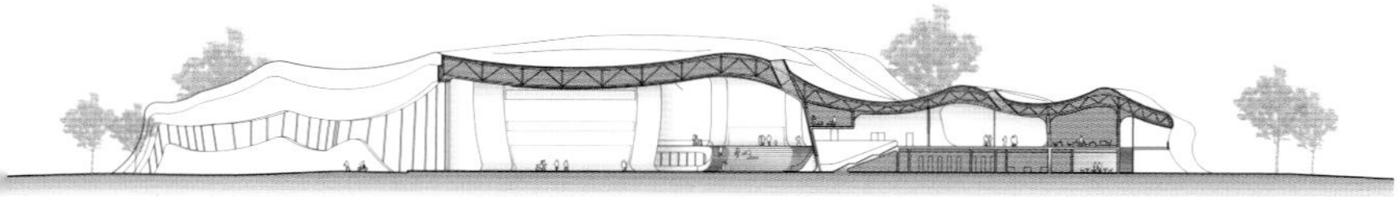

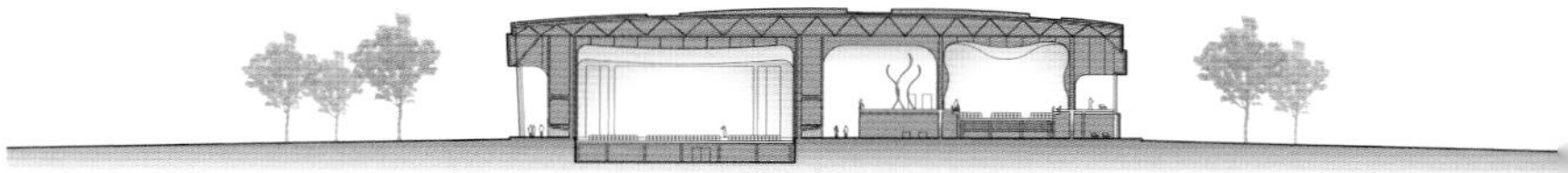

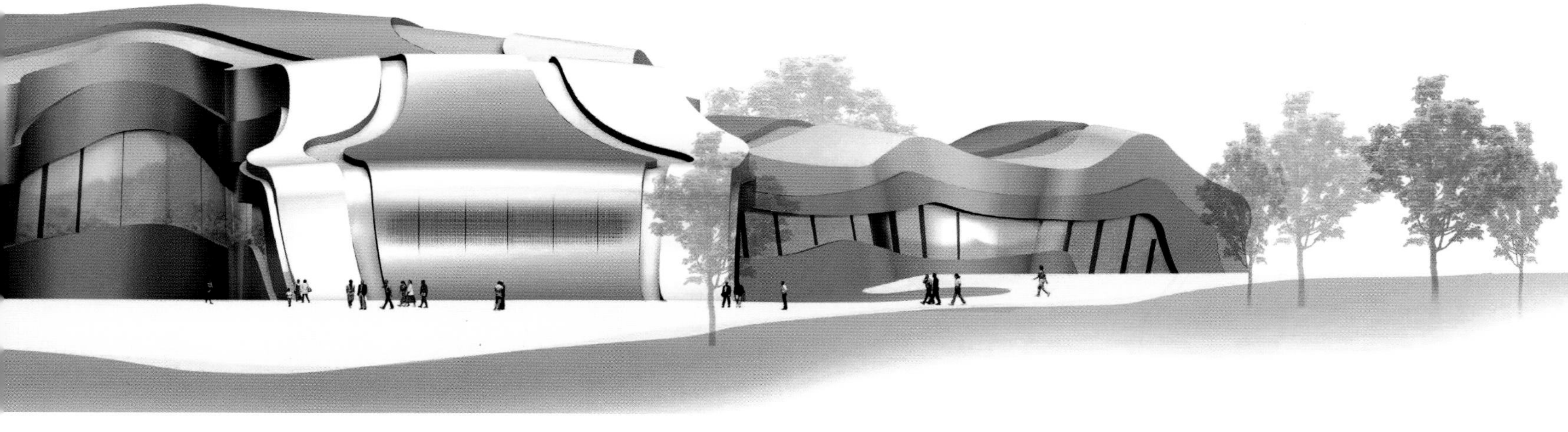

S11

OFFICE BUILDING, HAMBURG, GERMANY

CLIENT: COGITON PROJEKT ALTSTADT GMBH, HAMBURG

PROJECT DATE: 2007–09

J. MAYER H.
PROJECT TEAM: JÜRGEN MAYER H., HANS SCHNEIDER, WILKO HOFFMANN, MARCUS BLUM

ARCHITECT ON SITE: IMHOTEP, DONACHIE UND BLOMEYER, BERLIN
STRUCTURAL ENGINEERS: WTM, HAMBURG
BUILDING SERVICES: ENERGIEHAUS, HAMBURG,WITH SINE-PLAN, HAMBURG
MODEL: WERK5, BERLIN

The "Steckelhörn 11" project is located in the old center of Hamburg, close to the prominent new "HafenCity" development. It replaces a ruinous building and fills the gap between two historic premises. The triangular-shaped lot stretches across the city block, thus allowing for a narrow façade of about 1.3 m width facing the harbor and a main elevation of about 26.4 m oriented toward Steckelhörn street. The vertical design and soft setbacks of the latter pay tribute to the massing of the surrounding structures, as well as to local building-height regulations. The top floors provide additional outside space, offering a spectacular panoramic view over the city of Hamburg.

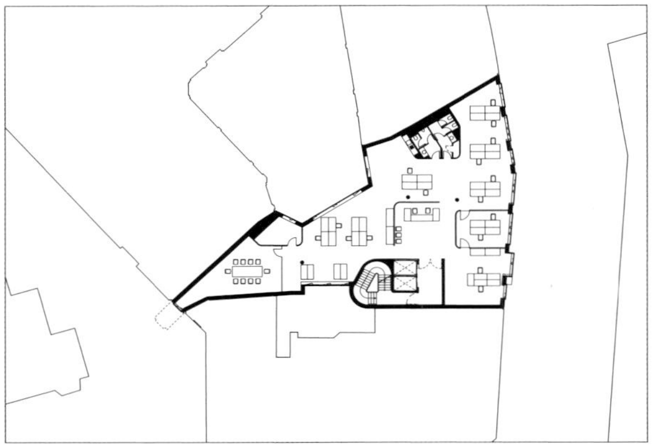

3RD FLOOR

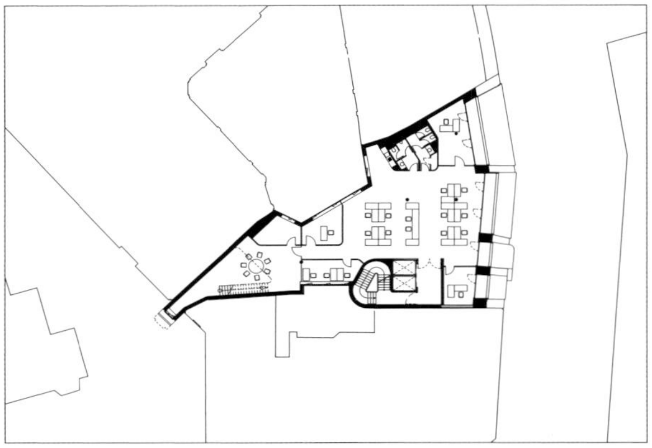

7TH FLOOR

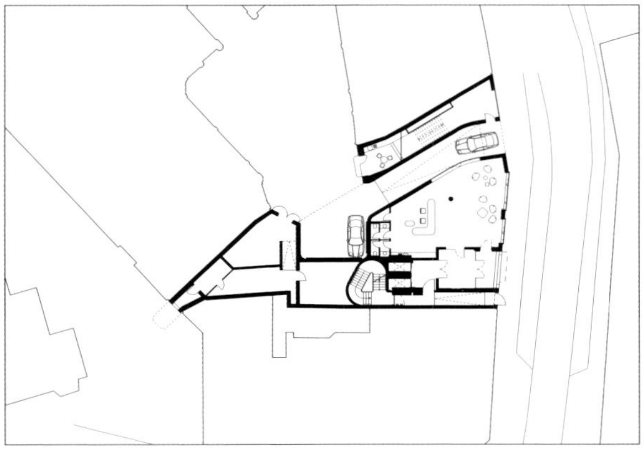

GROUND FLOOR

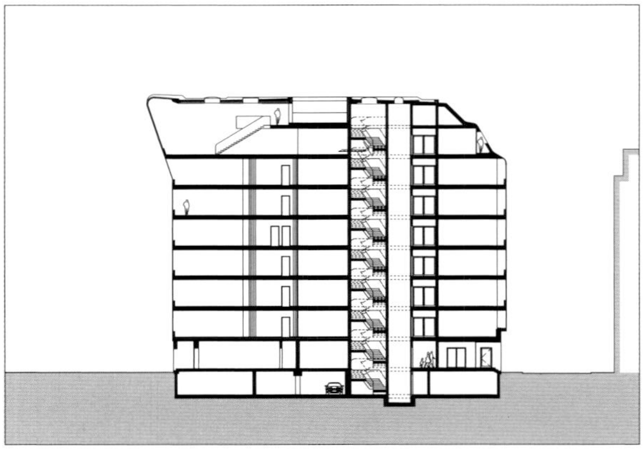

SECTION

DHL

THE DECISION OF ARCHITECTURE

JOHN PAUL RICCO

By virtue of the gift and the incessant sharing of the world one does not know where the sharing of a stone or of a person begins or ends. The delineation is always wider and at the same time more narrow than one believes when one grasps it (or rather one grasps quite well, as long as one is attentive to what extent the contour is trembling mobile and fleeting). — Jean-Luc Nancy [1]

Around: the architectural. This is the spatiality at hand, not only here in this brief excursus on the work of J. MAYER H., but in terms of the architectural "as such." Not only because any thinking, speaking, and writing of the architectural will always be "about" and "around" it, but even more so because the architectural is that which is always (in an ontological sense) *around*. In other words, to speak of the architectural is always to speak in terms of the peri-architectural. The peri-designates, then, not that which lies around and surrounds us, as though in a peripheral relationship to architecture, but rather is the name for the "becoming-architectural."

This peri-spatiality that comes to define the ontological priority of the architectural is, as I shall attempt to demonstrate, incapable of being appropriated or fully grasped—perhaps even by architecture itself. Something like this might have been expressed in Louis Kahn's definition of great architecture as that which begins and ends with the immeasurable, but only to the extent that the peri-architectural is understood as rendering impossible any definitive sense as to architecture's beginnings and ends. For rather than taking the measure of its own immeasurability, the distinction of J. MAYER H.'s work lies in its presentation or exposition of the extent to which the immeasurability of the peri-architectural—the leeway, orbit, and ease of architecture—remains immeasurable. We might refer to this as the ethical field of the architectural, and perhaps even as the "archi-ethical." Not in the sense (in either case) of an ethics of architecture, but in terms of the architectural as one of the ways in which ethical decision is staged. *For an ethical relation to architecture lies in the decision to take care of and to sustain this immeasurable spatiality, as opposed to taking its measure.* The work of J. MAYER H. sets the stage for this decision.

My concept of "taking care" as the performative praxis of architecture, while clearly drawing upon Martin Heidegger's notion of *Besorgen* as inextricable from what it means to be in the world,[2] involves a certain deconstruction of this duality of *Vorhandenheit* ("at-hand-ness" or "presence-at-hand") and *Zuhandenheit* ("handiness" or "ready-at-hand"). For, while both terms name a relation to things, as Derrida points out in his reading of Heidegger, *Vorhandenheit* marks a "relation to the thing as subsisting and independent object" while *Zuhandenheit* is "related to the thing as maneuverable tool," that is, as usable thing. Heidegger contrasts the latter with the unhandy or unusable thing: that which runs the risk of sliding down the slippery slope from conspicuousness to obtrusiveness to obstinacy to dead matter or waste. What is curious—although not terribly surprising—about Heidegger's thinking on unhandiness, is that it can be the result of something being missing or in need of repair *but it can also* bear a relation to that which is *not* missing or unusable at all, meaning: all-too handy.

"In associating with the world taken care of, what is unhandy can be encountered not only in the sense

1 Jean-Luc Nancy, **The Creation of the World or Globalization,** trans. François Raffoul and David Pettigrew, SUNY Series in Contemporary French Thought. (Albany, N.Y., 2007), p. 110.

2 "Strictly speaking, to talk of putting ourselves in the place of taking care is misleading. We do not first need to put ourselves in the place of this way of being in associating with and taking care of things. Everyday Da-sein always already **is** in this way," (original emphasis). Martin Heidegger, Dennis J. Schmidt, ed., **Being and Time,** trans. Joan Stambaugh, SUNY Series in Contemporary Continental Philosophy (Albany, N.Y., 1996), p. 63.

of something unusable or completely missing, but as something unhandy which is *not* missing at all and *not* unusable, but 'gets in the way' of taking care of things" (original emphasis).[3] In other words: the unhandy is that which is at once too handy and not handy at all. In turn, the deconstruction of handiness lies in this aporia, such that handiness can neither be missing something and in need of repair, nor can it be completely without something missing and completely usable.

For Heidegger, at hand or presence-at-hand (*Vorhandenheit*) is derivative of handiness or ready-at-hand (*Zuhandenheit*), and taking care of things occurs in our association with them in their handiness or being ready-at-hand. These things are then deemed useful, as things "in order to ..." and always in relation to other useful things, in a way that involves finding accommodation (spatial, architectural—surroundings) within a field of references (region). The kind of seeing involved here is circumspective. In contrast, Heidegger conceives of at-hand-ness or presence-at-hand as a theoretical and thematizing association with things, which can occur when the handy and usable thing is broken and in need of repair—that is to say, is unhandy. If such an at-hand-ness involves a taking care of things, it is only in the sense of looking or staring at the thing, and even then in a specifically non-circumspect way.

Yet, I wish to put forward a concept of taking care as our relation/association to things that is not dictated by the demands of equipmental use (praxis)—and thereby threatened by a fear of the unusable or useless—nor (derivatively) reducible to a mere theoretical postulation. Instead, one might begin to think of taking care as the performative praxis of the immeasurability of the immeasurable, the incessant worklessness at the heart of work. This happens nowhere other than "around," a peri-space that is non-circumspective (without predetermined ends) but that exists as a constitutive opening. Not derivative—including in the sense of the broken thing in need of repair—this would be a relation to the thing as irreparable, yet not in the sense of the thing-in-itself (i.e. Descartes's *res extensa*). Nor would this involve a withdrawal and receding of the object and its materiality either, but instead would be a matter of its shine, glow, and vibration—an inessential supplement that is, in turn, distinct from any presumption of enlightened illumination. In sum, the peri- is the space that is at once between and prior to the Heideggerean duality of "at-hand-ness" (*Vorhandenheit*) and "handiness" (*Zuhandenheit*), where "to take care of ..." means to sustain this space of mediality as a means without end.

If we understand handiness to be the measure of usability and of distance removed from conspicuousness—a taking care of architecture that will always amount to settling, finalizing, and completing the sense as to where architecture begins and ends—then I propose that the work of J. MAYER H., in its performative praxis, is a taking care of architecture that is neither conspicuous nor inconspicuous, handy nor unhandy, but is the exposition of an infinite relation to the finite (as the very surface of things) that affirms the ending(s) of architecture to be never-ending.

So, not handling but rather gesture, in the sense that the latter has been theorized by Giorgio Agamben as the pure praxis of mediality: neither means nor ends, use or exchange. Agamben, in taking a cue from Mallarmé's *milieu pur*, writes that "what is relayed to human beings in gestures is not the sphere of an end in itself but rather the sphere of a pure and endless mediality."[4] Gesture, then, is the performative praxis of the difference and distance between "at-handness" (*Vorhandenheit*) and "handiness" (*Zuhandenheit*). Gesture is a taking care of the spatiality that *is* peri-, or around. Gesture retains the hand only to the extent that it is attached to a mode of thinking irreducible to concept, and in the process of which extends itself without either giving or taking. This sense of gesture is closely aligned with Derrida's reading of Heidegger's hand, in which he writes: "If there is a thought of the hand or a hand of thought, as Heidegger gives us to think [in *Being and Time* as discussed above], it is not of the order of conceptual grasping. Rather this thought of the hand belongs to the essence of the gift, of a giving that would give, if this is possible, without taking hold of anything."[5] It is in this way that we can speak of gesture as non-possessive and non-appropriative praxis, a taking care that would be nothing more than an inconspicuous and imperceptible encounter and a tiny displacement—not a state of things or affairs, and perhaps even less than an event, gesture bears upon the post-medium periphery of things.

Rather than using or repairing that which it encounters, gesture is what we mean when we talk about *putting a shine on* something. While casting a certain kind of glow, this is not the work of illumination, enlightenment, or the revelation of a secret, but is instead a polishing, sanding, waxing, or cleaning that un-finishes the irreparable finish of every surface. It is also a tangential inflection of things that occurs through a carefully orchestrated collision of mobile and stationary objects as when, in the game of billiards, one speaks of putting a shine on the ball by hitting it in such a way that it moves in a trajectory that is as decided as it is unexpected.

Such an art of surfaces renders all of us dermatologists, in the capacity of which the finitude of the world—its very sense—is staged as its never-ending mediality. Gesture opens up and stages the ethical in, and as the sustaining and care of, this peri-spatiality, which is also the relational space of decision.

Halo, is another name for this inappropriable and immeasurable sphere of pure mediality and poten-

3 Ibid., p. 69.

4 Giorgio Agamben, **Means without End: Notes on Politics,** trans. Vincenzo Binetti and Cesare Casarino, Theory out of Bounds series (Minneapolis, Minn., 2000), p. 58. "The gesture is the exhibition of a mediality: it is the process of making a means visible as such."

5 Jacques Derrida, "**Geschlecht** II: Heidegger's Hand," in John Sallis, ed., **Deconstruction and Philosophy: The Texts of Jacques Derrida** (Chicago, 1987), p. 173.

6 Giorgio Agamben, **The Coming Community**, trans. Michael Hardt, Theory out of Bounds series (Minneapolis, 1993), p. 56.

7 As quoted in Agamben, **Means without End: Notes on Politics,** p. 75.

8 Agamben, **The Coming Community**, p. 57.

tiality that is disclosed by putting a shine on what is already irreparable or perfectly finished. As an inessential supplement that, in its very conception, seems to be a recasting of the historical limits of the medieval and the modern, the halo is at once Aquinas's notion of "an unraveling or an indetermination,"[6] of the limits of each beatific singularity, and also figures architecturally in Merrifield's description of the Crystal Palace as "perhaps the only building in the world in which the atmosphere is perceivable ... by a spectator situated either at the west or east extremity of the gallery ... where the most distant parts of the building appear wrapped in a light blue halo."[7]

Each of these historical instances are relayed to us by Agamben, and it is Aquinas who provides him (and us) with the strongest conceptualization of the finishing and unfinishing that is the immeasurability of each and every thing in its singularity. As Agamben explains: "One can think of the halo, in this sense, as a zone in which possibility and reality, potentiality and actuality, become indistinguishable. The being that has reached its end, that has consumed all of its possibilities, thus receives as a gift a supplemental possibility ... This imperceptible trembling of the finite that makes its limits indeterminate and allows it to blend, to make itself whatever, is the tiny displacement that every thing must accomplish in the messianic world."[8]

The work of J. MAYER H. is full of halos. The "smart-dust" sensory outfits of Body.Guards amount to full-body halos, while Corridor is one single stretched -and-folded halo. In its use of cinematic surfaces of projection, the space generates a series of afterglow colors and light images, and the ceiling is a halo made of pixels of light and color that inspire us to think of it as a kind of "light noise." One can say that the light poles in the plaza of the Stadthaus Scharnhauser Park project, in their mobile response to the wind, function as inscriptive devices and write temporary halos of light on the ground. Seasonscape (not realized), in its topographic doubling of the lake and beach, can be understood as a "haloing" of the landscape, and while technical problems have impeded its realization, the intention was for the outside walls of Dupli.Casa to be waxed on a triennial basis.

In each of these instances, one encounters the peri-architectural as architecture's halo, and begins to understand the way in which, by deciding to put a finish or shine on the wall, surface (whatever)—that is, by the gesture that is neither handy nor unhandy, usable nor unusable—the finish or end of architecture is disclosed as never-ending and its pure potentiality is once again at hand. This, then, would be a way of grasping the uncircumscribability of the architectural by sustaining its syncopated rhythm and taking care of the super-thin wall that separates its waxing and its waning.

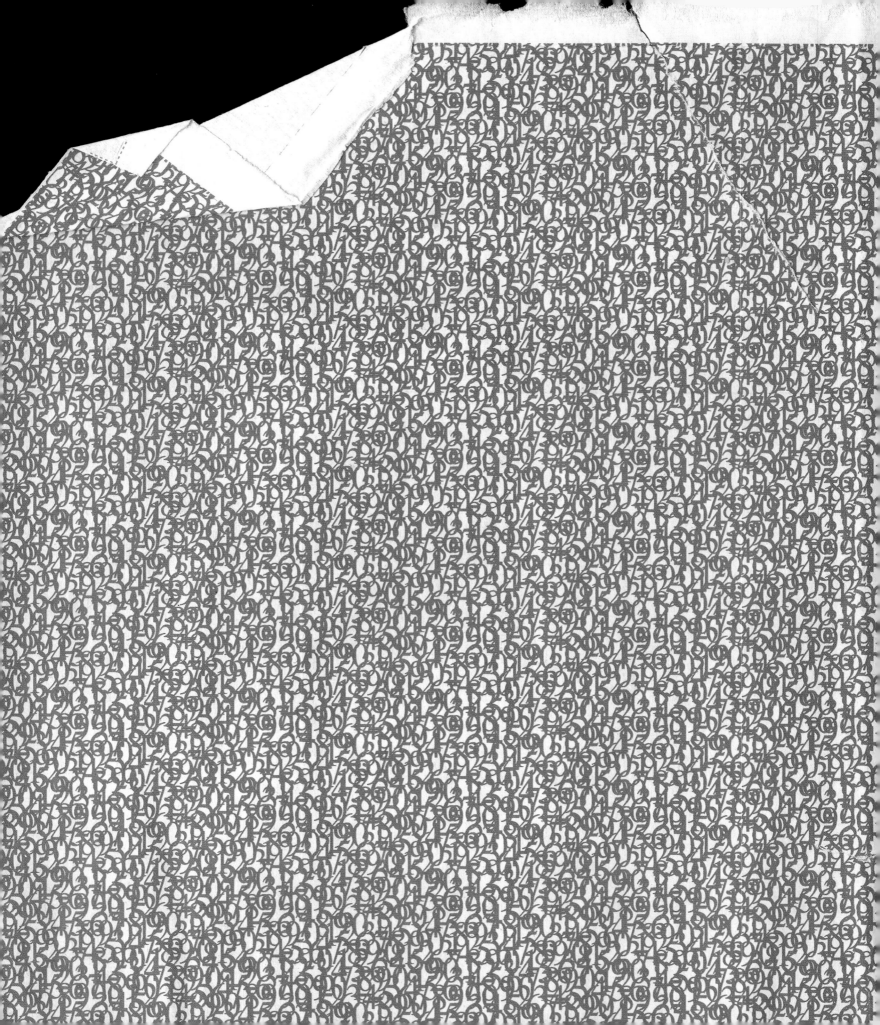

UIA STYLEPARK LOUNGE

CLIENT: STYLEPARK, FRANKFURT, GERMANY
LOCATION: BERLIN, GERMANY

PROJECT DATE: JULY 2002

J. MAYER H.
PROJECT TEAM: JÜRGEN MAYER H., SEBASTIAN FINCKH

COLLABORATION: SIKKENS, GIRA, DORNBRACHT, GARPA

The temporary Stylepark meeting lounge was specifically designed for the intersection of the UIA Congress and the Plancom Fair. The integral concept of the stand programs the linoleum floor surface into an undulating topography to meet different functional requirements. Communication areas and interactive elements fuse into each other and connect all programmatic elements into a homogeneous but spatially structured configuration. The conventional categories of furniture, wall, and multimedia are transformed into a communication landscape.

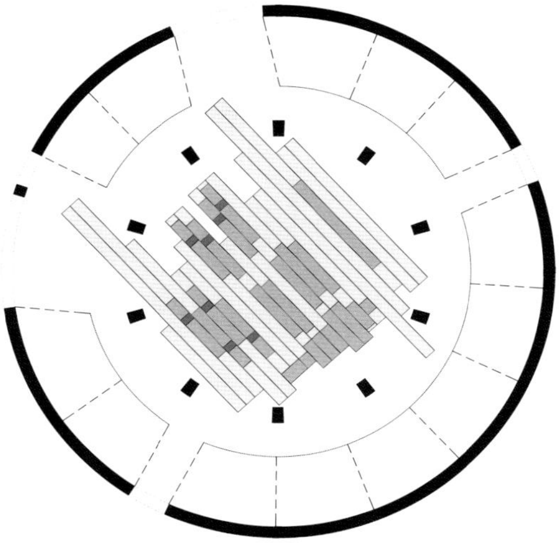

FLOOR PLAN

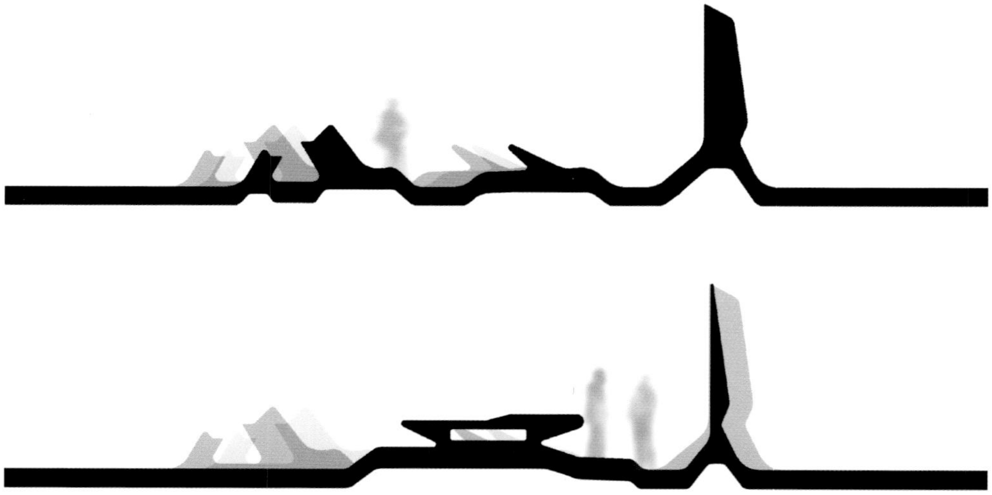

SECTIONS

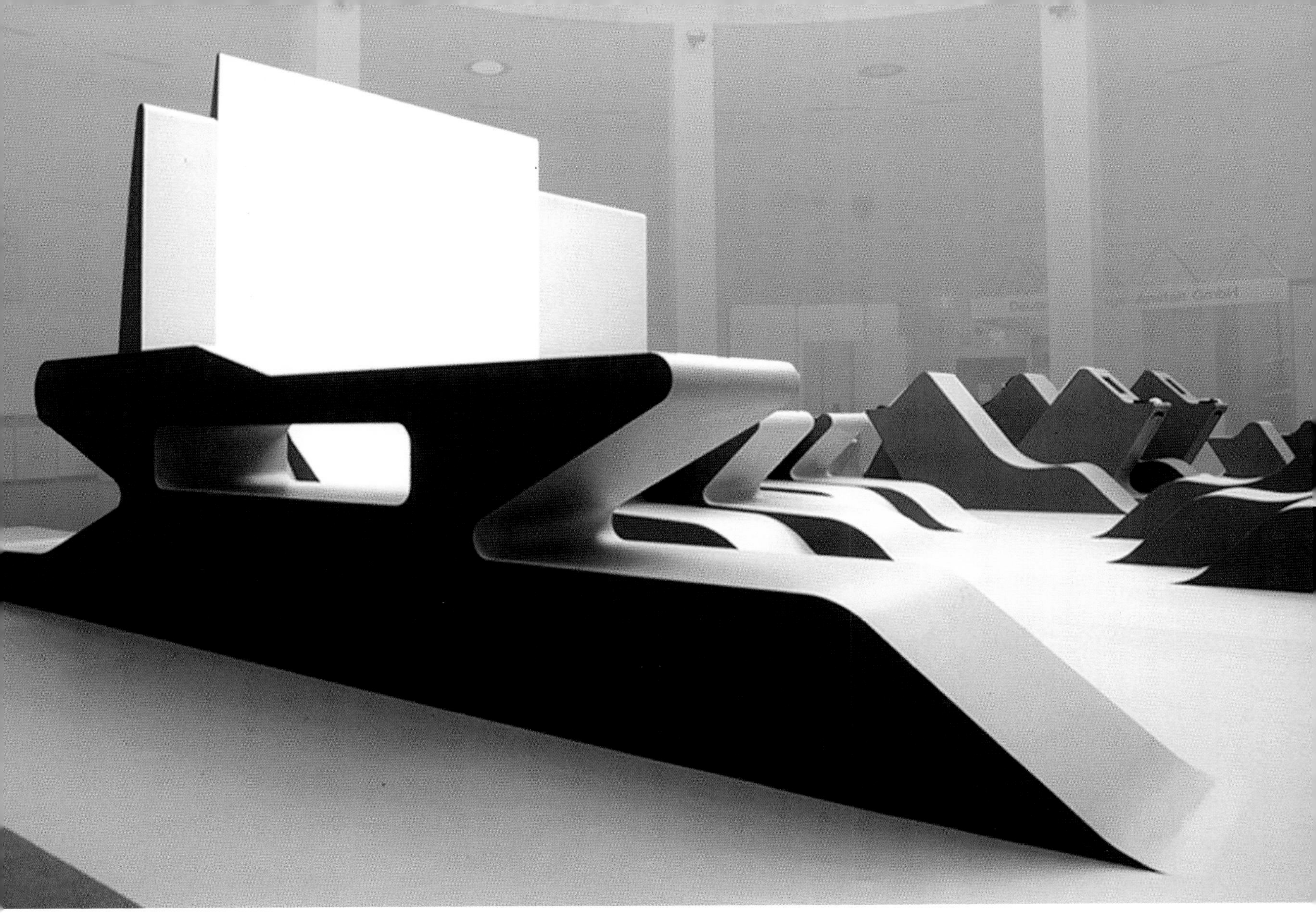

BUTTON.BUDS

CLIENT: MERTEN GMBH & CO. KG, WIEHL, GERMANY

PROJECT DATE: 2005

J. MAYER H.
PROJECT TEAM: JÜRGEN MAYER H., JAN-CHRISTOPH STOCKEBRAND

Button.Buds is a switch-and-technical-communication unit that constantly grows and modifies its form, shape, location, and function. Button.Buds relate more to the human body of their user than to the architecture from which they stem. Their sensory effects and haptic qualities attract interaction. On an index scale with endless possible programmatic and formal mutations, Button. Buds demonstrate differentiation in the articulation of a body-technology interface within a family of objects.

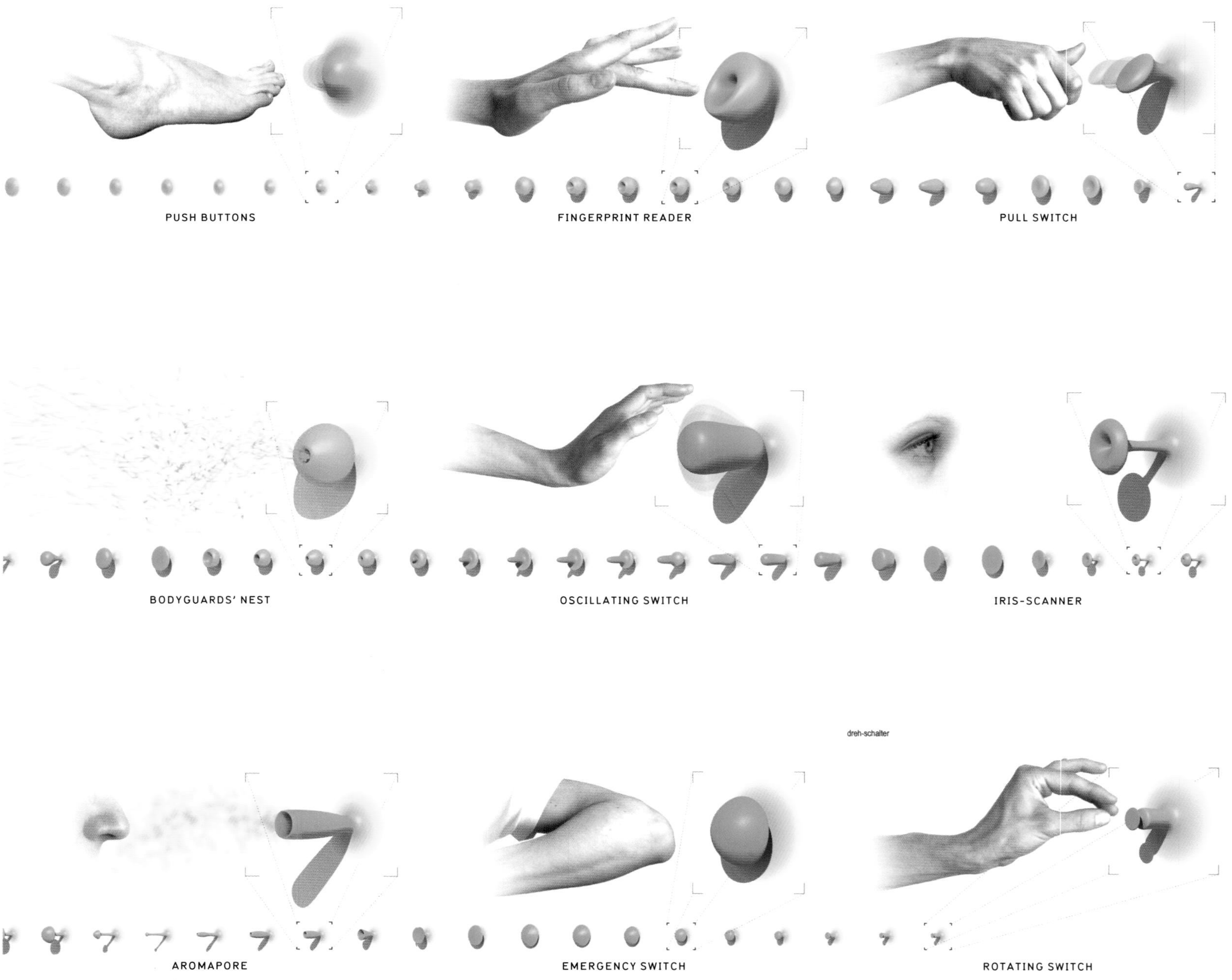

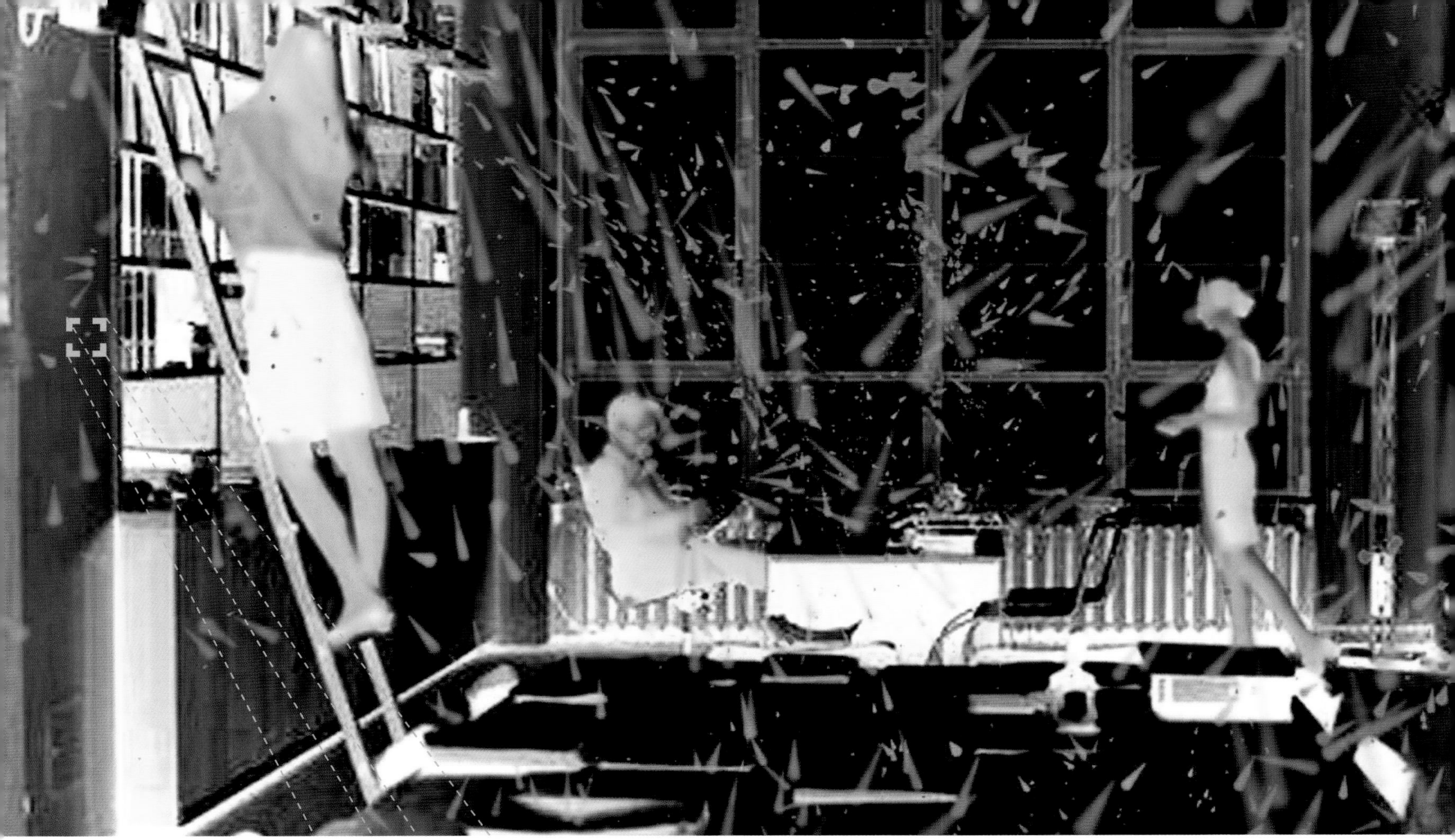
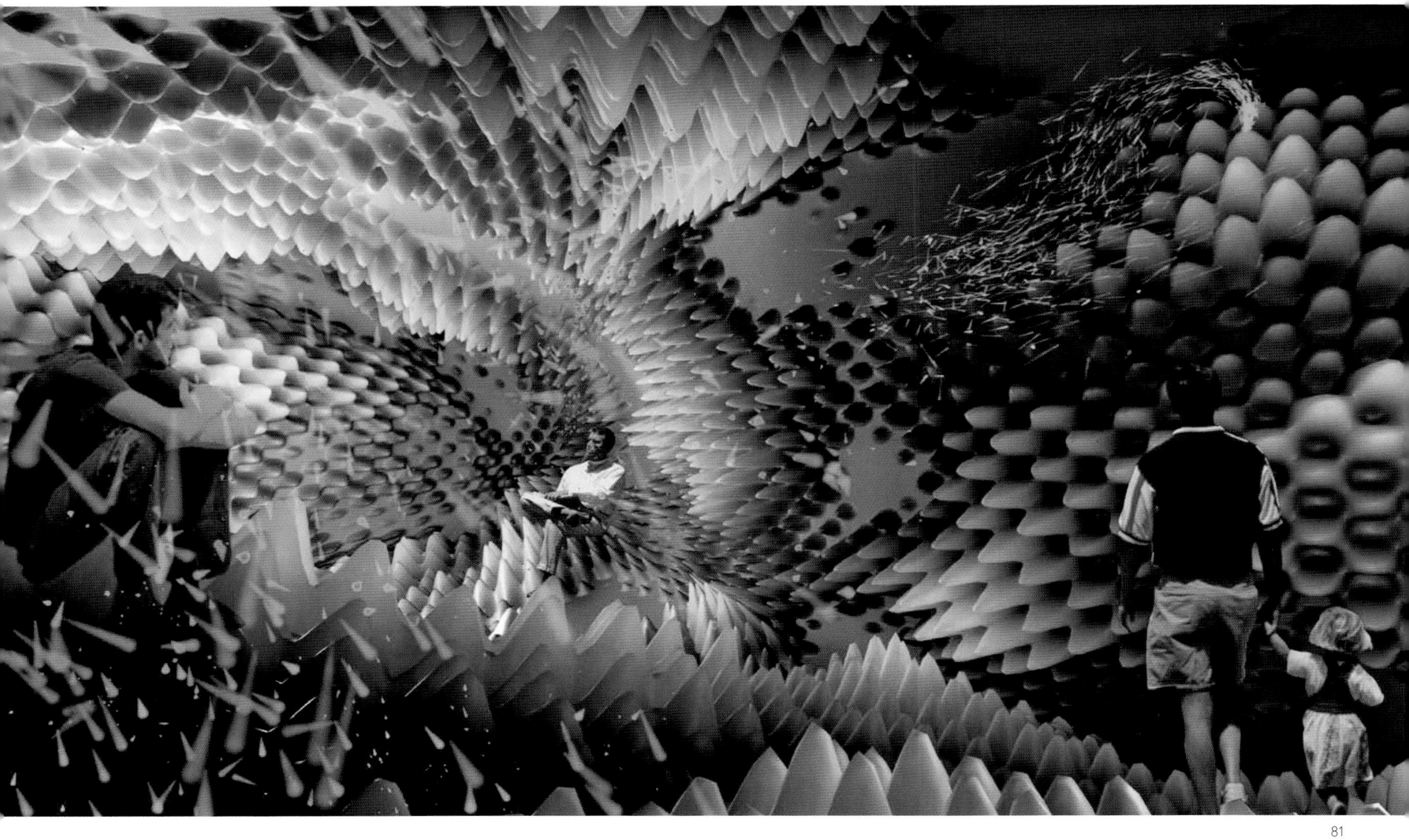

SOFT MOSAIC

GLASS MOSAIC ON POLYURETHANE FOAM

CLIENT: BISAZZA S.P.A, ITALY

PROJECT DATE: 2003–08

J. MAYER H.
PROJECT TEAM: JÜRGEN MAYER H., HEIKE PREHLER, WILKO HOFFMANN, SIMON TAKASAKI

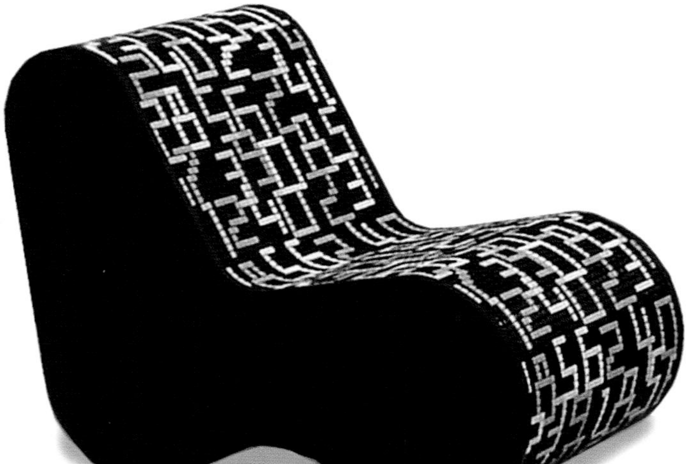

PRE.TEXT / VOR.WAND NEW MUSEUM

DATAPROTECTION PATTERN IN SHINGLE STYLE
NEW MUSEUM, NEW YORK, US

PROJECT DATE: JANUARY–APRIL 2003

J. MAYER H.

COURTESY MAGNUS MÜLLER GALLERY, BERLIN, GERMANY

Various lines of demarcation, or even better "façades of countenance," have always separated the personal and the public. And in the case of information, the relationship between public and private becomes a complicated set of liabilities. It is a contract of confidentiality. By the beginning of the twentieth century, information control had generated a visual pattern called "Data Protection Pattern," or DPP, that helped to veil personal information in print media. Ingredients of information-construction, such as letters and numbers, were used in excess in order to create a speechless form of covering text—almost a textual "slurry."

The very patterns used to obscure private information have concealed their own technological development. Only a few traces remain to provoke my speculation about their origins. When producing a book, repeated test prints are made on the same sheets, during which process text over text is formed—and the repeated use of carbon paper can create a pattern that may also be considered a predecessor to the data-protection pattern.

Until now, the oldest known example of the DPP technique appears to be the Berlin printing company Berthold, which offered lead plates to be used as data-protection patterns in their catalogue from 1913. Through the invention and usage of carbon paper, written information could be stored simultaneously as an original and as copies on various stacked and covered layers. The technical processes of multiple copy-forms required a procedure of printing on the cover page in order to black out certain areas that were used to convey information. Superficially, an excess of text transforms this "private information" through a mad storm of numbers and letters into a state of apparent nonexistence. However, by this very process the private is established. Data-protection patterns guarantee the indecipherability of the information until it reaches the intended receiver.

Today, a new global network of unsecured data transfer remains to be resolved. While DPP continues to proliferate in print media it also provides the model for carriers of electronic information, which are physically erased by overwriting the entire data carrier—or at least its used sections—with a confusion of pattern-making.

The sheer, infinite spectrum of specific data-protection patterns—ranging from letters, numbers, and logos to organic, camouflage, and ornamental graphics—can be read as an Ursuppe, a "primordial soup," for our times, preceding meaning and yet constituting a strategic field from which to generate an ambivalent space, to thicken the "skin" of discretion, and to inhabit the flatness of exposure.

ROTVERSTECK

DATAPROTECTION PATTERN AND RED FILM
MÜLLERDECHIARA GALLERY, BERLIN, GERMANY

PROJECT DATE: MAY–JUNE 2002

J. MAYER H.

COURTESY MAGNUS MÜLLER GALLERY, BERLIN

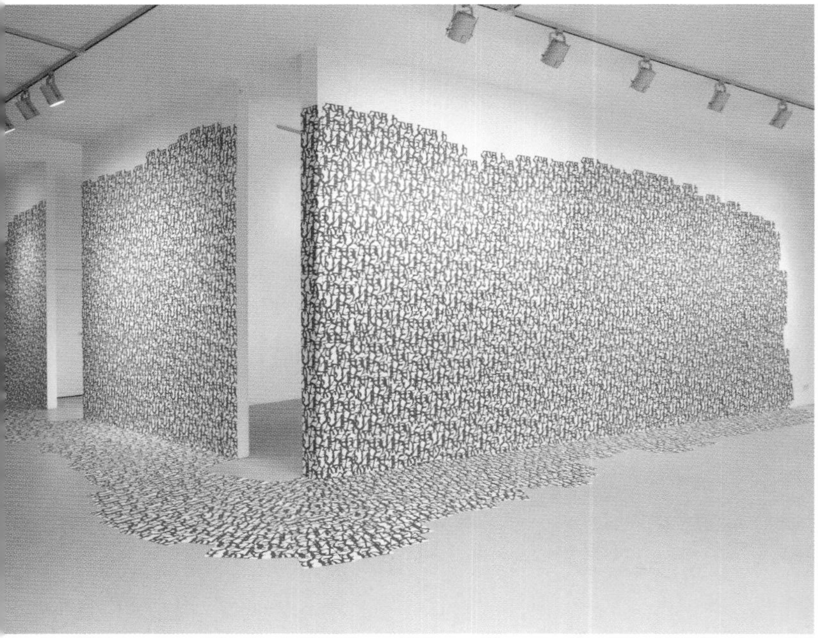

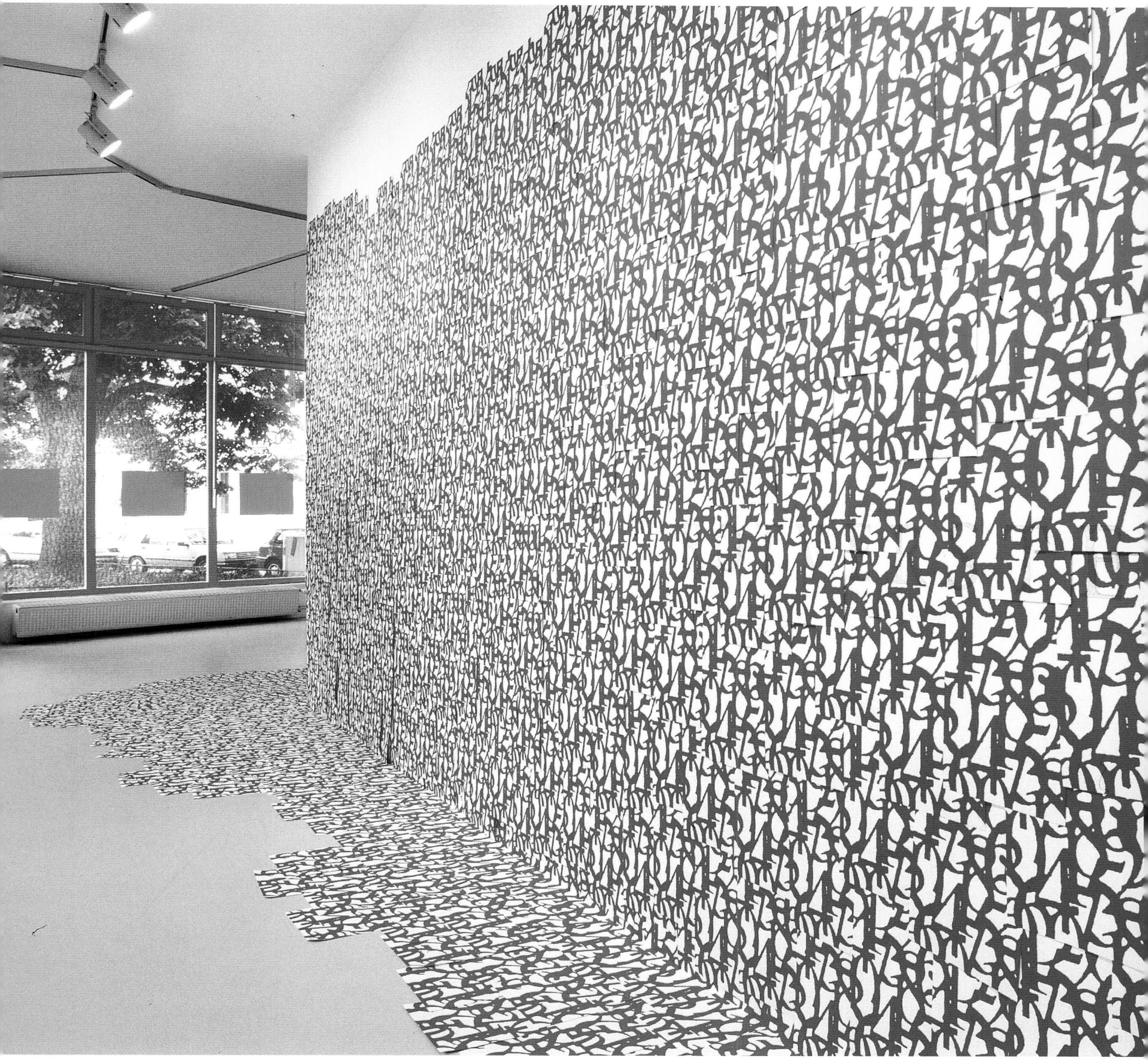

PRE.TEXT / VOR.WAND SFMOMA

DATAPROTECTION PATTERN FLOCK PRINT
GLAMOUR, GROUP SHOW
SFMOMA, SAN FRANCISCO, US

PROJECT DATE: 2004

J. MAYER H.

COURTESY MAGNUS MÜLLER GALLERY, BERLIN, GERMANY

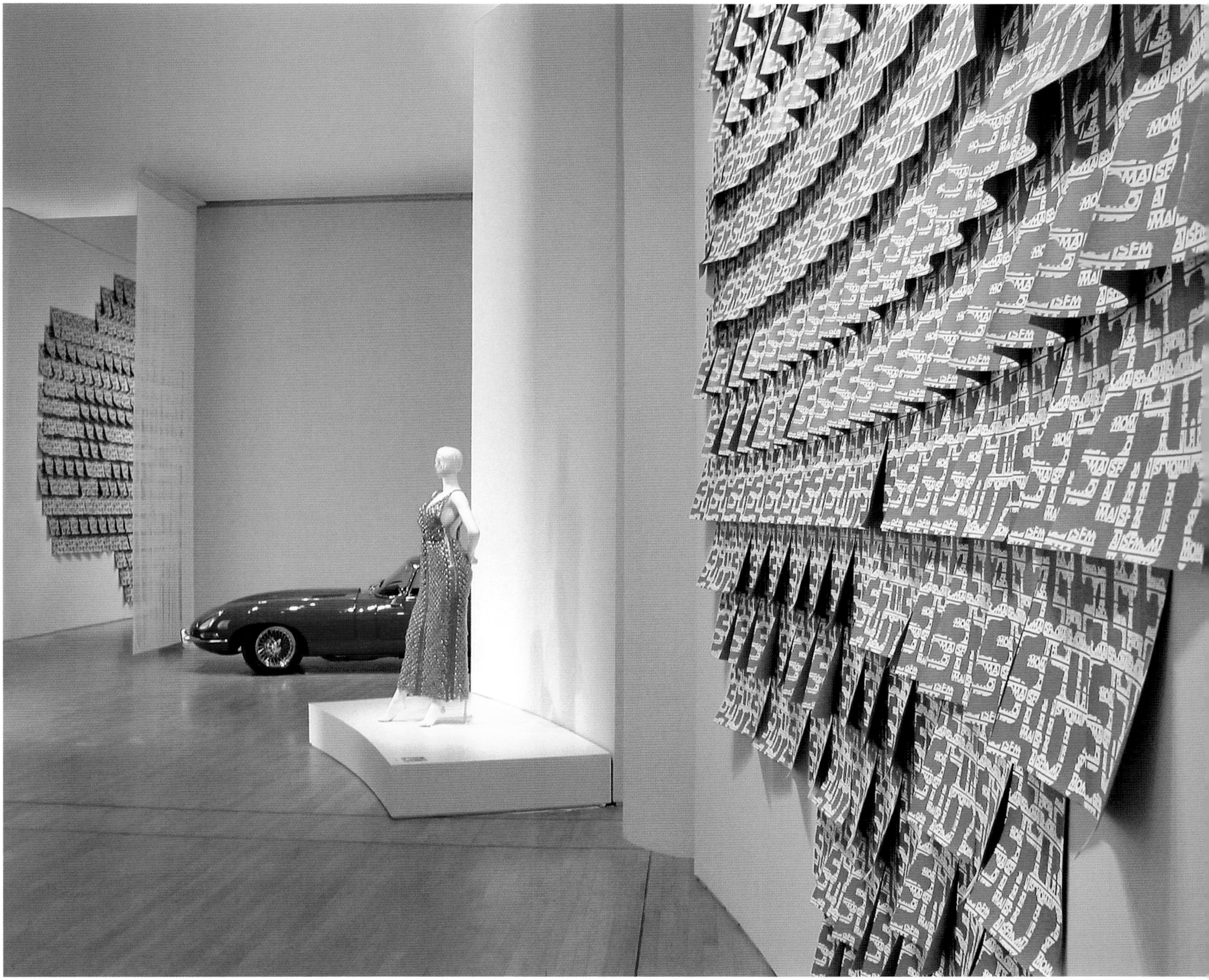

LIE

BED SHEETS, TEMPERATURE-SENSITIVE
DATA-PROTECTION PATTERN ON COTTON
HENRY URBACH ARCHITECTURE GALLERY, NEW YORK, US

PROJECT DATE: 2006

J. MAYER H.

COURTESY MAGNUS MÜLLER GALLERY, BERLIN, GERMANY

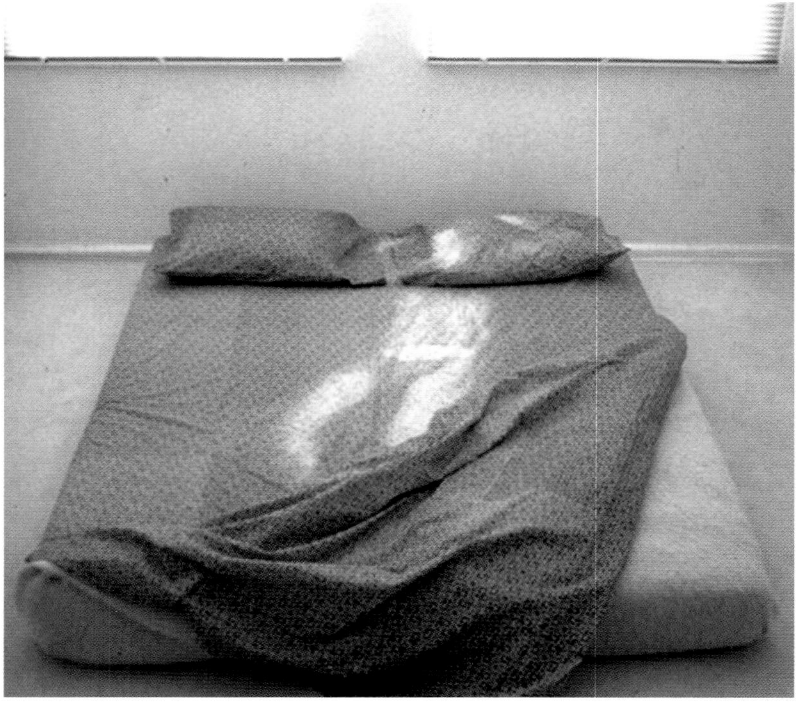

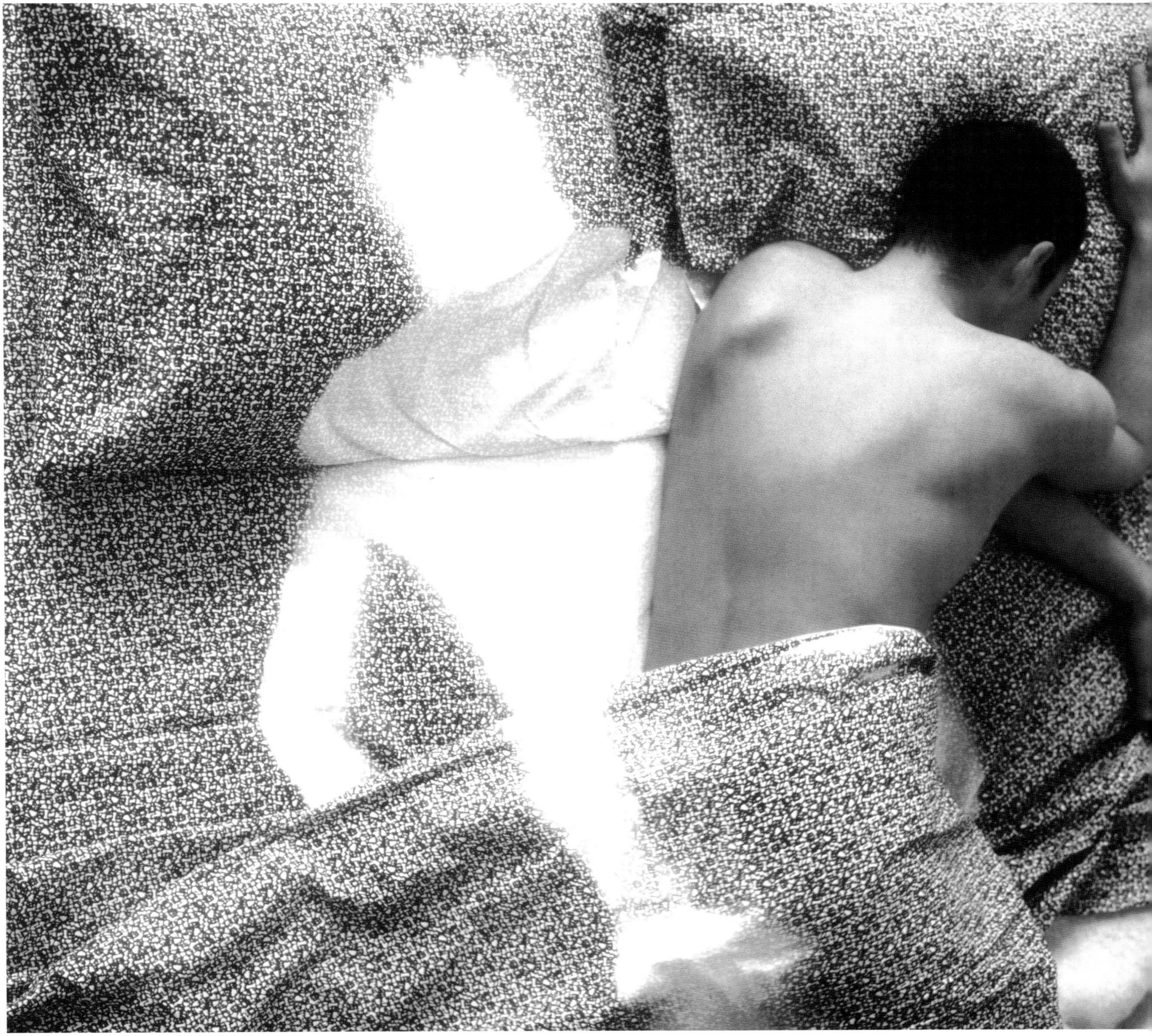

DATOO

TATTOO PARLOR CURATED BY TOBIAS WONG, JOSÉE LEPAGE, AND ARIC CHEN
LOCATION: MIAMI DESIGN, FLORIDA, US

TATTOOED ON JEFFREY NEWBURGER

PROJECT DATE: 2007

J. MAYER H.
PROJECT TEAM: JÜRGEN MAYER H., WILKO HOFFMANN

FADING FUTURE: JÜRGEN MAYER H. AND THE SEVENTIES

PHILIP URSPRUNG

One evening in the early seventies—I was about ten years old—my father brought home a copy of the book *The Limits to Growth*. The book had a tremendous impact— particularly in the German-speaking countries, where it helped to trigger the environmentalist movement. My father told us gravely about the radical changes that were occurring throughout the world. Our entire planet was endangered, humanity was consuming too much energy, the population was growing too quickly, and supplies of natural resources were coming to an end. The Earth, we learned, was not an inexhaustible source of raw materials but a closed system that was fragile and vulnerable, and the consequences of this were already visible. Oil prices skyrocketed, wages plunged, many lost their jobs, and the economy developed into an unfortunate mixture of inflation and stagnation, so-called "stagflation." In fall 1973, Germany and Switzerland (the country to which my family had moved from the United States) forbade the use of cars on Sundays. People went for walks on the empty highways. I liked it, but my parents were as worried as they were when they talked about the Watergate hearings, the war in Vietnam, and the threat of an economic recession.

Obviously, something had changed. The optimism of my parents' generation had turned into a fear of things to come. Instead of new frontiers to be conquered, an abyss opened under our feet. Steven Spielberg's dark thriller *Jaws* (1975) was the most successful motion picture of the decade. In the world of popular music, the outward-looking spirit of Woodstock was replaced by a retreat into the disco. As energy became more expensive, factories closed and unemployment rose; the walls of private homes became thicker, the windows smaller, the furniture heavier; clothing became longer, and even the hair of both men and women seemed to grow longer and thicker. In the family albums and on the streets, the brilliant Ektachrome blues and reds of the sixties faded away and earthy colors such as orange, brown, beige, and green appeared. Space seemed to shrink—air travel became affordable for the middle classes in the West, labor markets opened up and forced many to leave their countries. On the other hand, time seemed to expand and run more slowly—some had more free time, but most were threatened by unemployment and had little hope for change.

The Limits to Growth opens with a quote by U Thant, the former Secretary General of the United Nations, who said that the problems had to be addressed "within the next decade" or else they would be "beyond our capacity to control."[1] The authors of the book foresaw that the limits to growth would be reached "sometime within the next one hundred years,"[2] and the United Nations conferences on the protection of the environment held since the so-called "earth summit" in Rio de Janeiro, in 1992, each set a new time horizon. While earlier, modernist utopias had promised a better life in the future to compensate for the misery of the present, we were told that *our* future would *not* be better. My generation grew up with the paradoxical feeling that time and space were taken away from us, that it was not *our own* time, and not *our own* space which we could shape, define, and experience, but that everything depended on the temporal and spatial regime of our parents' generation—as if we were the leftover of an earlier project, so to speak, without its own potential. Most people misunderstood the Punk slogan "No future," coined by the Sex Pistols

1 Donella Meadows, Dennis Meadows, Jorgen Randers, William W. Beherens III, **The Limits to Growth, A Report for the Club of Rome's Project on the Predicament of Mankind** (New York, 1972), p. 17.

2 Ibid., p. 23.

in 1977, as a nihilistic statement. Rather, it was a protest precisely against the time regime that excluded a whole generation from its temporality. In fact, up to the present day, "youth culture" is dominated by the culture of the sixties—the Rolling Stones are still on tour, and "contemporary art" is firmly based on the artistic canon of that decade.

Who was to blame? In the propaganda of the seventies the scapegoat was Nature. The perceived problems were "naturalized." Scarcity was explained as a function of the mysterious "oil crisis," namely the idea that oil reserves were ending, and not as an effect of the political and economic strategy for accumulating profits. Unemployment was presented as if it were due to "overpopulation" and "unbalanced" growth, not as the result of automation and deregulation. We were made to believe that there were simply not enough resources, not enough space, and not enough time left for us to continue life as before. And we were even made to feel guilty ourselves. It was not easy to understand the irony of Sheikh Zaki Yamani, the oil minister of Saudi Arabia from the 1960s to the 1980s, who is said to have stated: "The Stone Age did not end for lack of stone, and the Oil Age will end long before the world runs out of oil."[3] We internalized the narrative of the natural reasons for scarcity, although we sensed that progress now meant regression; that the computers in the factories and offices did not make workers' lives easier, but rather made them obsolete; that the surveillance cameras did not protect us from what we feared, but actually produced fear; that the shipping containers and the just-in-time production not only saved us time and space, but also absorbed them and made time and space discontinuous. Much ink flowed on the question of the relationship between time and space—from Henri Lefebvre's concept of the "substance," Jean-François Lyotard's idea of topology and the Möbius curve, Gilles Deleuze's and Félix Guattari's concepts of "folds," to Fredric Jameson's idea of "depthlessness." However, it took a long while before we became aware that we were in the midst of a struggle about the control of time and space. Hence, there is only now an emerging critique against the effects of globalization; and hence, there is the longing for "presence," "identity," and "orientation."

Jürgen Mayer H. has been addressing these issues since the late nineties. His affinity with the design ethos of the seventies is obvious, and he makes it very clear that he intends to build on this "unfinished project."[4] However, what makes his work unique is that he neither simply mimics the formal vocabulary of the past—the colors, patterns, shapes, surfaces, and materials that might currently be *en vogue*—nor radically condemns the authoritative structure related to it. Rather, Jürgen Mayer H. expresses the ambivalence and internal contradiction of this phase, makes clear how we are part of it—even somehow responsible for it—and articulates both its beautiful and its uncanny dimensions. His interest, I would argue, lies precisely in the complex relationship between the human subject and its spatial and temporal environment. If we are constantly controlled by cameras why not play with them and turn them into an entertainment device, like the installation Wind.Light that J. MAYER H. produced in front of his Stadthaus Scharnhauser Park building in Ostfildern? Here, glass-fiber cables, hanging from poles, project points of light onto the ground—and J. MAYER H. had initially planned that built-in webcams would send images of these changing patterns into the Stadthaus (town hall) and onto the City of Ostfildern's website. If we are still haunted by the modernist ideology of "transparency," why not strike back with transparency's own emblem? In the hands of J. MAYER H., transparent glass sheets are not means to make phenomena clearer, or democratic, but devices of separation and control. He turns them into observation machines, as in his Stadthaus Scharnhauser Park or in the office complex AdA1 in Hamburg. If the protection of written data is assured with special patterns—the very opposite of transparency—why not appropriate these as ornaments that both hide and reveal? If the public and the private spheres blur, why not produce furniture for the city like that in his Kerykes Activity Tool for Athens or in the Metropol Parasol project for Seville?

The beautiful and the abysmal are inseparably linked in the work of J. MAYER H. The Heat.Seats, which temporarily conserve the traces of its users is both a playful device and a *memento mori*, reminding us of the fragility of our bodies and our surroundings. As I sat on a prototype of Pixy.Pieces, elastic glass-mosaic furniture the tactile experience was both softer and harder than expected. And I could not help but perceive the tesserae as pixels, as if I had tried to penetrate the screen of a television set. The furniture, which would not adapt to my body, had an interface that was comparable to a television screen: a membrane, both repugnant and attractive, that simultaneously links us to and separates us from the world; that both makes us see and makes us blind, entertains and bores, isolates us passively in our private homes and lets us participate actively in the public sphere. Similarly, J. MAYER H.'s Mensa Moltke in Karlsruhe is certainly one of the most elegant and thrilling buildings to be seen on a campus in the last few years, yet its wax-like, yellowish surface has an uncanny effect. Does it recall the repressed memory of the green-yellow oil paint that was traditionally used in schoolhouses and factories alike because it is easily washable? In other words, does it remind us not only of the shiny surface of boutiques and lounges but also of the fact that a university canteen, in the end, is nothing more than a functional place where students and faculty

3 For an excellent study of the "oil crisis", see Midnight Notes Collective, **Midnight Oil, Work, Energy, War 1973–1992** (Brooklyn, New York, 1992).

4 "Seventies architectural language is not really revived yet. There is still something left behind, not tested. There is still a potential that I want to explore, take on and rethink for the future." Jürgen Mayer H., "In Anticipation, Jürgen Mayer H. in discussion with Bostjan Vuga," in **Activators, J. Mayer H.,** Design Document Series, 19, (Seoul, 2006) pp. 12–23, here: p. 19.

can eat cheaply? Or, if one were to adopt the crude language of Marxism, that the canteen is a place where the worker can feed, and thus reproduce himself or herself as labor power?

If we are indeed trapped, as many theoreticians tell us we are, in the temporal regime of an eternal present, where the past shrinks and the future is condensed, where prognosis is impossible and history suspended, then at least there is the advantage that we can move about freely and return to earlier phases without becoming nostalgic or reactionary. If *déjà-vu,* the loop, and the Möbius strip are emblematic of our perception of time, then the past is also open for reconsideration and change. J. MAYER H.'s retroactive projects allow us to travel back in time in order to correct the mistakes of our forebears, reconsider the past, experience pleasurable moments of presence, and shape our own future.

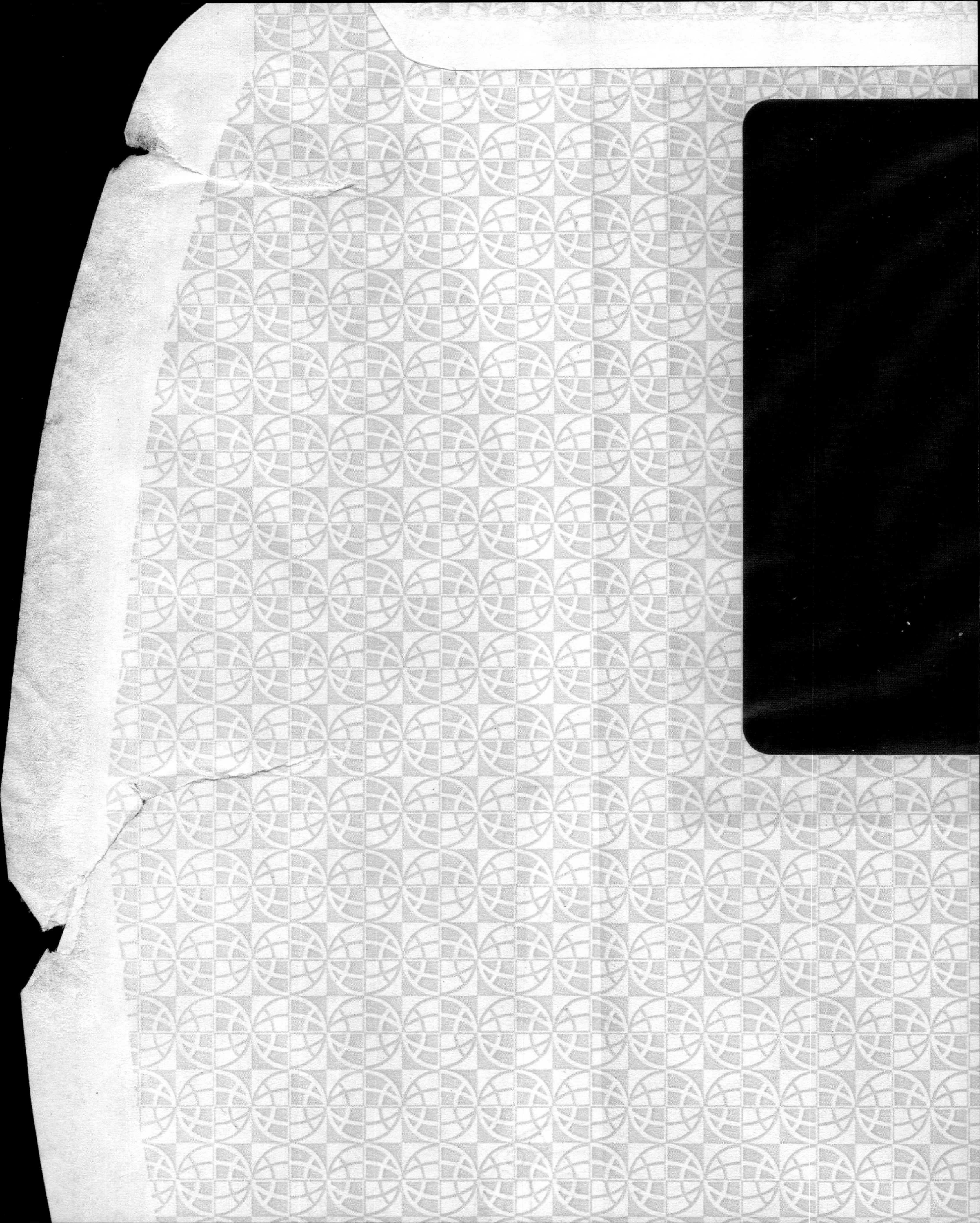

E.GRAM

PROJECT DATE: 2000

J. MAYER H. WITH SEBASTIAN FINCKH

PERMANENT COLLECTION OF THE MUSEUM OF MODERN ART, NEW YORK
VENICE BIENNALE 2004, ARSENALE AND GERMAN PAVILION

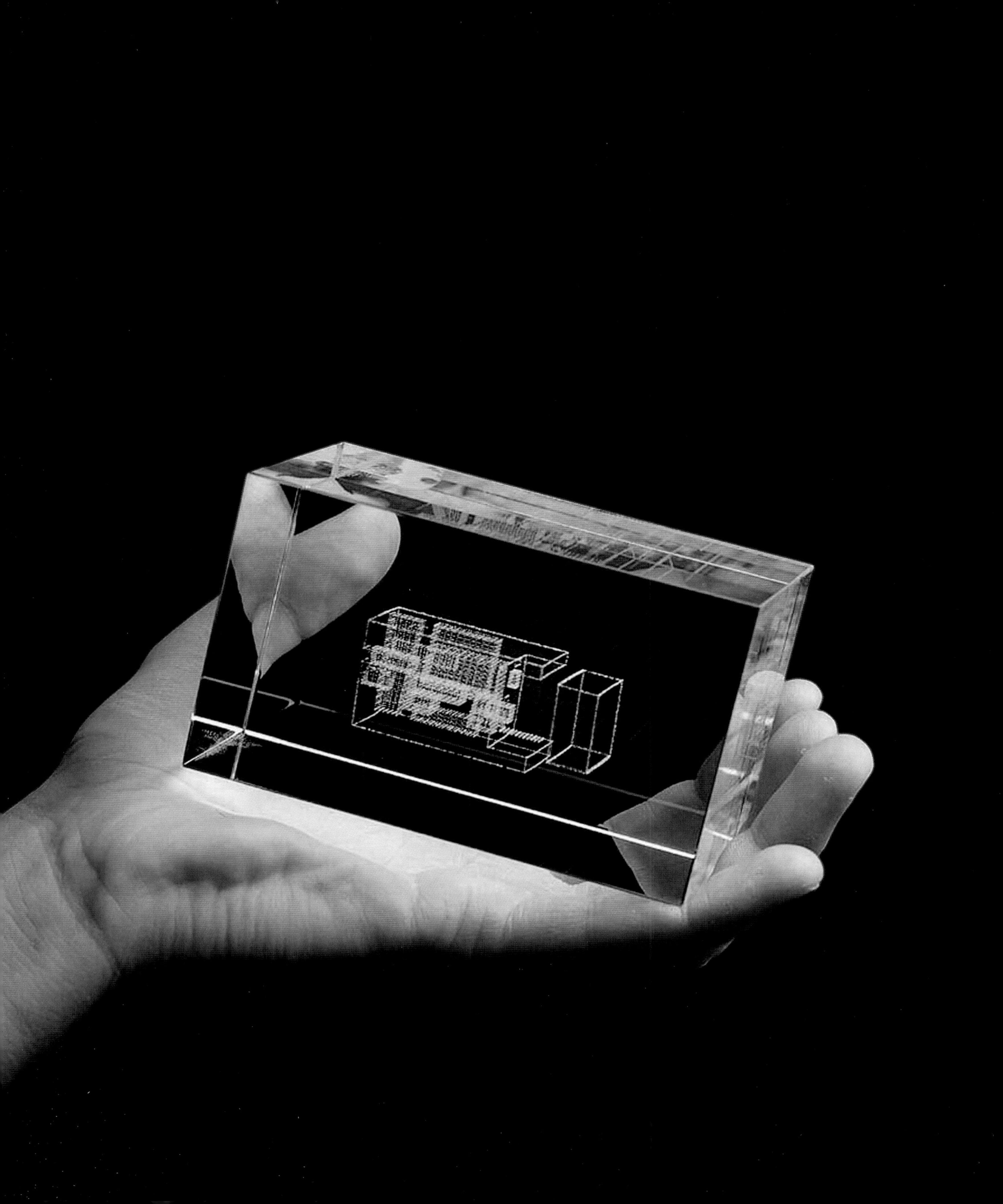

STADTHAUS SCHARNHAUSER PARK

MIXED-USE CIVIC CENTER, OSTFILDERN, GERMANY

CLIENT: CITY OF OSTFILDERN

INTERNATIONAL COMPETITION: 1998, 1ST PRIZE
PROJECT DATE: 1998–2001

J. MAYER H.
PROJEKT TEAM: JÜRGEN MAYER H., ANDRE SANTER, SEBASTIAN FINCKH, ANDREAS BERZBORN, MARKUS BONAUER, STEFAN DAMBACHER, ROBERT FRENZEL, MARTIN KÜHFUSS, KATE LEMMEN, PETER MARTIN, MARCELLO MAZZEI, SASCHA NIKOLAUSCHKE, JULIA OLSSON, DIRK REINISCH, GABRIELE ROY, GUNDA SCHULZ, JÖRG STOLLMANN, GEORG VRACHLIOTIS, HANS WEIBEL, PHILIP WELTER, SONJA WIESE, CHRISTOPH ZELLER

ARCHITECT ON SITE: ULRICH WIESLER, STUTTGART
STRUCTURAL ENGINEERS: MÜLLER + MÜLLER, OSTFILDERN
SERVICE ENGINEERS: WETZSTEIN, HERRENBERG
BUILDING PHYSICS: DR. SCHAECKE UND BAYER, WAIBLINGEN
LANDSCAPE ARCHITECT: KLAUS WIEDERKEHR, NÜRTINGEN
LIGHTING ENGINEERS: LUNA LICHTARCHITEKTUR, KARLSRUHE

The Town Hall, located at the center of the urban development zone of Scharnhauser Park, is a public building designed to accommodate multiple functions. In addition to administrative spaces and a magistrate's office, an international competition in 1998 also called for classrooms for a music school and a night school, and for exhibition spaces. This diversity of functions has been bundled into a "box" with a dramatically overhanging roof—a structure whose initial appearance is one of simplicity. A second glance, however, reveals that this functional container has been slanted backwards by a few degrees—just enough to generate a mild sense of unease, and to endow its seemingly orthogonal volume with an aesthetic tension. The color scheme of the external cladding—with its stepwise progression from a pale strip below to a dark one above—runs counter to expectations, thereby heightening an effect of defamiliarization. The ribbon windows run around the building like stripes, yet without exposing the structure's internal subdivisions.

3RD FLOOR

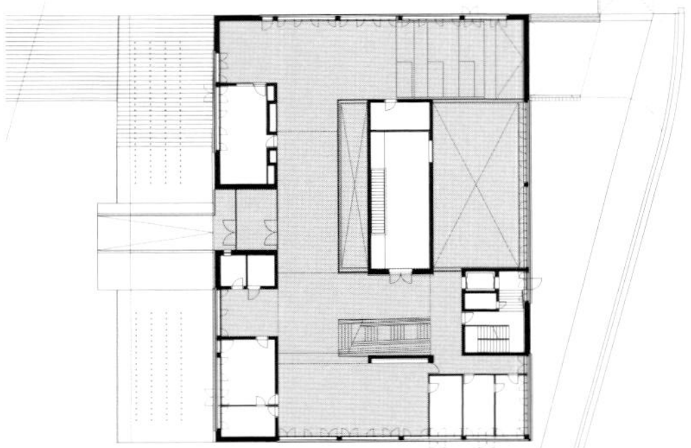

GROUND FLOOR

The building's articulation is guided by the volumes housing its various functions, which are set like individual boxes within the plan. The intermediate zones lying between them serve as areas for public circulation, but are far more spacious than those usually encountered in such buildings. The structure's gentle slant is also perceptible on the large staircase—although here the incline is set spatially into the transverse axis, rendering it hardly noticeable at first glance. The main stairs can be seen as an internal connector for the openings formed by incisions in the spatial shell. These acquire a certain tension in conjunction with the inclinations of the surrounding vertical walls. All the other conventional elements of a functional public building, such as symmetry and long unobstructed corridors, which serve to provide orientation and transparency are redefined here and displaced to produce relationships of tension. They thereby emblematize the possibility of radically novel approaches to designing such buildings. With its computer-programmed rain curtain (Pitter.Patterns) and Wind.Lights, the exterior of the Town Hall also represents a new approach to the insertion of public buildings into public space. —Andres Lepik

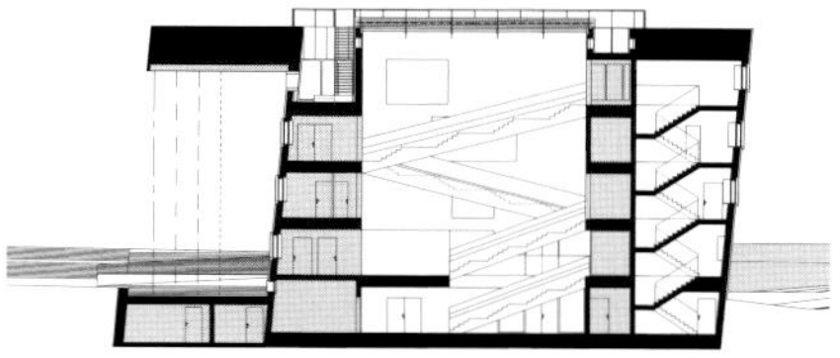

SECTION

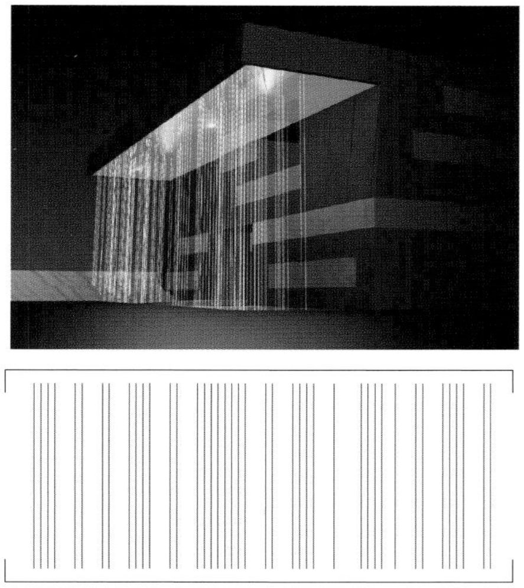

RAIN CODE

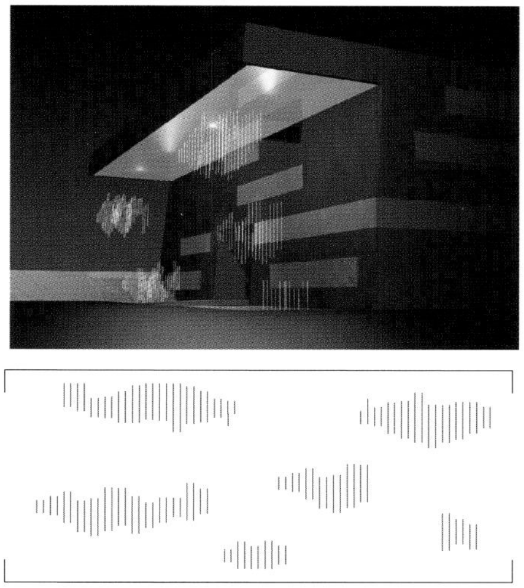

FALLING CLOUDS

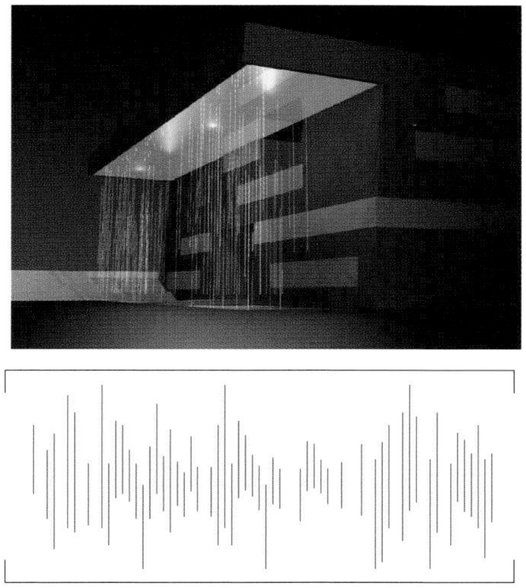

FREQUENCY SHOWER

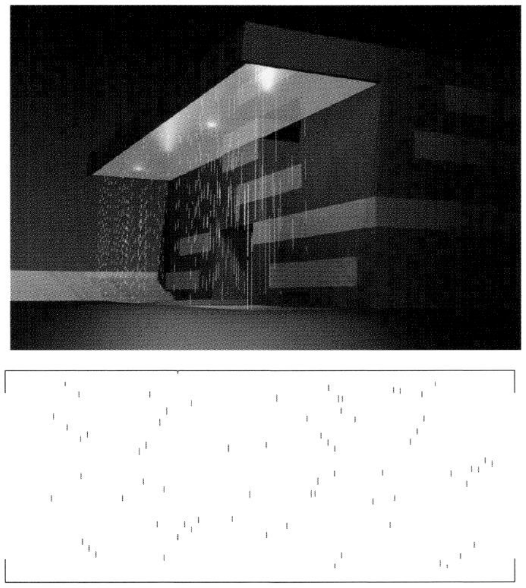

PIXEL POUR

RAIN BEAMS

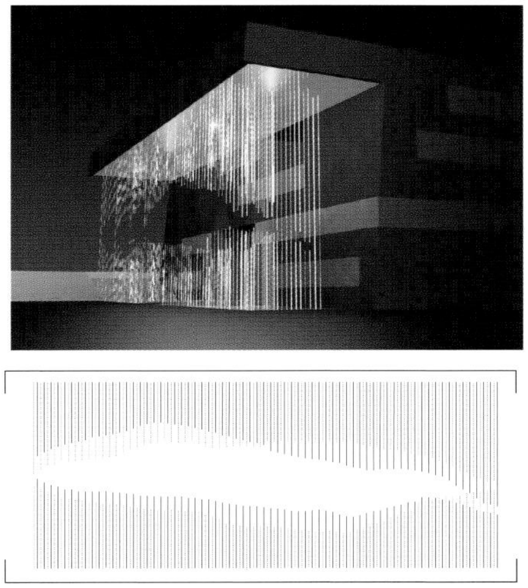

RAIN CAVE

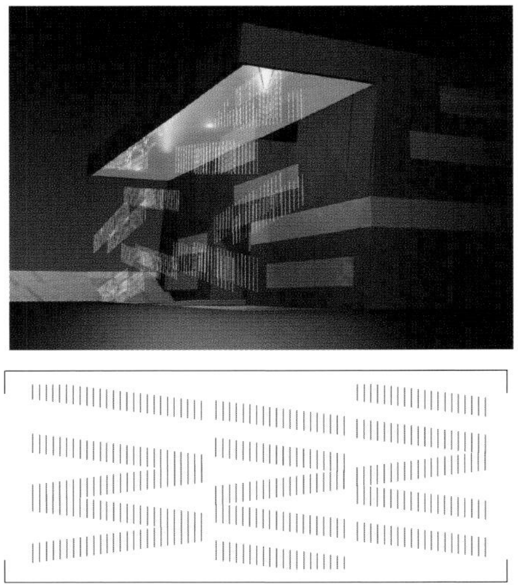

ZIG ZAG

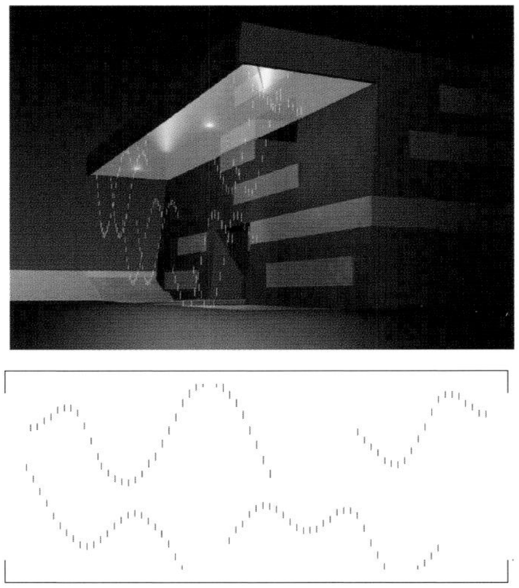

SINUS DROPS

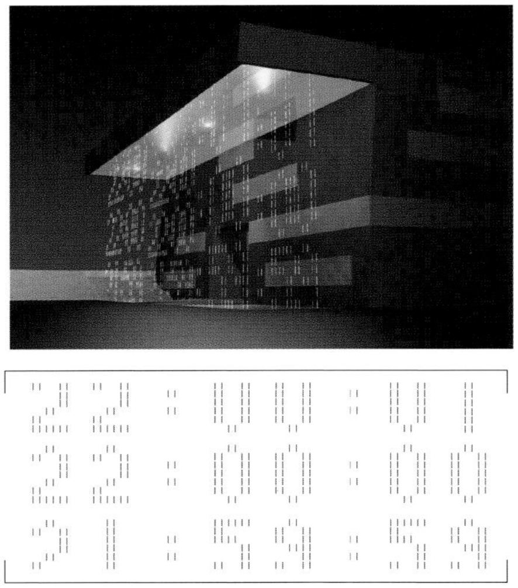

TIME DROPS

SERVICE
BÜRGERSERVIC

HEAT.SEAT

TEMPERATURE-SENSITIVE FURNITURE
ARCHILAB, ORLÉANS, FRANCE

PROJECT DATE: 2001

J. MAYER H.
PROJECT TEAM: JÜRGEN MAYER H., MARCUS BONAUER, HANS WEIBEL

PERMANENT COLLECTION OF SFMOMA, SAN FRANCISCO, US
COURTESY MAGNUS MÜLLER GALLERY, BERLIN, GERMANY

FACE

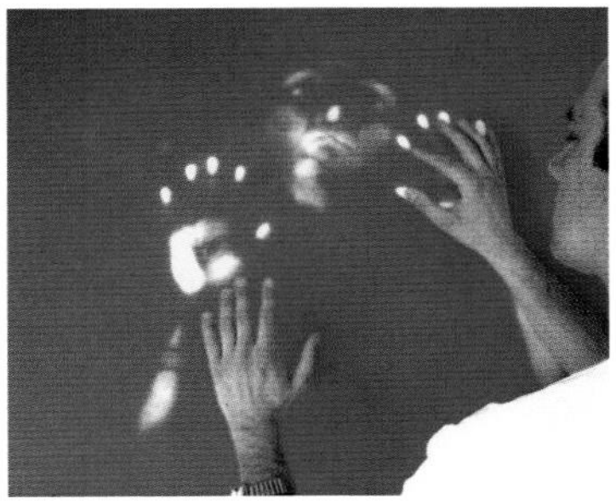

POLAROIDS OF FACE PRINTS ON TEMPERATURE-SENSITIVE SURFACES

PROJECT DATE: MARCH–APRIL 1998

J.MAYER H.

COURTESY MAGNUS MÜLLER GALLERY, BERLIN, GERMANY

The upholstered canvas of Face is painted with a heat-sensitive red color. By pressing one's face into the cushion, the participant leaves behind a thermo-print on the surface. Although the portrait on the cushion fades as it cools, a Polaroid photograph conserves the impression.

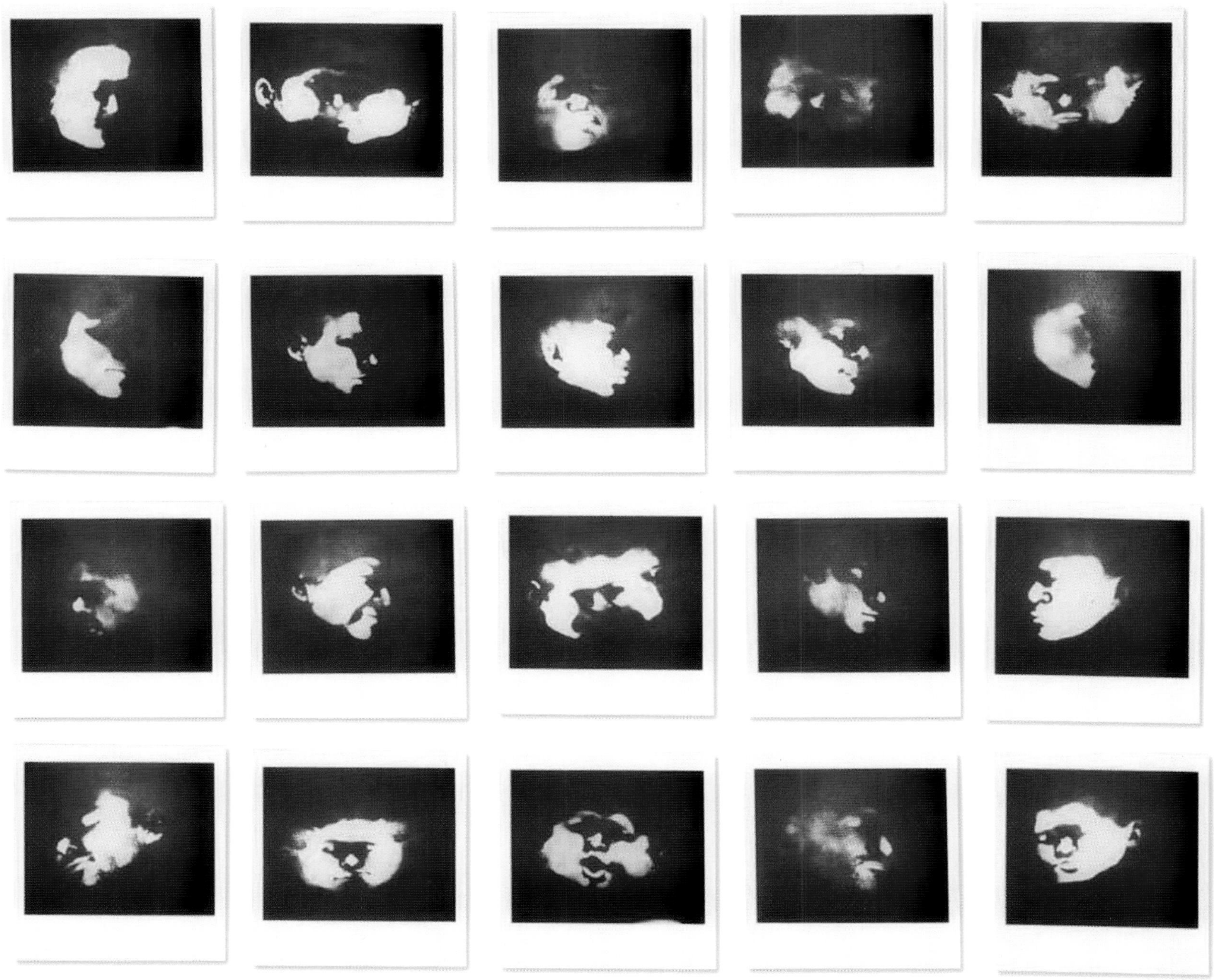

HOUSEWARMING II

PROJECT DATE: 1995

J. MAYER H.

COURTESY MAGNUS MÜLLER GALLERY, BERLIN, GERMANY

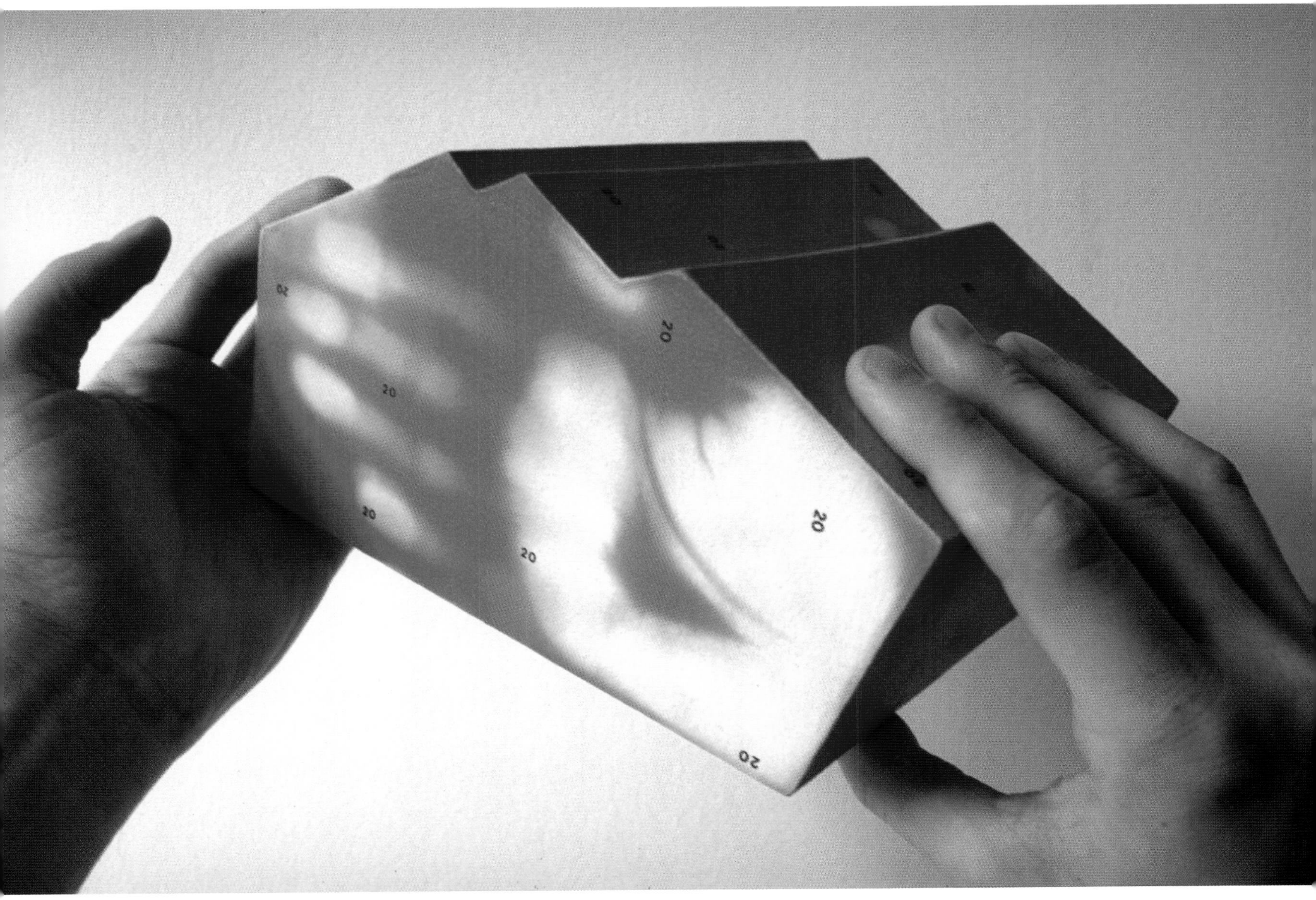
20
20
20
20
20
20

HOUSEWARMING MYHOME

VITRA DESIGN MUSEUM, WEIL AM RHEIN

PROJECT DATE: JUNE–SEPTEMBER, 2007

J. MAYER H.
PROJECT TEAM: JÜRGEN MAYER H., JONATHAN BUSSE, MARCUS BLUM

COURTESY MAGNUS MÜLLER GALLERY, BERLIN, GERMANY

Housewarming MyHome is part of a larger group show at the Vitra Design Museum. The exhibition focuses on contemporary questions concerning the affects of living with and amongst a collection of various installation works. Housewarming MyHome extends the Museum Café into the exhibition area with a large supergraphic displayed on the floor, walls, and ceiling, thus blurring their spatial boundaries. Referencing the architectural language of Frank O. Gehry's deconstructivist buildings, Housewarming MyHome echoes and intensifies the interior space. Certain zones of the wall and seating surfaces are covered with a heat-sensitive coating which turns white upon being warmed. Built in hot wires are programmed to turn on and off, creating temporary ornamental clusters of parallel white lines, which unexpectedly appear and disappear in rhythm with their heating and cooling.

As visitors of the Museum and the Café make contact with the installation, they leave temporary traces, imprints of the temperature-landscape of their bodies. The temperature-sensitive surfaces become the interface of interactivities, coming both from external stimuli via touch and from internal stimuli via the built-in hot wires. As such, the architecture actively participates in relation to the human body.

WARM-UP TABLE

TEMPERATURE-SENSITIVE FURNITURE

PROJECT DATE: 2002

J. MAYER H.

COURTESY MAGNUS MÜLLER GALLERY, BERLIN, GERMANY

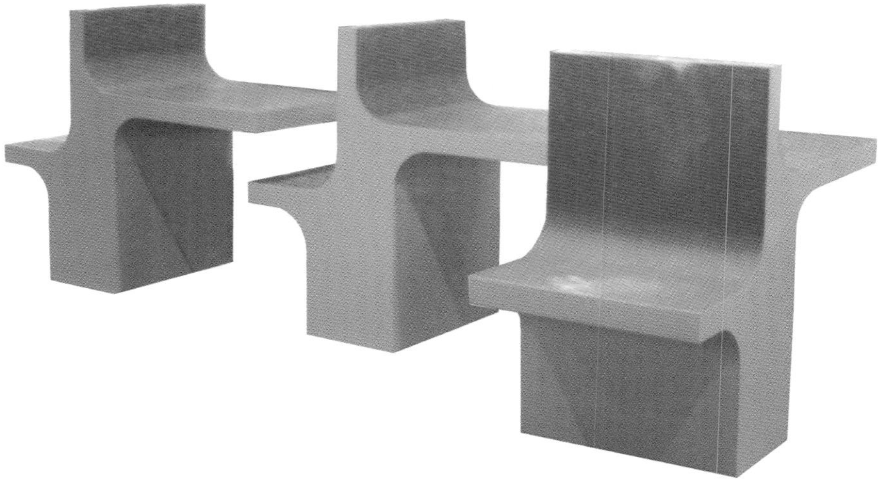

IN HEAT

HENRY URBACH ARCHITECTURE GALLERY, NEW YORK, U.S.

PROJECT DATE: APRIL–MAY 2005

J. MAYER H.

...stems from Friedrich Kieslers design for the 1947 Blood Flames exhibition at the Hugo Gallery, New York. His radical new concept proposed merging art, architecture, and the viewer into a continuation of painted walls and floors which hosts and interconnects the artwork. In Heat develops this fusion of art, viewer, and space in an even more radical way by introducing thermosensitive coatings as interactive paintings so that the viewer creates a temperature shadow by touching and melts into the overall exhibition design. Everything becomes flattened into an architectural surface with depth in time.

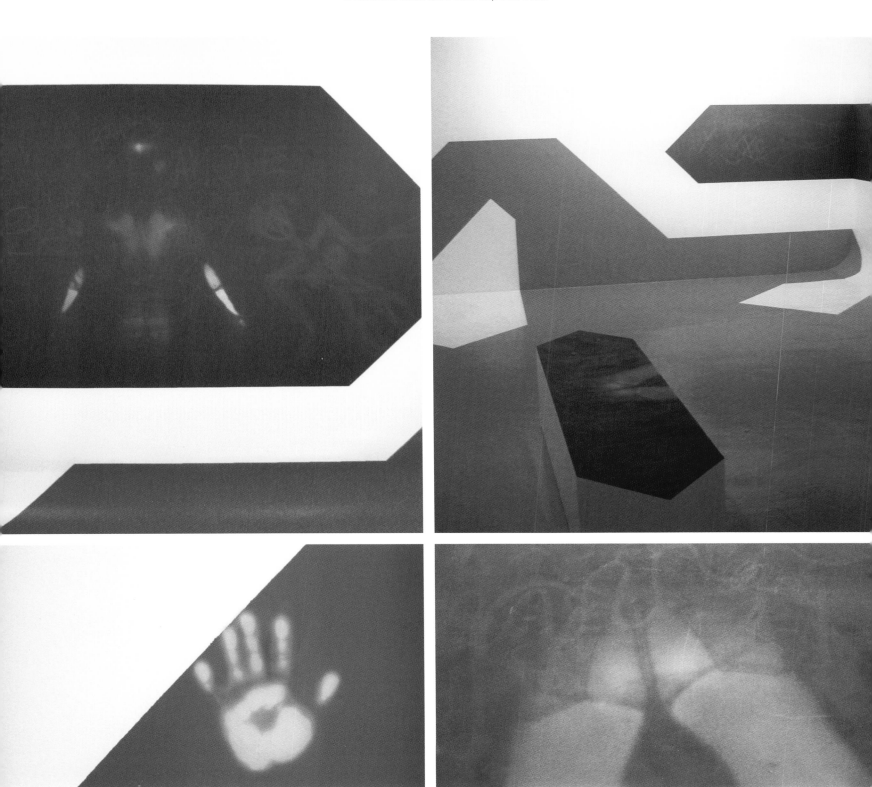

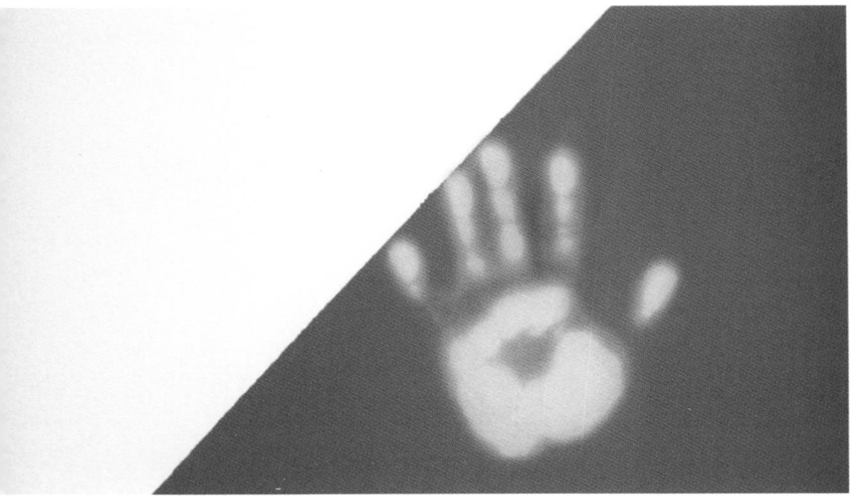

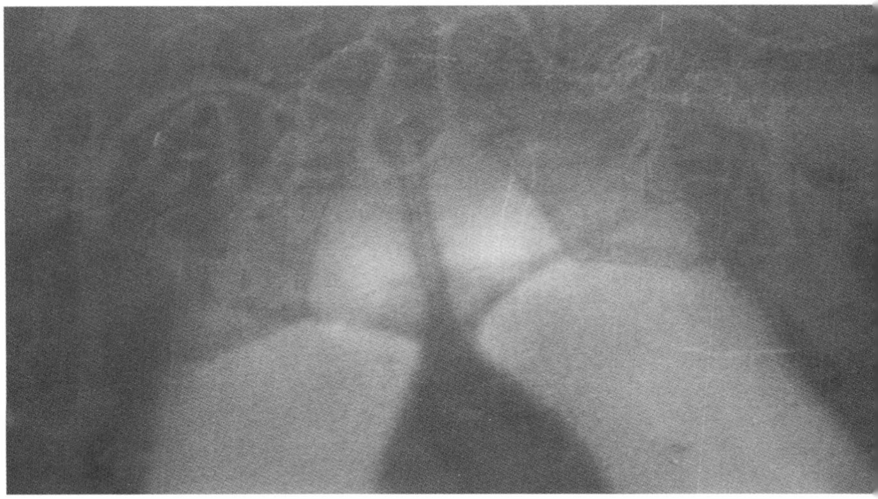

LO GLO

LIGHT-SENSITIVE ELASTIC FURNITURE

CLIENT: VITRA EDITION 2007, WEIL AM RHEIN, GERMANY

PROJECT DATE: 2007

J. MAYER H.

PROJECT TEAM: JÜRGEN MAYER H., MARCUS BLUM

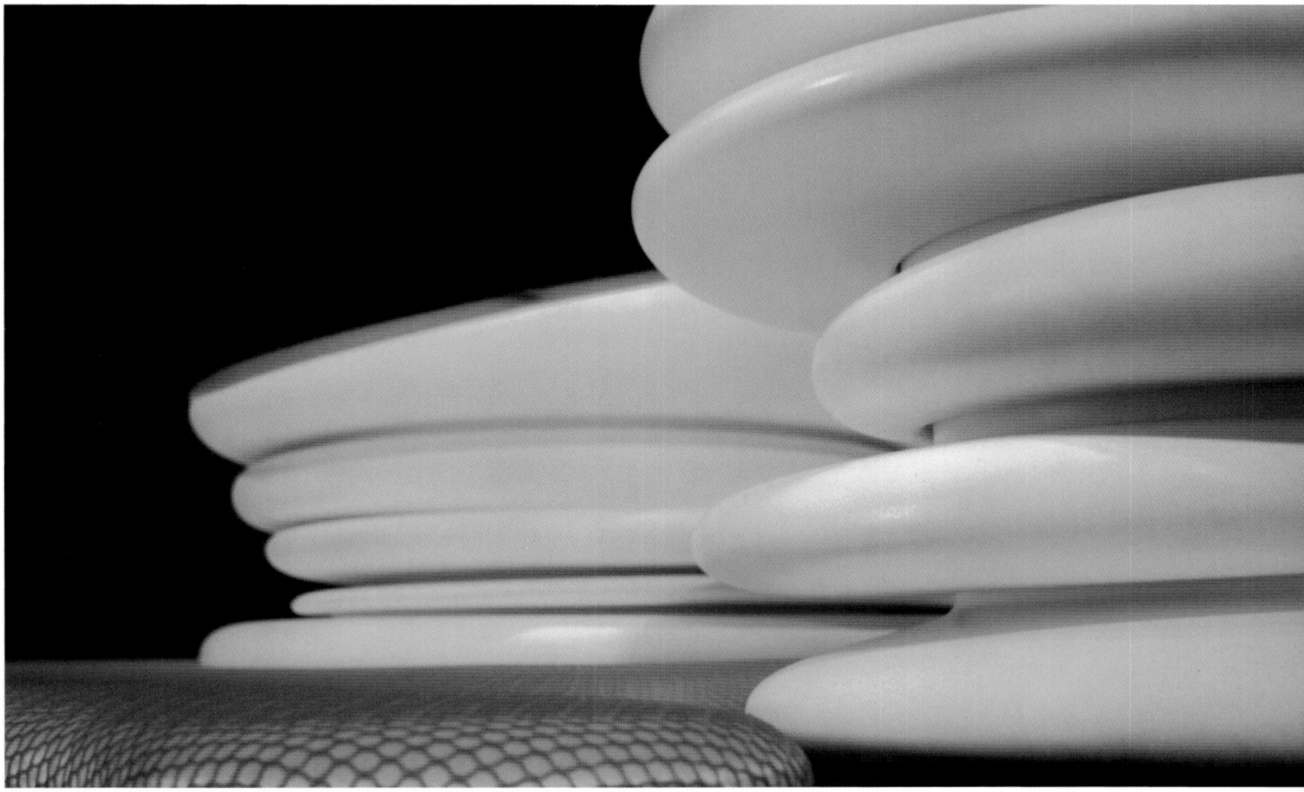

KERYKES

ACTIVITY TOOL FOR THE 2004 CULTURAL OLYMPICS, ATHENS, GREECE

CLIENT: CITY OF ATHENS

INTERNATIONAL COMPETITION: 2003, HONORABLE MENTION

J. MAYER H.
COMPETITION TEAM: JÜRGEN MAYER H., DOMINIK SCHWARZER, SASCHA NIKOLAUSCHKE

STRUCTURAL ENGINEERS: LYDIA THIESEMANN, HAMBURG
COST CONSULTANT: ELWARDT & LATTERMANN, BERLIN

Kerykes are "possibility structures," designed as multifunctional platforms which generate a broad variety of programs and events. In peripheral areas, where shopping, production, and living activities lack a cultural institution or social space, Kerykes offer a new location as a meeting place for local citizens and visitors to the Cultural Olympics alike. These event-structures have a daily rhythm that adjusts to everyday patterns like shopping and commuting as well as to special events and leisure activities. With Kerykes as activity generators, community activity and tourist events merge into one special moment of interaction.

WATERSLIDE-MODE

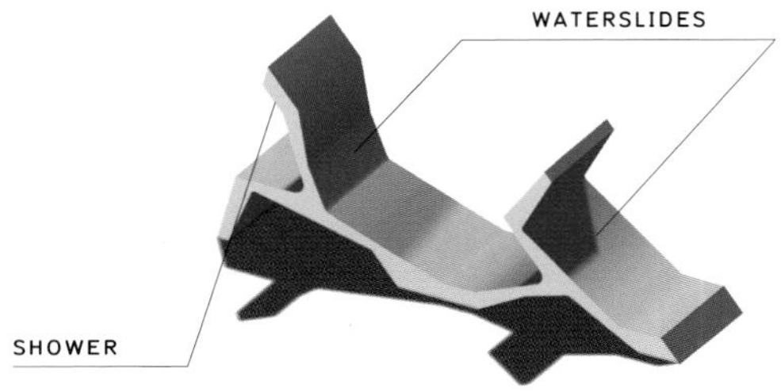

CINEMA-MODE

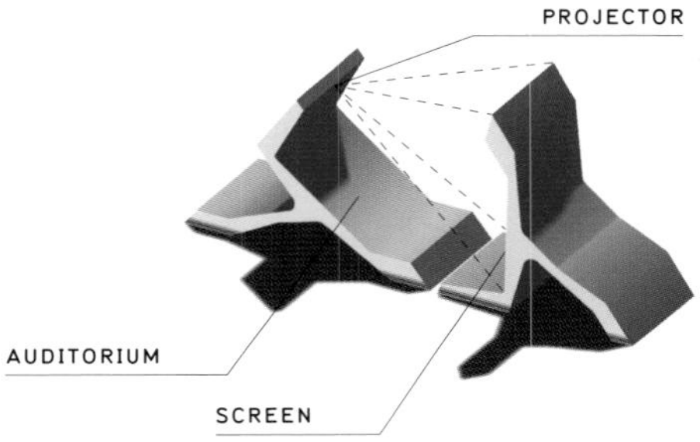

CLIMBWALL-MODE

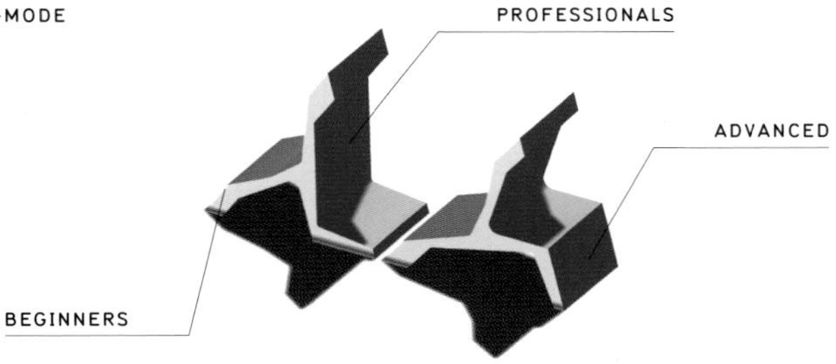

HALFPIPE-MODE

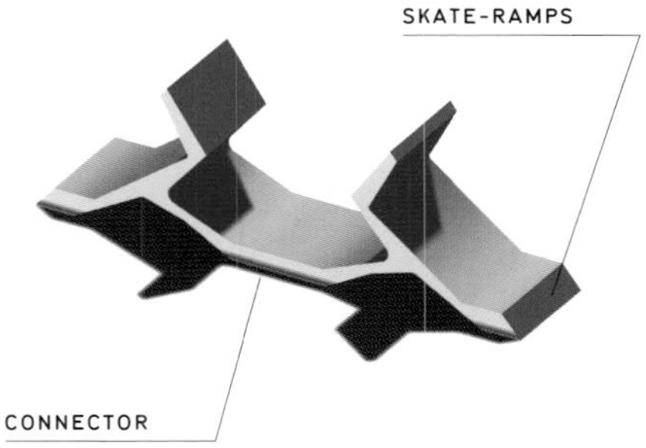

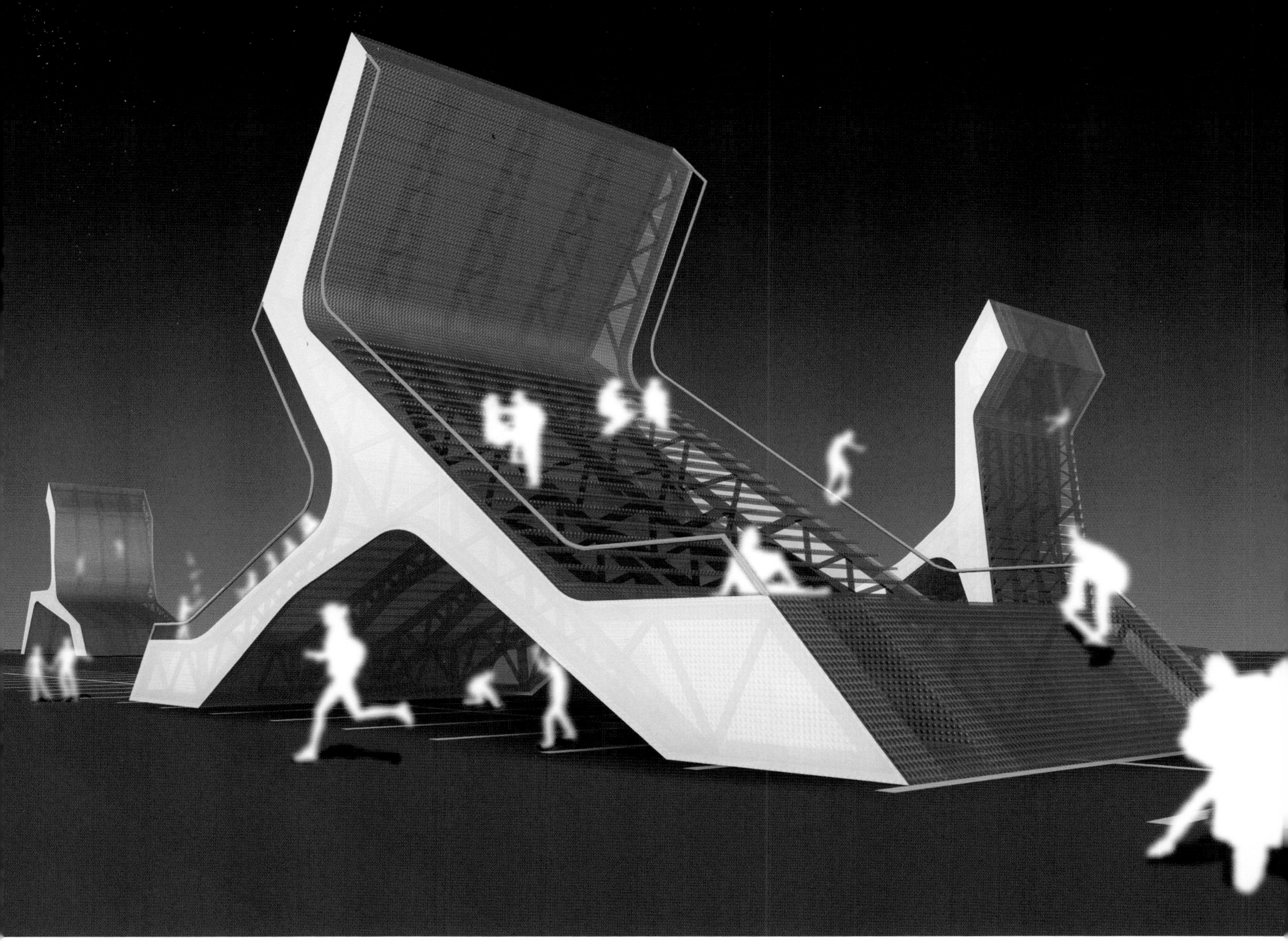

POSITIVE.NEGATIVE

REMODELING OF KICKEN GALLERY, BERLIN, GERMANY

CLIENT: KICKEN GALLERY, BERLIN

PROJECT DATE: 2008

J. MAYER H.
PROJECT TEAM: JÜRGEN MAYER H., SEBASTIAN FINCKH

Positive.Negative is a strategic intervention into the existing gallery space. A dynamic object in two parts, consisting of frame and infill, remakes the space into various configurations for possible exhibitions. The mutability of the gallery opens up unexpected possibilities for rethinking the conventions of "white cube" art spaces as a static framework. Positive.Negative probes deeply into new forms of presenting photography.

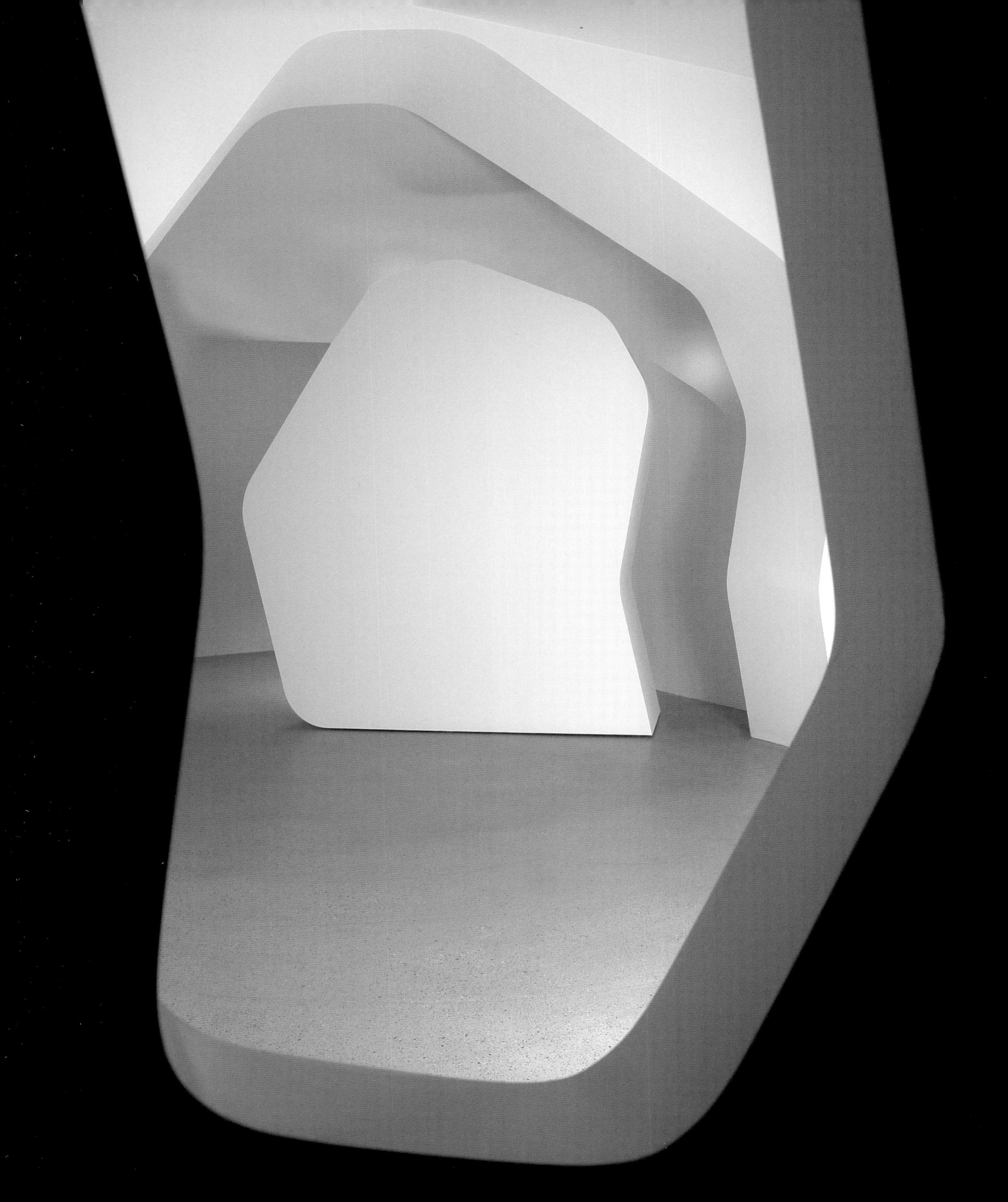

PATH.LOGIC

EXHIBITION ARCHITECTURE, CRTL.SPACE,
ZKM KARLSRUHE, GERMANY

CLIENT: ZKM—CENTER FOR ART AND MEDIA, KARLSRUHE

PROJECT DATE: OCTOBER 2001–FEBRUARY 2002

J. MAYER H.
PROJECT TEAM: JÜRGEN MAYER H., SEBASTIAN FINCKH

The objective of all surveillance is to acquire the most comprehensive possible overview and the greatest insight. In many cases it is not a question of the gaze as such, but instead of an omnipotent capacity for engaging in observation. The exhibition architecture establishes a field (surface), which is modulated by the program of exhibited objects and thematic areas. Thickenings, pockets (interiors), and platforms are thereby generated. Various modes of surveillance are strategically located on this modulated surface. The selection of information and the superabundance of data go hand in hand.

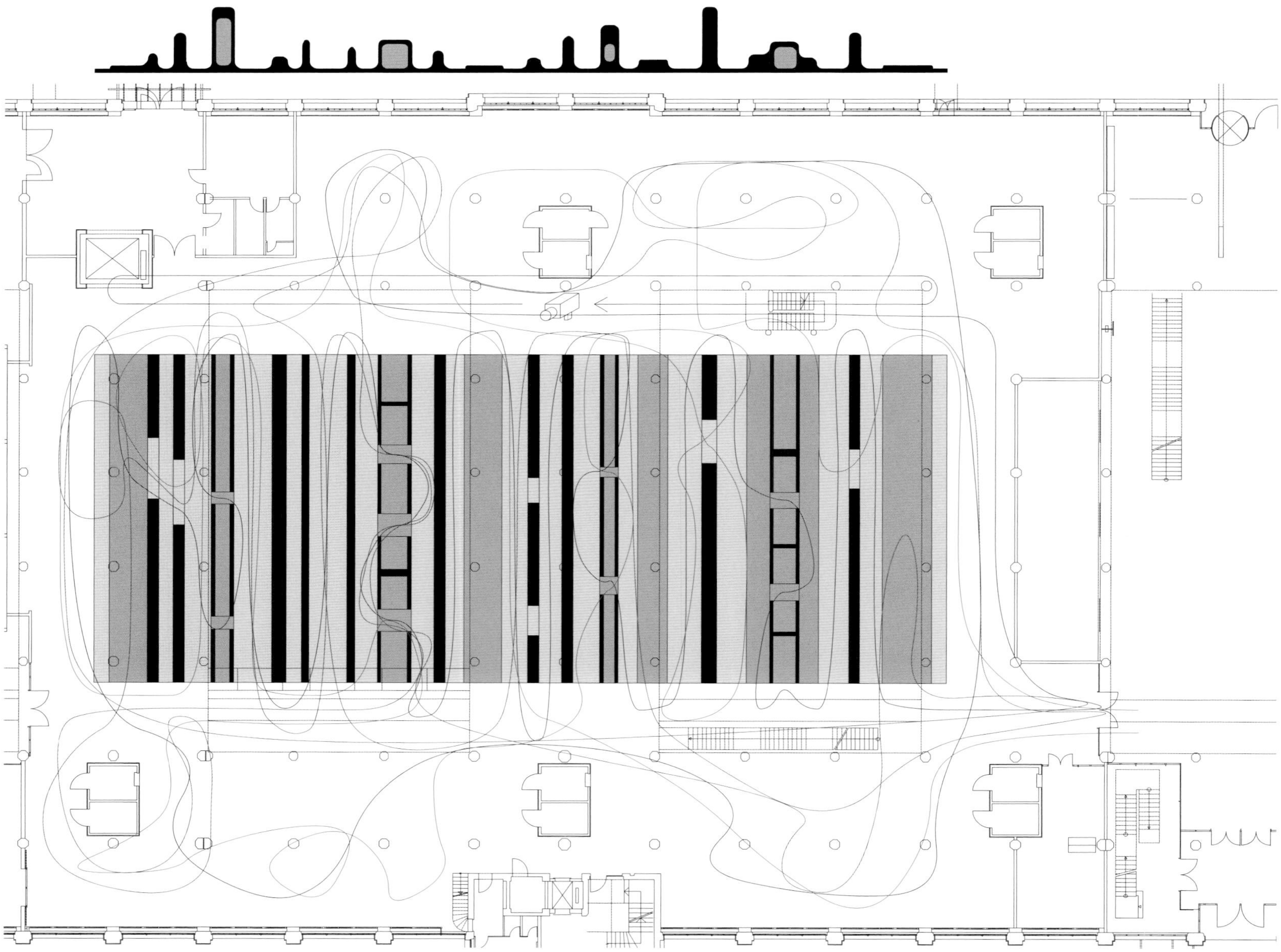

ACCUMULATED WALKING MAP

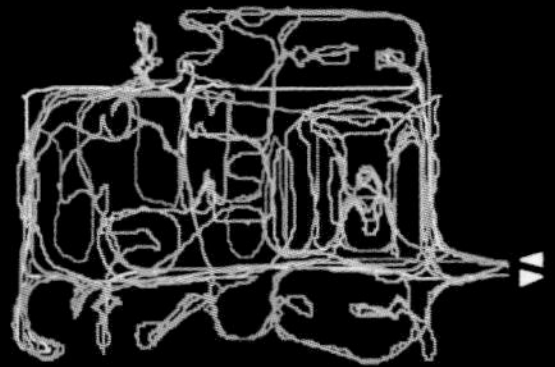

VISITOR A: STROLLING

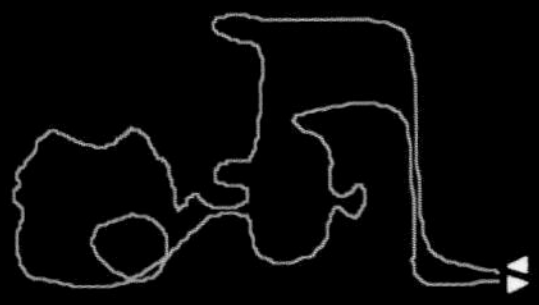

VISITOR B: SPECIAL INTEREST

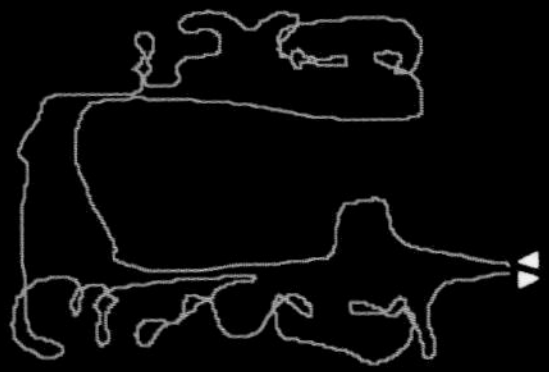

VISITOR C: ONLY HIGHLIGHTS

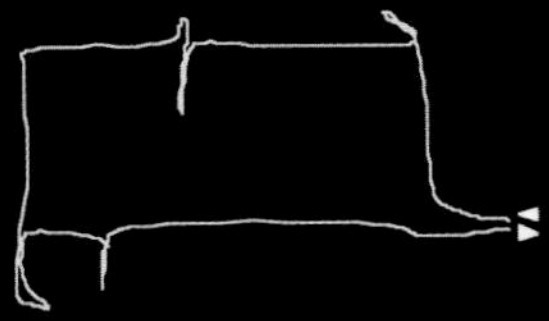

VISITOR D: SHORT ATTENTION SPAN

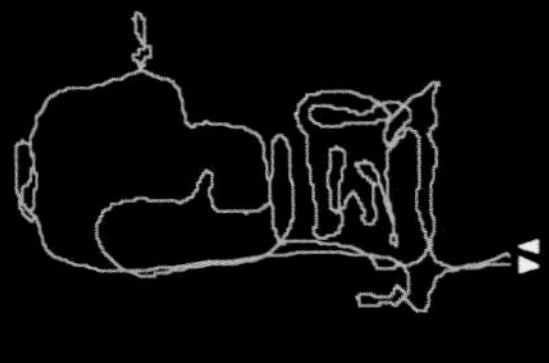

VISITOR E: STRATEGEIG SELECTION

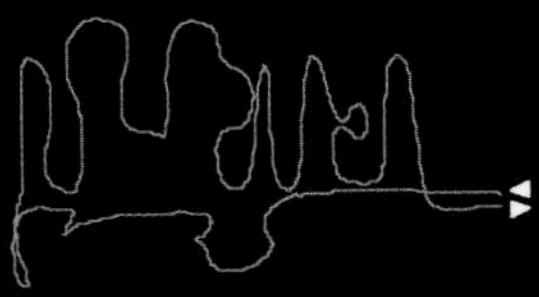

VISITOR F: OVERALL

SMART SURFACE

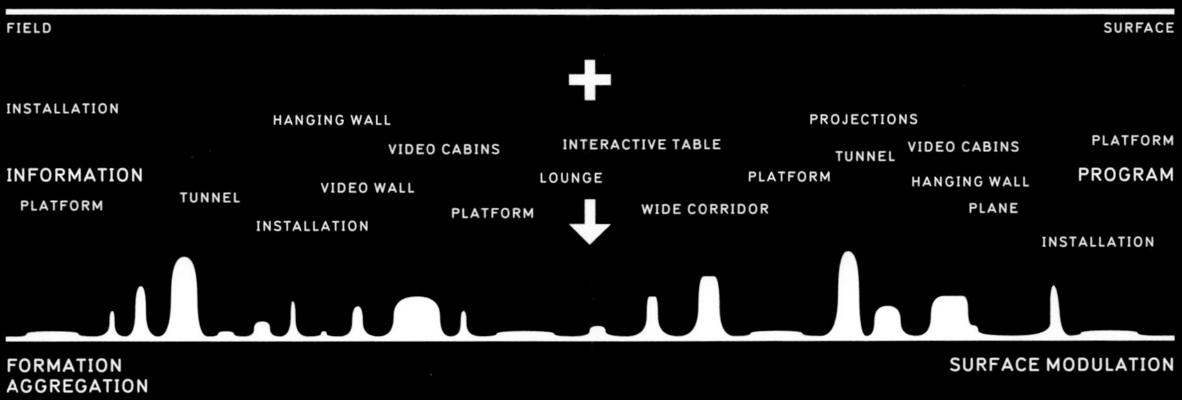

CONTROL SPACE

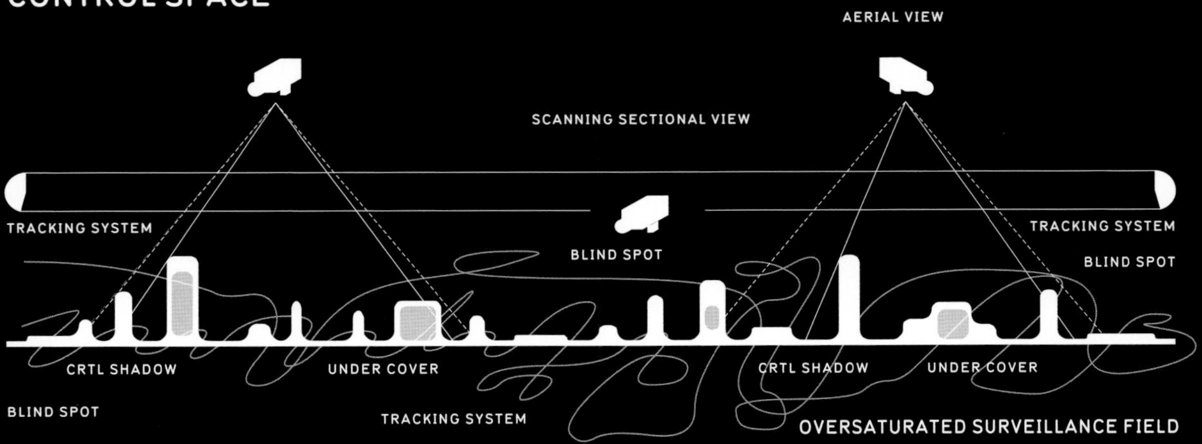

TRACKED INDIVIDUAL WALKING PATTERN

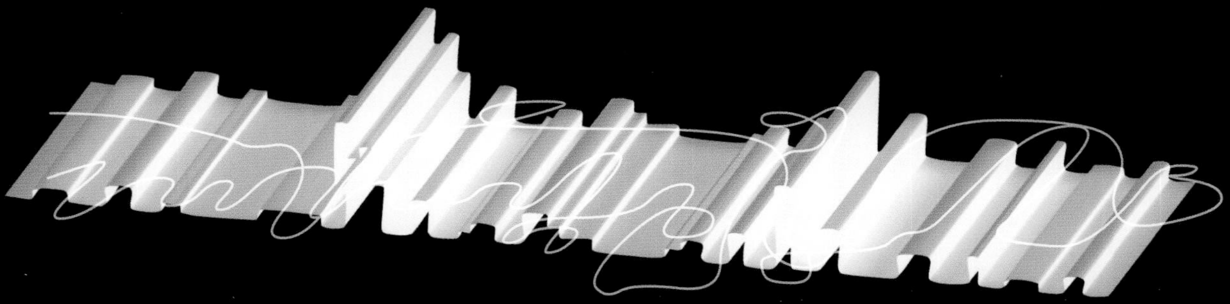

BODY.GUARDS

MONITOR MAGAZINE

PROJECT DATE: 2004

J. MAYER H.

PROJECT TEAM: JÜRGEN MAYER H., JAN-CHRISTOPH STOCKEBRAND

Body.Guards is a new kind of outfit that uses "smart dust" as a sensory device. Nearly invisible airborne particles build up a dynamic, intelligent cocoon for testing, warning, spying, scouting, communicating, guarding, and protection. So far only used in military technology, these nano-devices will very soon expand their field of operation into most aspects of our everyday life. Body.Guards function as scouts that constantly investigate the environment, identifying physical, biological, chemical, or radioactive hazards.

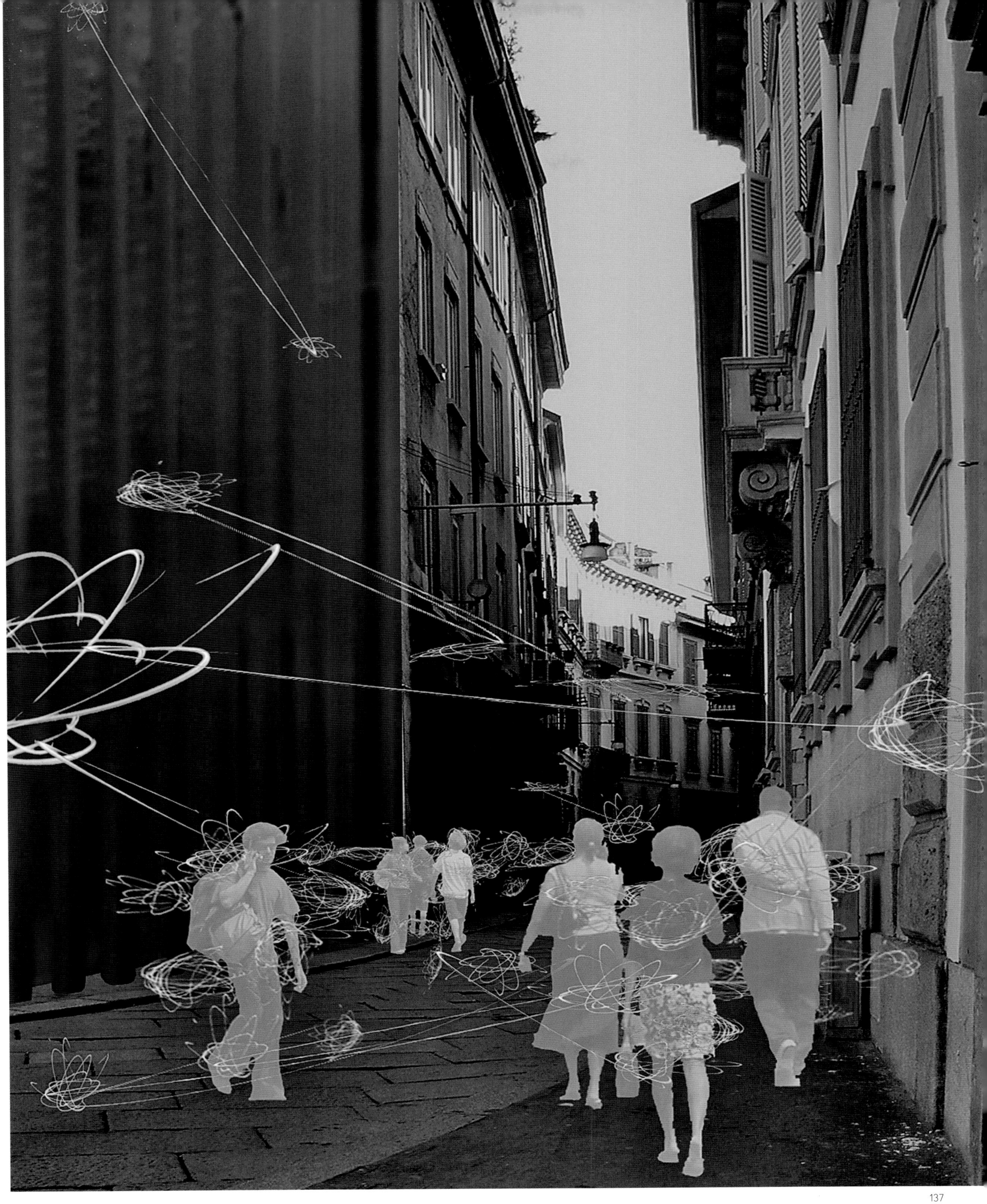

ROTOR

PENTHOUSE, COPENHAGEN, DENMARK

CLIENT: PRIVATE

PROJECT DATE: 2004–06

J. MAYER H.
PROJECT TEAM: JÜRGEN MAYER H., SEBASTIAN FINCKH, GÜVENC ÖZEL, JAN-CHRISTOPH STOCKEBRAND

ARCHITECT ON SITE: TOMAS QUISTORF SOERENSEN

Rotor is a space-continuum, which pulsates around a central, rotating media column. Each of its four programmatic pockets is centered on panoramic views onto the city. The media column at the center incorporates various technological devices for entertainment, control, information, and communication. By rotating, these different media services blur the fixed program into a dynamic space-continuum. In combination with new media and technological effects, extra-sensory elements straddle the space between comfort and surprise.

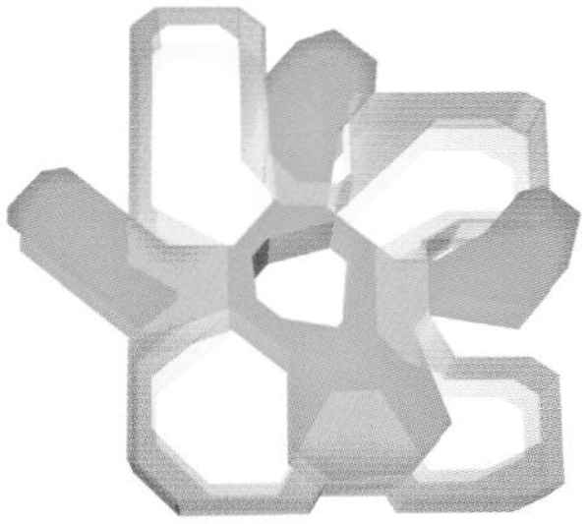

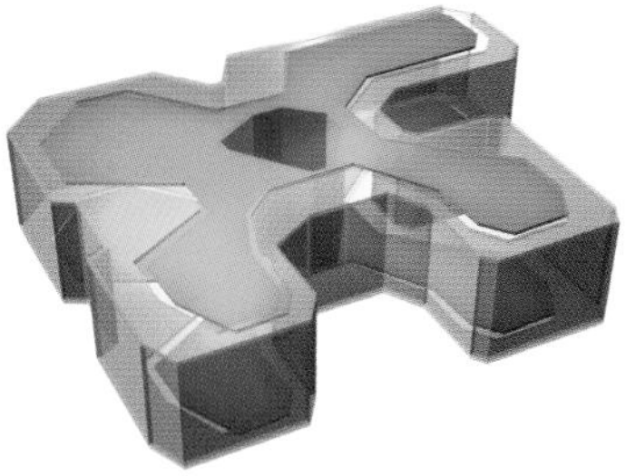

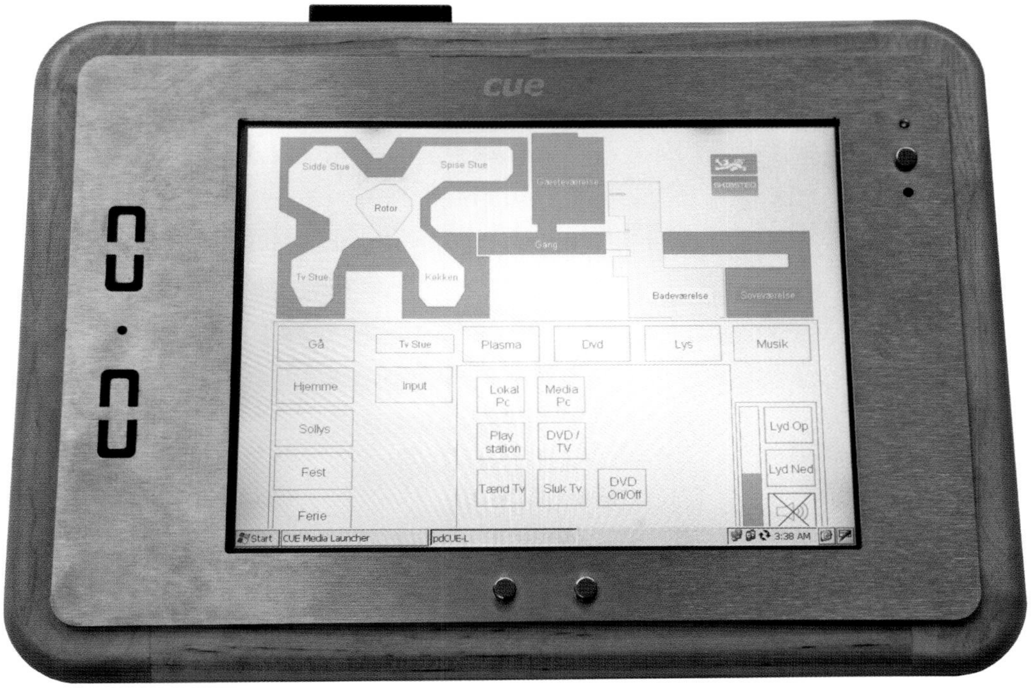
cue
Sidde Stue
Spise Stue
Rotor
Tv Stue
Gang
Badeværelse
Gå
Tv Stue
Plasma
Dvd
Lys
Musik
Hjemme
Input
Lokal Pc
Media Pc
Sollys
Play station
DVD / TV
Fest
Tænd Tv
Sluk Tv
DVD On/Off
Ferie
Lyd Op
Lyd Ned
Start
CUE Media Launcher
3:38 AM

WEATHER.HOUSE

OR "INSIDE THE WEATHER CHANNEL": RETHINKING COMFORT IN THE DOMESTIC AIR-STAGNATION POCKET
PRINCETON UNIVERSITY, NEW JERSEY, US

PROJECT DATE: 1994

J. MAYER H.

With the advent of technological control in the nineteenth century, climate in the domestic interior lost its dependency on the outside. Deflected with the major wind direction, the inside of this house, however, is animated by certain weather conditions. The program—which is usually divided into specific functions such as living room, dining room, or kitchen—is now defined according to its climatic condition: spaces for normal clothing, light clothing, and no clothing. The weather becomes the selected landscape, without the intention of safety.

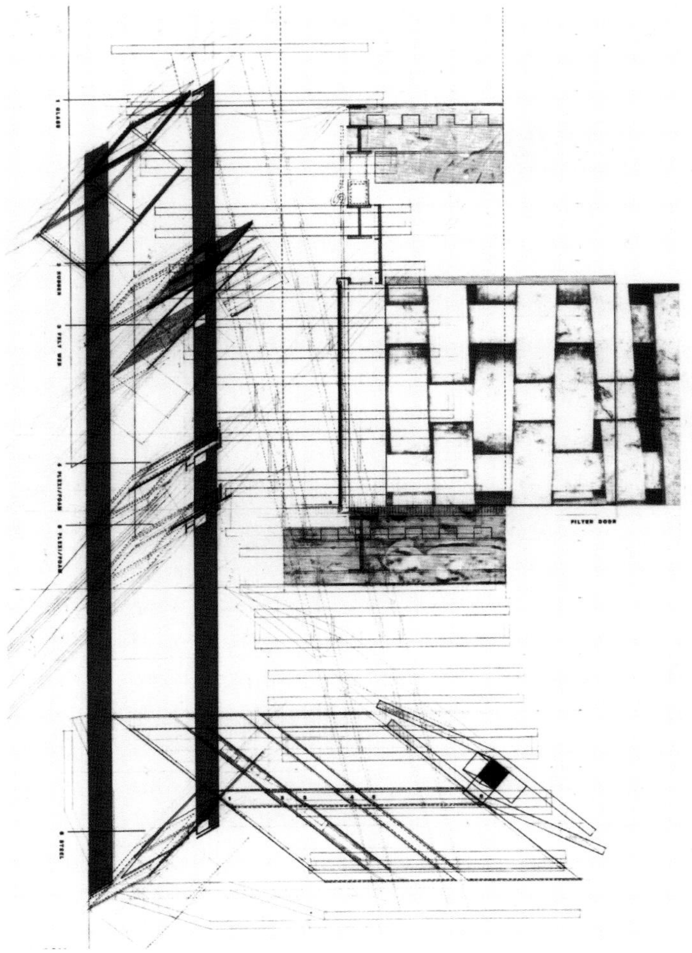
1 GLASS
2 RUBBER
3 FELT WEB
4 PLEXI/FOAM
5 PLEXI/FOAM
6 STEEL
FILTER DOOR
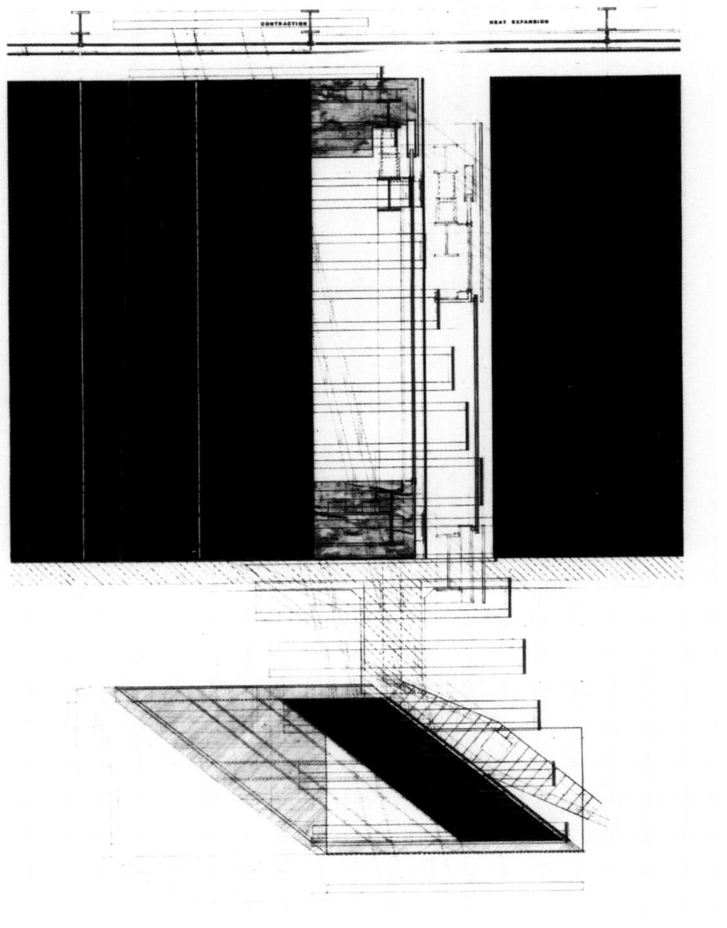
CONTRACTION
HEAT EXPANSION
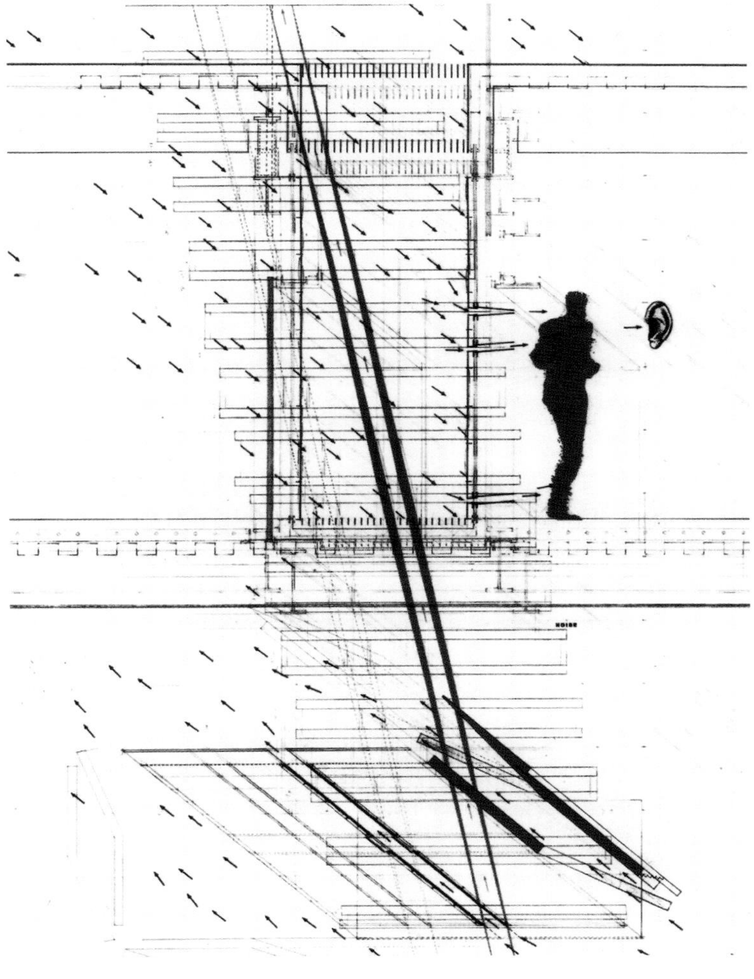
NOISE
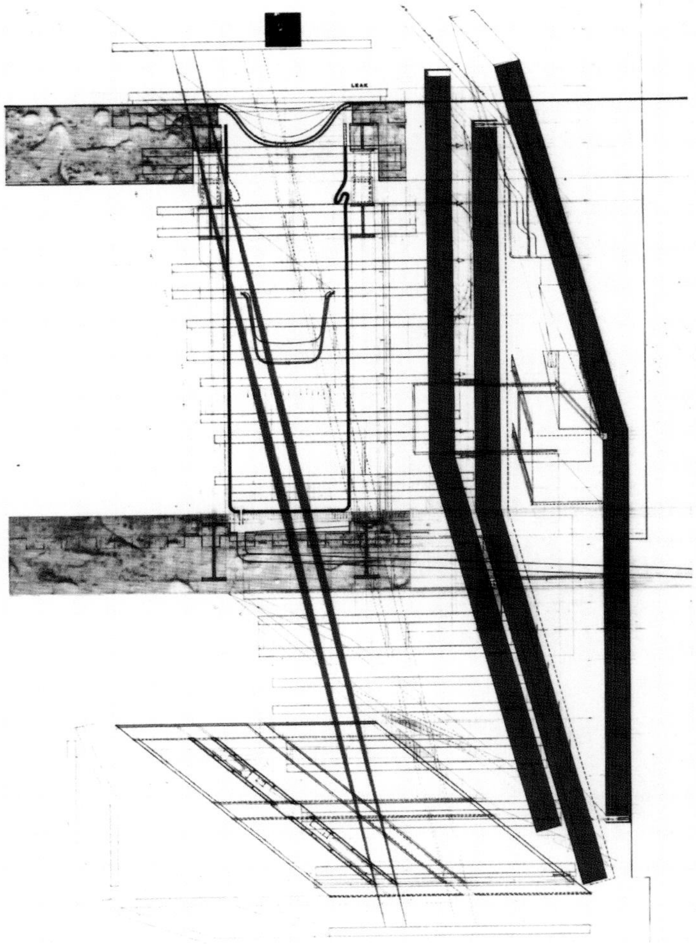
LEAK

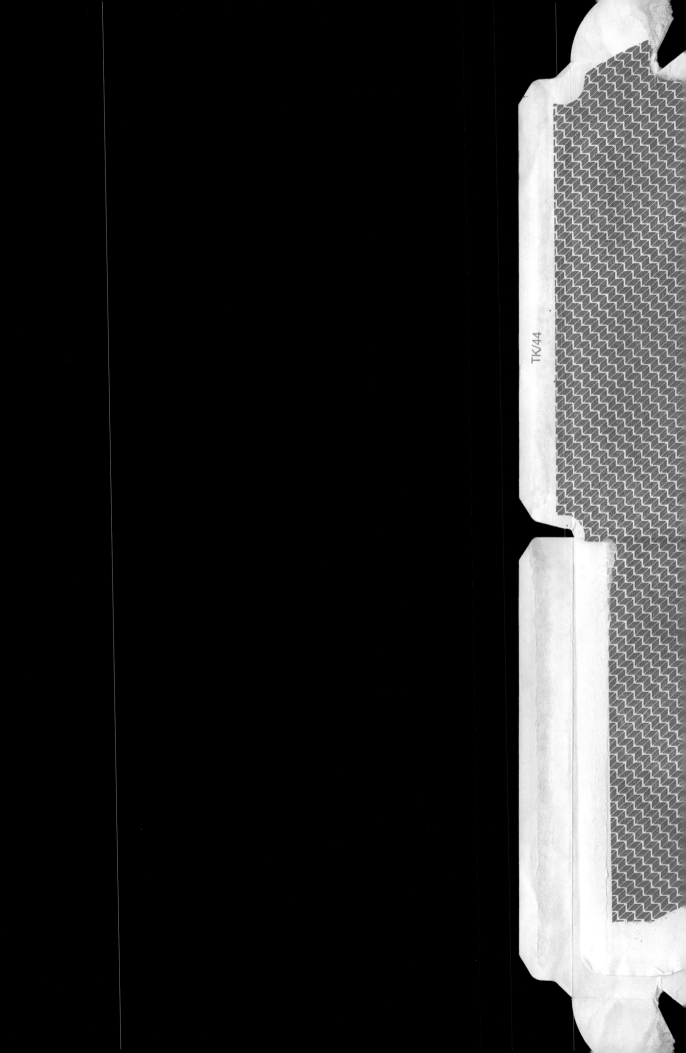

Bitte haben Sie Verständnis dafür, dass wir wegen der elektronischen Datenverarbeitung nicht immer verhindern können, dass Sie mehrere Briefsendungen an einem Tag von uns erhalten. Das Zusammensortieren aller Sendungen für denselben Empfänger wäre aus Zeit- und Kostengründen nicht zu vertreten.

Dieser Umschlag wurde aus chlorfreiem Papier hergestellt.

TK

LOBBY TALK

ROLF FEHLBAUM IN CONVERSATION WITH JÜRGEN MAYER H.

Milan, April 18, 2008, 8 a.m.
Grand Hotel Et De Milan, Italy

Jürgen Mayer H.: This conversation is well timed, since our collaboration has lasted for almost two years now. I remember very well when you called me in August of 2006. After twenty years, you wanted to reactivate the theme of limited-edition furniture, because space for innovation in the furniture industry had shrunk progressively as an effect of the subjection of large editions to international norms. You were interested in seeking out new approaches concerning the real significance of furniture in the environmental sense; you were concerned with spatial atmosphere in relation to context, and the possibilities of research. Of course, I immediately said yes to such an exciting and important project! Exactly one year ago, shortly before the actual opening and presentation in Weil am Rhein in early June of 2007, all of the designers for this project met in Milan to discuss the results and the installation of the MyHome exhibition in the Vitra Museum. Since then, the limited-edition furniture has been displayed at various locations, currently at the Milan Triennial Building. But let's start at the beginning: why did you come to us? What sparked your interest?

Rolf Fehlbaum: It was the project Metropol Parasol in Seville. It grabbed me right away. I realized that you didn't simply remain with the building itself, but instead worked on an object. I had also seen that in your lounges something happened with the furniture, which you integrated into a kind of performance. Your approach reminded me of Denis Santachiara, who had made a performance-influenced contribution to our first edition. I was attempting to renew this performative aspect. After the nineteen-eighties, astonishingly, the dream of intelligent furniture, furniture which, for example, was capable of emitting signals, was neither continued nor realized.

JMH: Some of the ideas were almost "impossible": objects that turned red, for example, when you called out to them ...

RF: ... or robot furniture that came up to you when you entered the room.
I'm delighted that we were able to continue, and that our collaboration led to two results last year: a group of objects and an installation.

JMH: With the nocturnally illuminated furniture Lo Glo, the gaze begins with the object and continues into the surrounding space—comparable to a set that continually propagates itself and assumes various functions and formations on the basis of various shapes. With the temperature-sensitive installation Housewarming MyHome, things are reversed: here the space develops from a three-dimensional supergraphic, which makes a direct reference to the building of the Vitra Museum "down" to an interactive surface that can be sat upon and occupied. Both outcomes show the same research-oriented access to space, to furniture, and to the body, in relationship to architectural and functional surfaces—and clearly show diverse results.

RF: Yes, since the one is reproducible, and the other is not. I am fascinated by the fact that the space in the Vitra Museum became something completely different by means of this intervention. The graphic quality of your work, a kind of casting mold that clearly distinguished itself, spoke strongly to me, and was highly effective in medial terms. The

Moltke Dining Hall in Karlsruhe is an additional instance of this.

JMH: Regarding responses to the dining hall, I noticed that the striking exterior of the building constituted a kind of promise, one that becomes a three-dimensional experience when you enter. Precisely the materiality, the special haptic quality, is important to us. In Karlsruhe, the "skin" is not simply an ordinary surface. By means of the somewhat rubber-like polyurethane coating, the elastic conception of the building becomes palpable. The surface becomes a bearer of meaning. With other projects, other surface qualities stand in the foreground. With the temperature-sensitive furniture pieces known as Heat.Seats, the body temperature of the user leaves behind temporary color changes, and in the nocturnally illuminated Lo Glo pieces, the user's presence is recorded as a shadowed contour. New discoveries, temporal displacements, surprises, and hence new worlds of experience are constantly being opened up. The time spent working with Vitra was characterized precisely by the search for the new, by the consistent realization and further development of conceptual approaches.
During the period when I was recruited into the "Vitra family," I noticed that personal connections played a big role. Soon, there were three or four generations of interrelationships, mutual interest, and intensive collaboration. I soon realized that, on the one hand, relations were highly familial and based on trust, but on the other were also extremely professional, structured, and characterized by high levels of mutual respect. How is this corporate culture articulated in your everyday activities?

RF: For me, it's the essence of what makes this company special. Charles and Ray Eames provided us with a new definition of design, and also of the designer as a personality. Before them, the designer was someone who beautified objects on behalf of the industry. Charles and Ray Eames, but also George Nelson and others, are "author designers" who, to be sure, take on commissions, but who bind these to their own visions of the world, creating objects which are on the one hand functional, but which on the other also represent their sense of individuality.

JMH: Do you also see Lo Glo in those terms? When I showed you sketches of it, they reminded you of a German *Baumkuchen* (literally: "tree cake"). And you brought *Baumkuchen* with you on your visits to Charles and Ray Eames in Santa Monica—a nice anecdote, which embeds Lo Glo in the history of Vitra.

RF: There is a famous essay by Isaiah Berlin, which deals with two different personality structures. In "The Hedgehog and the Fox," Berlin distinguishes between the fox—who does, knows, and attempts a variety of things—and the hedgehog— who only knows one thing, but knows it extremely well. Clearly, I am a fox who brings together a variety of things.

JMH: It's a question, then, of the multiplicity of discoveries rather than of refining one thing and discovering its essence?

RF: Yes, those are the two attitudes. You, too, are an architect as well as a designer and an artist. For Le Corbusier, it was also completely natural to work simultaneously as a painter, sculptor, designer, architect, and city planner. I find the dissolution of boundaries to be very interesting.

JMH: In my everyday activities as well, I don't notice such boundaries: everything flows and exerts an influence on everything else. Ideas are developed, new ones are added, and are then shaped, transformed. Conceptual approaches to furniture on a small scale, or for installations, sometimes reemerge in similar form on a larger scale for buildings—and are then transformed into new parameters, and vice versa. Emerging consistently are similar questions concerning the relationships body/space, technology/nature, and communication/information. For me, questions of scale or of discipline are not that important—the media, on the other hand, attempts to classify me as a designer, an architect, or an artist. A piece of furniture produced by an artist has a very different significance than one produced by a designer or architect. These disciplines, then, really do exist! Interestingly, commentary on one and the same object can assume very different forms depending on whether it is part of an installation in an art museum or is displayed at a furniture fair.

RF: A commensurate level of functionality is expected of you as a designer. If you do not succeed in this regard, your work is regarded as a failure. Expectations of art are very different.

JMH: A role is also played by political, social, and cultural themes, which demonstrates the seductive power of the market. Again and again, art expresses a critique of the market, interrogates its structures, and exposes its strategies. But I absolutely do perceive a potential for commentary in architecture and design as well.

RF: In contrast to design commentary, artistic commentary need not fulfill any practical purpose. That's why design practice is something entirely different. This became very clear to me last year during a visit to a sculpture project in Munster. On display there were small drawings at scales of 1:6 or 1:7, according to which the sculptures were then manufactured on the principle "that's it" or "it's like that." In design, such a drawing would only have been a point of departure; afterwards, there would be an initial prototype, then a second one, a third, a fourth, before the final product would eventually emerge ... This indicates a different attitude, namely that of "working things out." In collaboration with a manufacturer, the object is optimized step-by-step.

JMH: Of course, a single custom-made object is not comparable to a mass-produced one, which must conform to very different standards and criteria—and is then integrated into everyday life. A work of architecture, on the other hand, is almost always a kind of prototype, one that is developed as a rule for a precise location—also because the task is always relatively specific. There remains the possibility of mass-production on a larger scale, for example in the case of a row house. Previously, we had had relatively little to do with furniture design. For Bisazza, we made furniture which is now coming onto the market after four or five years. This serves as a reminder of how long the development phase actually lasts. The other furniture items were exhibited more as spatial installations in the context of art. Lo Glo was the first direct commission, which was developed from the very beginning as a collaboration between producer and designer: a new and very exciting experience for us!

RF: Of course, Lo Glo is an extreme case in the context of such collaborations, because normal uses and prices were not required; normal conditions, then, were put out of play. It would be interesting to see what might emerge under regular conditions.

JMH: The Lo Glo stool has an elastic backbone, on which one sits actively: not only is there an aesthetic experience, but the act of sitting itself is also affected. Do you see any potential in this approach for further developments in the direction of mass production?

RF: Definitely not for mass production. The image of movement and the spine-like construction can be realized as an idea in the framework of an edition project, but for serially produced furniture the expense is too great. There, other criteria apply: is there a reasonable relationship between the functional performance enjoyed by the user and the price he or she has paid?

JMH: I'd like to come back to the question of multidisciplinarity we spoke about earlier. With us, it is manifested in the variety of projects and scales. And of course, it also exists for you as a manufacturer, museum founder, and collector.

RF: Collecting and manufacturing are not only divergent activities; each requires an entirely different perspective. As manufacturer, I'm interested in good products with clear functional parameters. As a collector, I'm interested in manifestations of new ideas and new tendencies. There are many things I've included in the collection that I'd never actually use. And then there are the design highlights: the objects that make sense for collector and user alike, products in which the new has been manifested in an eminently practical manner.

JMH: At the beginning, we spoke about the media effect of our activities: Vitra is actually an ideal instance of this, having inserted accents into the development of architecture with buildings by Frank O. Gehry and Zaha Hadid. Surely the media responses were also calculated, but at the same time the enterprise was permeated by a spirit of exploration. You could see things there that were otherwise only vaguely perceptible on paper.

RF: The media presence was a desirable side effect; the project would have been no different in the absence of media attention.

JMH: Precisely as a collector, of course, you stand in a tradition. On the one hand, you observe what comes along; on the other, you have an image through the Eameses of how you might develop Vitra with regard to the present moment. At the same time, with the museum and in your work with children, you perceive a pedagogical task. That, too, is future-oriented; is important for the development of Vitra; and, most of all, shows how the relationship between aesthetics, the lived world, and furniture design has changed.

RF: I'm becoming conscious only now of the fact that our pedagogical work runs quite naturally alongside our everyday activities. This project was not planned strategically, it simply emerged.

JMH: It's like that with us as well: I'm always being asked about strategy. But I have none.

1/03

METROPOL PARASOL

REDEVELOPMENT OF THE PLAZA DE LA ENCARNACIÓN, SEVILLE, SPAIN

CLIENT: AYUNTAMIENTO DE SEVILLA AND SACYR

INTERNATIONAL COMPETITION: 2004, 1ST PRIZE
PROJECT DATE: 2004–10

J. MAYER H.
PROJECT TEAM: JÜRGEN MAYER H., ANDRE SANTER, MARTA RAMÍREZ IGLESIAS, JAN-CHRISTOPH STOCKEBRAND, MARCUS BLUM, ANA ALONSO DE LA VARGA, PAUL ANGELIER, HANS SCHNEIDER, THORSTEN BLATTER, WILKO HOFFMANN, CLAUDIA MARCINOWSKI, SEBASTIAN FINCKH, ALESSANDRA RAPONI, OLIVIER JACQUES, NAI HUEI WANG
COMPETITION TEAM: JÜRGEN MAYER H, DOMINIK SCHWARZER, WILKO HOFFMANN, INGMAR SCHMIDT, JAN-CHRISTOPH STOCKEBRAND, JULIA NEITZEL, KLAUS KÜPPERS, GEORG SCHMIDTHALS, DARIA TROVATO

MANAGEMENT CONSULTANT: DIRK BLOMEYER
TECHNICAL CONSULTANT FOR COMPETITION (2ND PHASE ONLY) AND MULTIDISCIPLINARY ENGINEERS FOR REALIZATION: ARUP GMBH
TECHNICAL SUPPORT FOR PLANTS—COMPETITION (2ND PHASE ONLY): COQUI-MALACHOWSKA-COQUI WITH THOMAS WALDAU
TRANSLATION COMPETITION TEXT: CARMEN DIEZ
PLEXI-MODEL: WERK 5, BERLIN
TIMBER-MODEL: FINNFOREST MERK, BREMEN

PERMANENT COLLECTION THE MUSEUM OF MODERN ART, NEW YORK, AND STAATLICHE MUSEEN ZU BERLIN, PREUSSISCHER KULTURBESITZ, BERLIN

With the Metropol Parasol, Seville acquires a new urban emblem at the heart of its historic center. The site is a plaza, the location of a former market hall whose southern part was demolished in the nineteen-fifties to provide space for a bus terminal—the remainder was razed in the seventies to accommodate a parking lot. The new structure redefines this important location and its urban context on a number of levels. The building is conceived as a large-roofed structure growing organically from the ground like an group of mushrooms, and creating a shadowed, slightly raised plaza beneath, which accommodates a range of public functions. Theater, music, dance, and other events can be scheduled beneath this roof during daytime or in the evening. Below the plaza, the market hall is reborn in a new form, once again serving as a center for the lively and densely settled neighborhood during the daytime.

The lowest level of the scheme, set beneath the market hall, contains an archaeological museum. This displays the remains of the Seville of antiquity, discovered here during excavation work, thus fostering an appreciation for the city's long history. Spacious openings in the floor of the market hall provide visitors with views below, rendering palpable their spatial proximity to the town's ancient origins. The load-bearing columns of the Parasol not only provide supports for the roof, but also contain the entrances and exits for both museum and market. One column contains the entrance to the accessible roof and the restaurant set there. From above, visitors enjoy spectacular views across the old town. Through its functional multiplicity and spectacular form, the Metropol Parasol represents a singular instance of how an urban texture that has evolved over centuries can be reanimated by means of a complex architectural ensemble.

—Andres Lepik

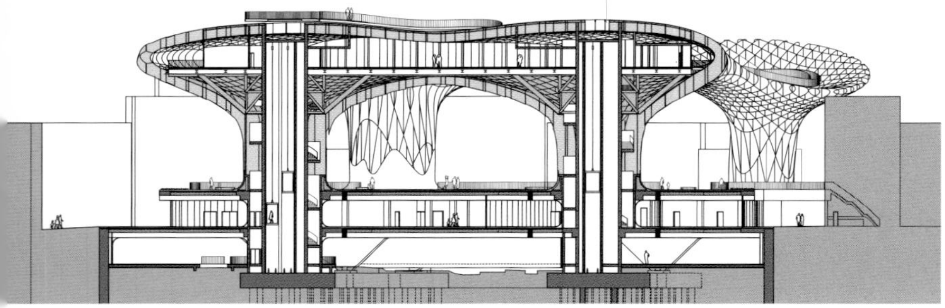

CROSS SECTION

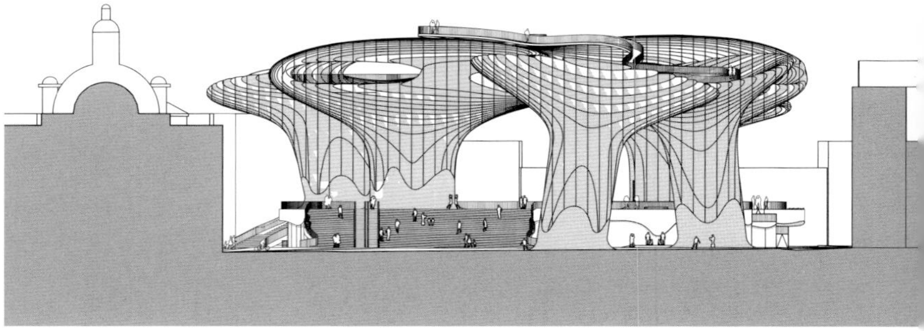

SOUTH ELEVATION

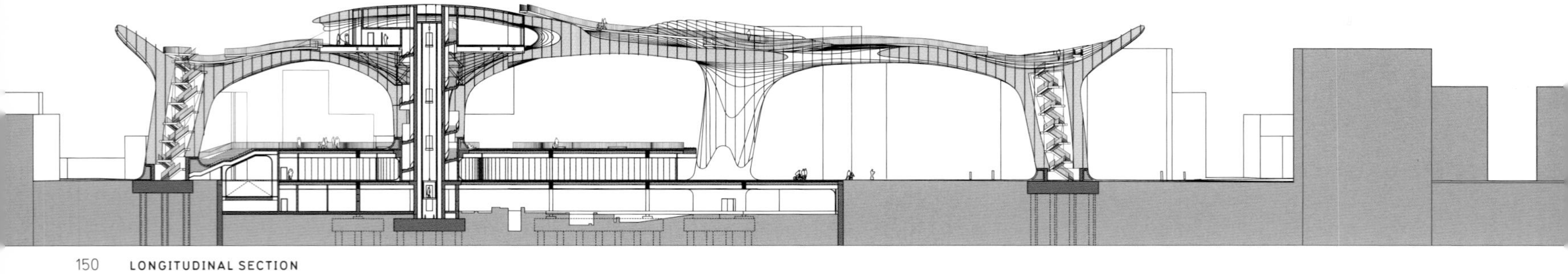

 LONGITUDINAL SECTION

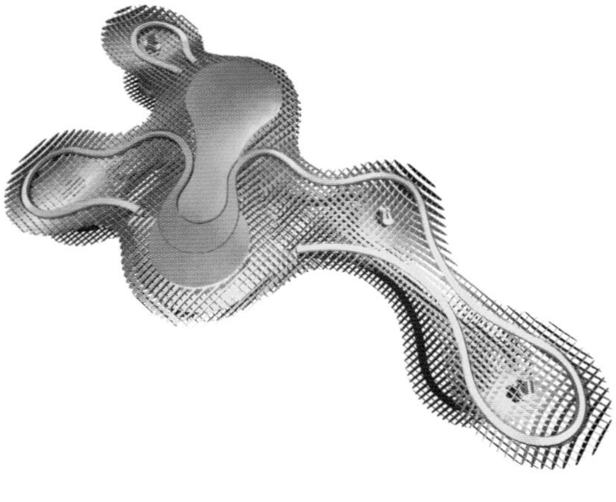

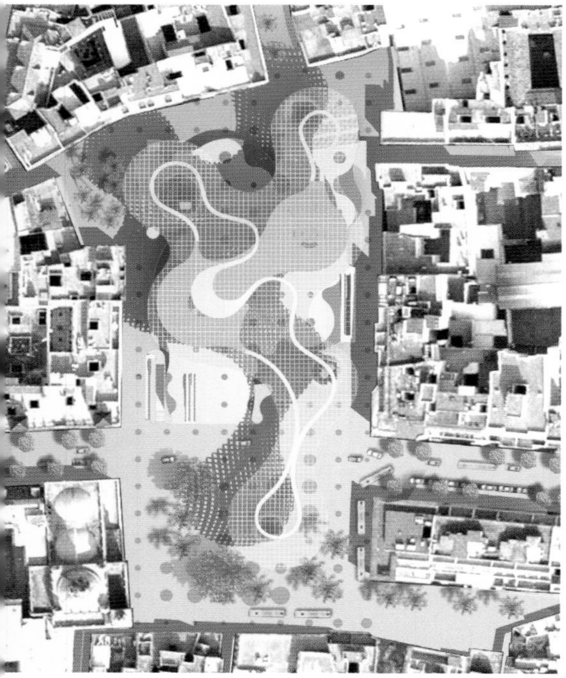

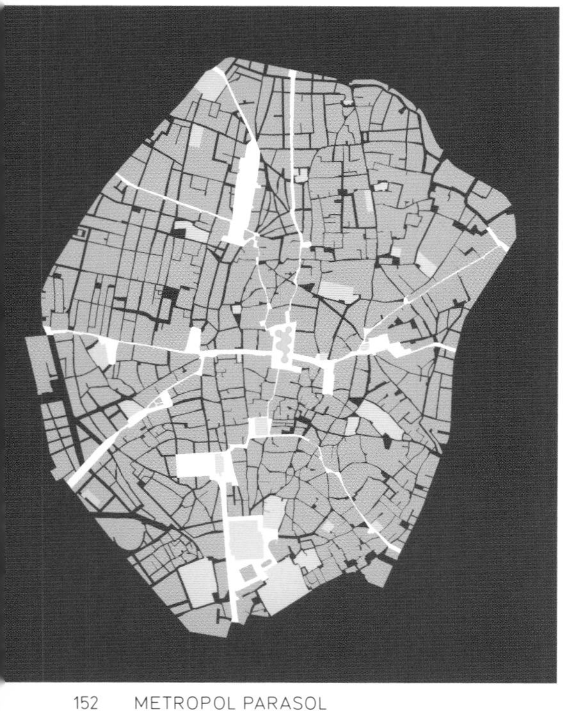

GENERAL OPTICA

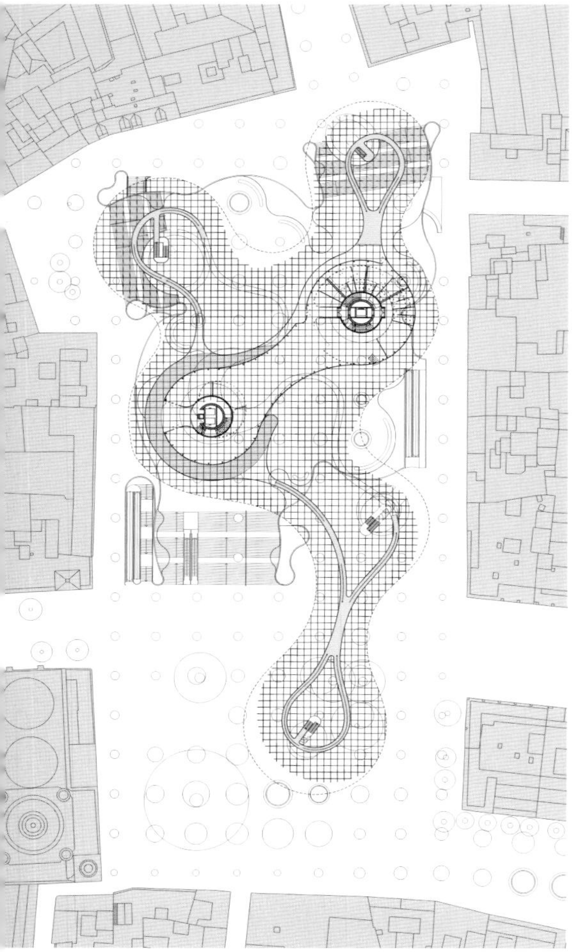

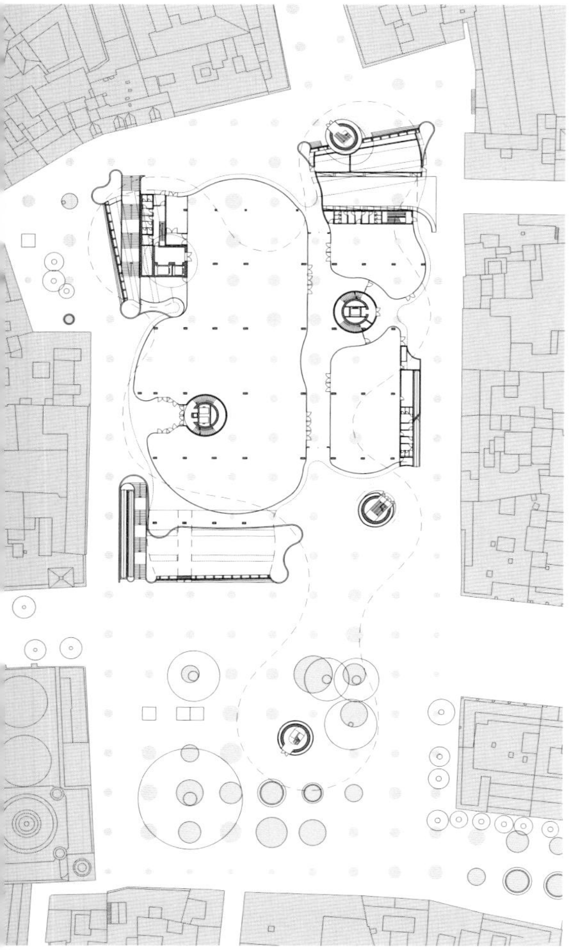

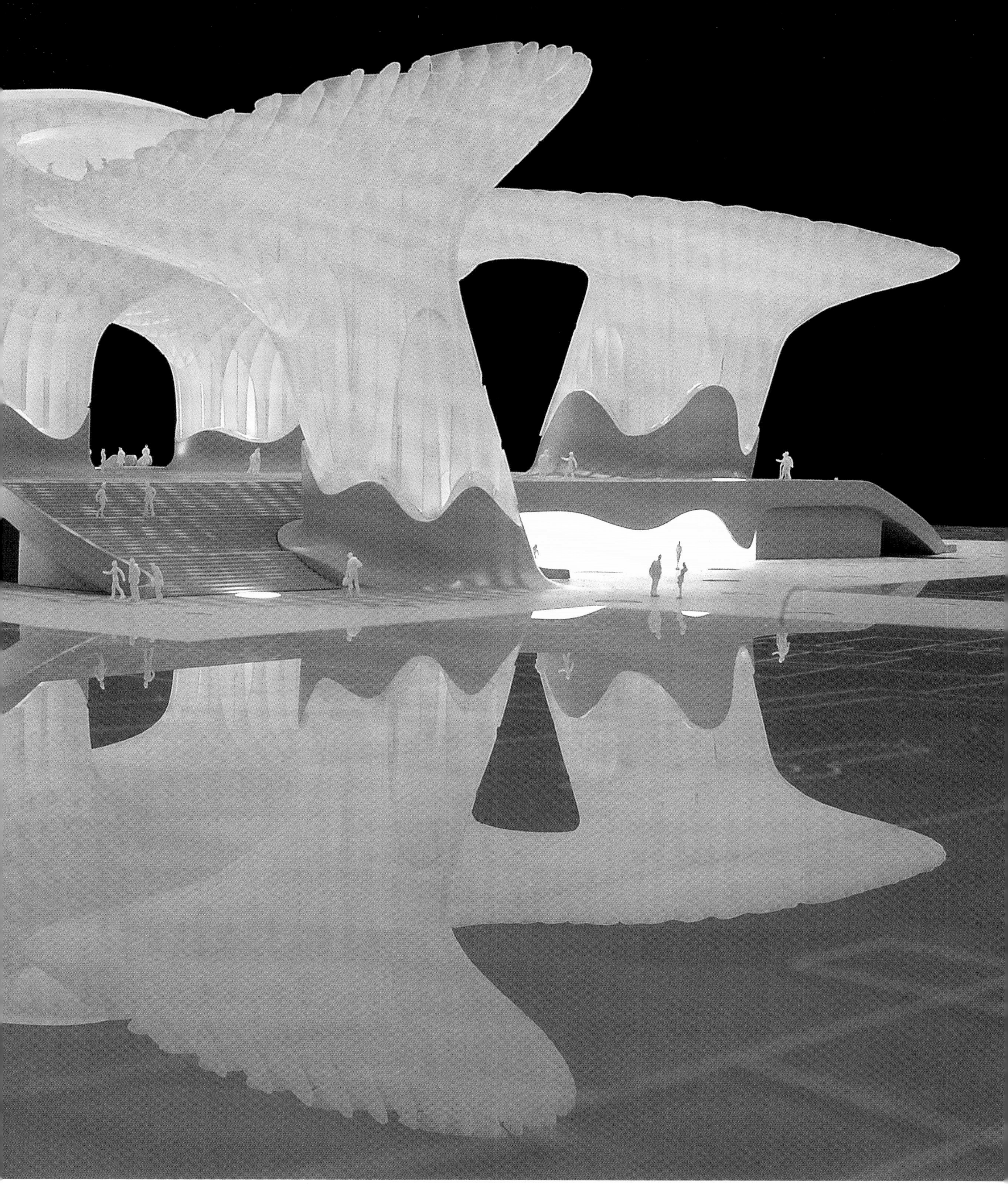

Sacyr

dp donpiso
piso 954 50 26 80 donpiso
PORTES

DRENTS MUSEUM

CLIENT: THE DRENTS MUSEUM, , THE NETHERLANDS

INTERNATIONAL COMPETITION: 2007

J. MAYER H.
TEAM 4 ARCHITECTEN, GRONINGEN
COMPETITION TEAM: JÜRGEN MAYER H., PAUL ANGELIER, MEHRDAD MASHAIE

COLLABORATION: TEAM 4 ARCHITECTEN, GRONINGEN
STRUCTURAL ENGINEERS: INGENIEURSBUREAU WASSENAAR BV, WASSENAAR
BUILDING SERVICES: ROYAL HASKONING, ROTTERDAM
MODEL: ARCHITEKTUR MODELLE BERLIN, BERLIN

The extension to the Drents Museum offers a unique opportunity to improve the role of the institution within the city of Assen. Its location in a park means that this project is a combination of landscape, exhibition platform, strolling destination, and underground exhibition building emerging on the urban surface. Externally, the museum extension offers a public 24-hour exhibition space for sculptures, performances, and projections. Inside lies an exhibition space capable of accommodating a wide variety of curatorial concepts.

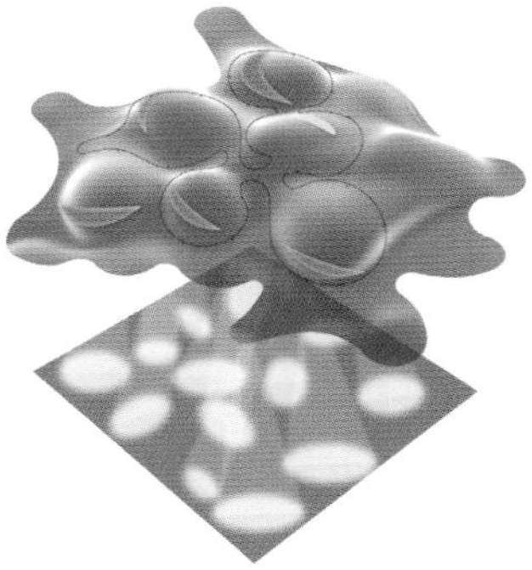

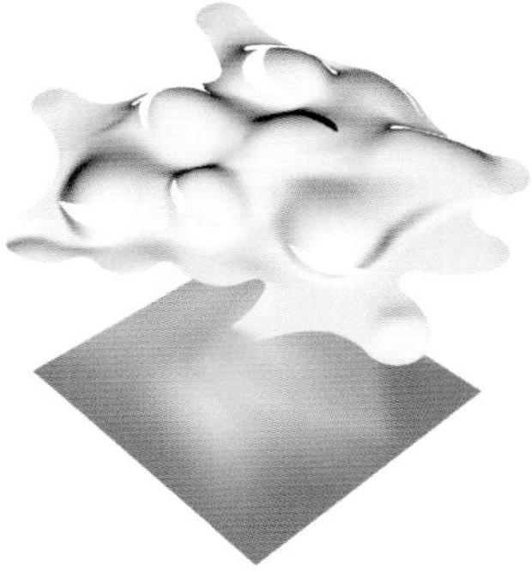

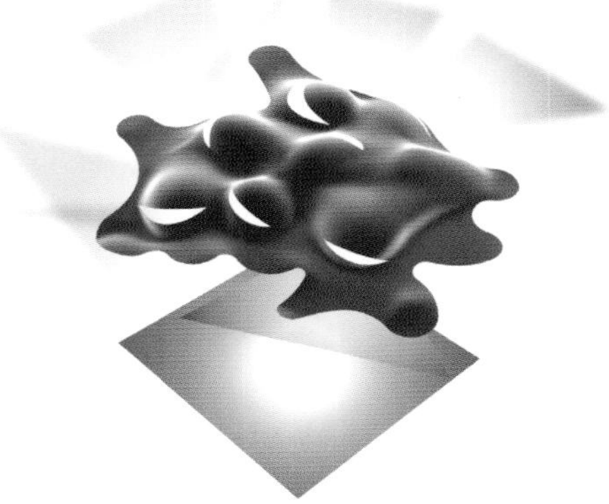

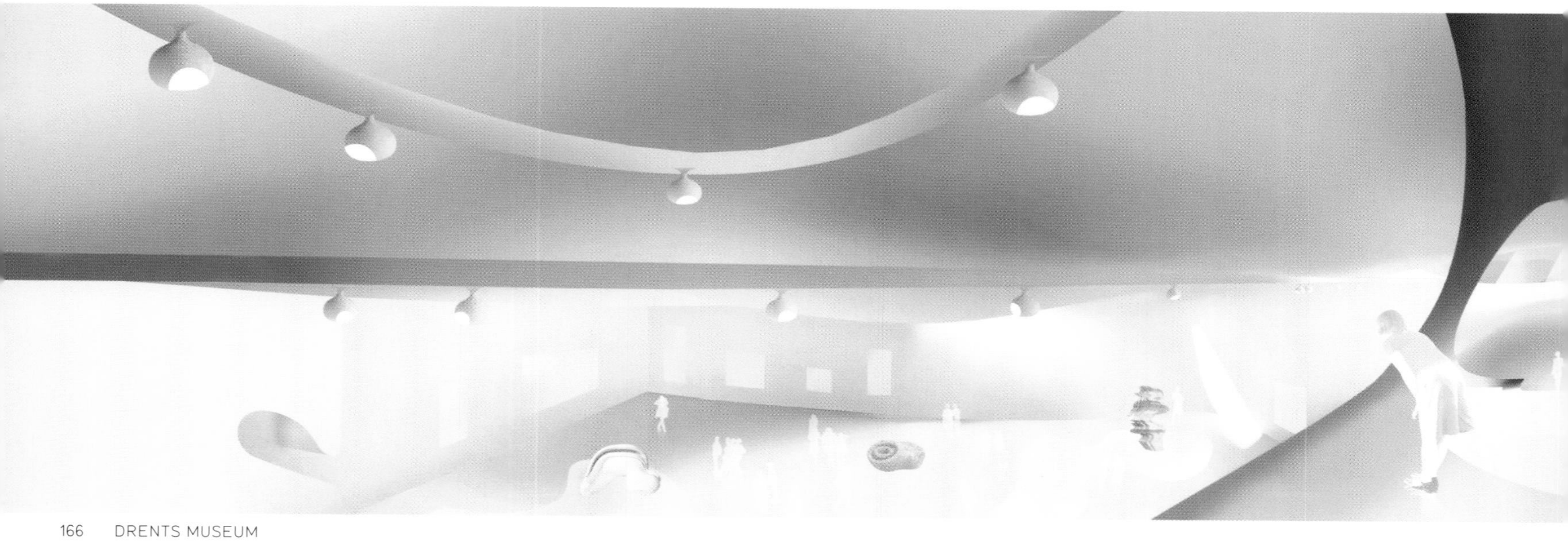

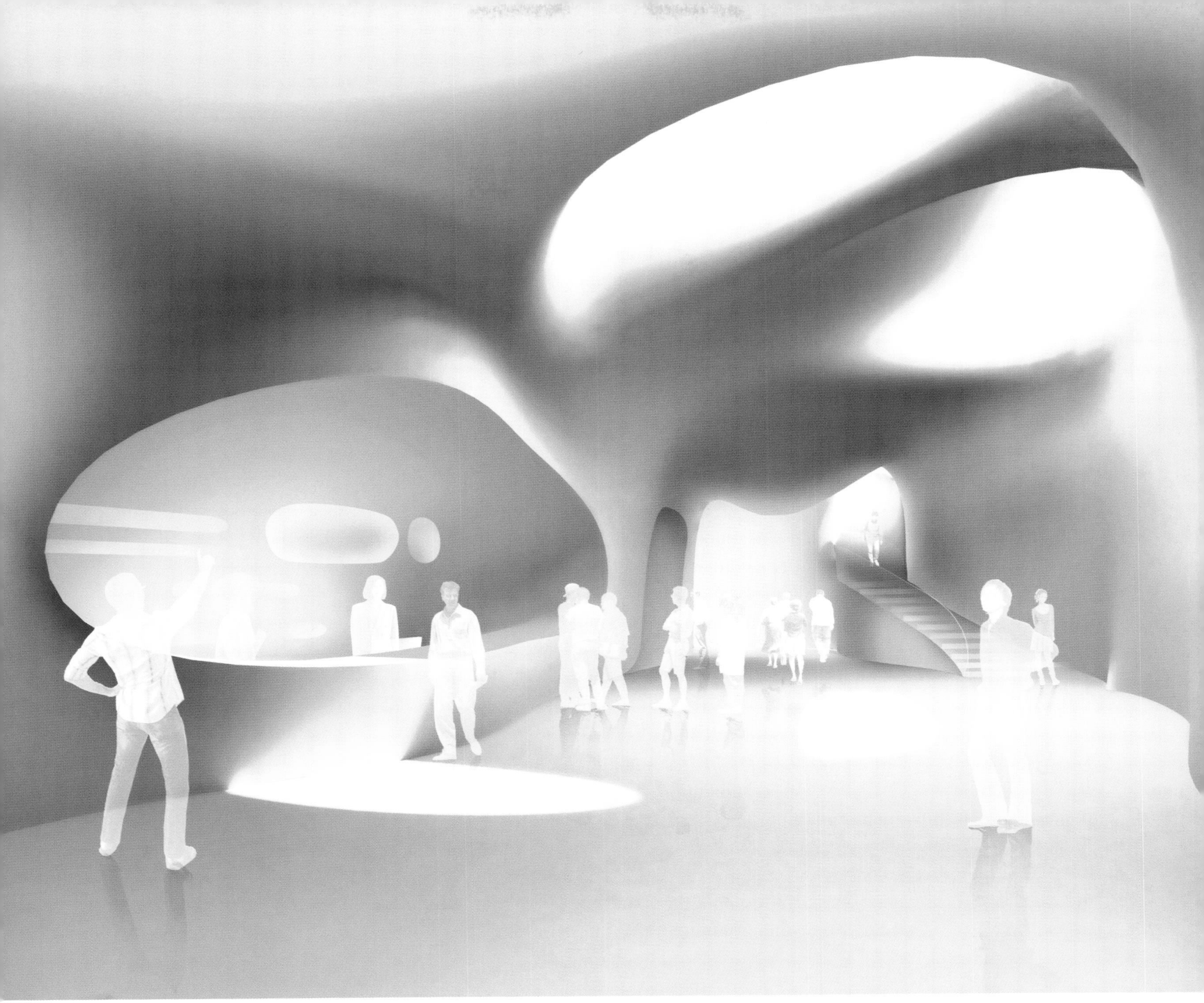

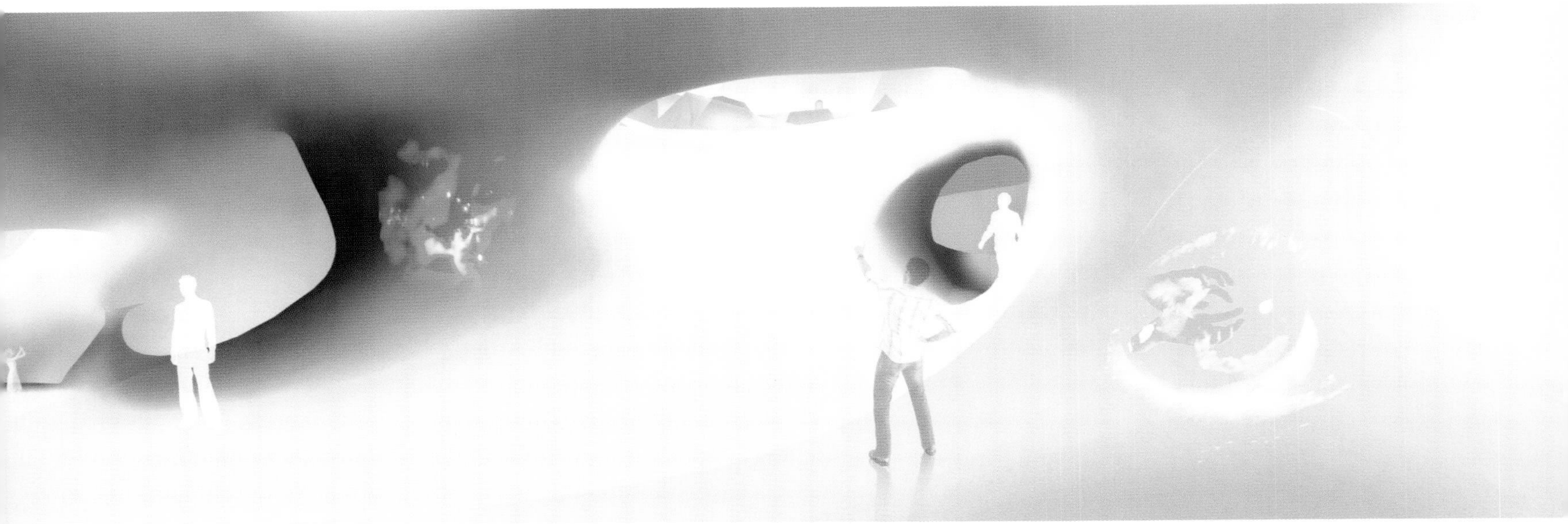

DUPLI.CASA

HOUSE NEAR LUDWIGSBURG, GERMANY

CLIENT: PRIVATE

PROJECT DATE: 2005–08

J. MAYER H.
PROJECT TEAM: JÜRGEN MAYER H., GEORG SCHMIDTHALS, THORSTEN BLATTER, SIMON TAKASAKI, ANDRE SANTER, SEBASTIAN FINCKH

ARCHITECT ON SITE: ULRICH WIESLER, STUTTGART
STRUCTURAL ENGINEER: DIETER KUBASCH, DITZINGEN
SERVICE ENGINEER: HANS WAGNER, FILDERSTADT
BUILDING PHYSICS: DR. SCHAECKE UND BAYER, WAIBLINGEN
LANDSCAPE ARCHITECT: KLAUS WIEDERKEHR, NÜRTINGEN

The private villa Dupli.Casa, set on a sloping site in the Neckar Valley near Ludwigsburg, enjoys views of the German Literature Archive in Marbach, which lies across the valley from it. The basic shape of the house was derived from its predecessor, owned by the client's family and standing here since 1984. That house had been extended via a variety of additions and expansions, but proved too dilapidated for reuse in a new construction. References to the basic form of the original structure generate programmatic allusions to the family's history in the area, and serve as a point of departure for a new beginning. While the building footprint at garden level reverts to the old ground plan, the same figure is repeated—now rotated and shifted—in the second upper story. This procedure creates a spatial tension between garden level and second story—one that is given visible form by the inclined wall elements of the intervening middle story. These slanting walls also reflect the transition between contrasting temporal layers. This story contains the main entry on the west side, an essentially open zone (with cloakroom), which accommodates social and communicative functions, such as living, cooking, and dining. A double-height lobby serves as a spatial and organizational junction between levels.

The uppermost story contains private areas, including guest- and bedrooms and an office. These appear in the plan as individually demarcated spaces, each "docked" onto a main line of the façade. Separating them at the core is a spacious buffer zone that allows each to be experienced as a separate unit. The panoramic window on the east side features a view of the Neckar Valley. The garden level serves as a residential zone for the children, and is also a "wellness" level with swimming pool. The villa accommodates all of the needs associated with a residence designed for a large family, while at the same time displacing individual functional elements into a dynamic spatial configuration.

—Andres Lepik

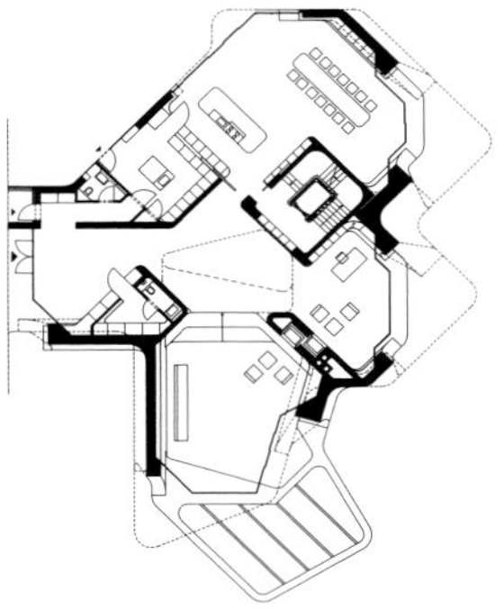

GROUND FLOOR

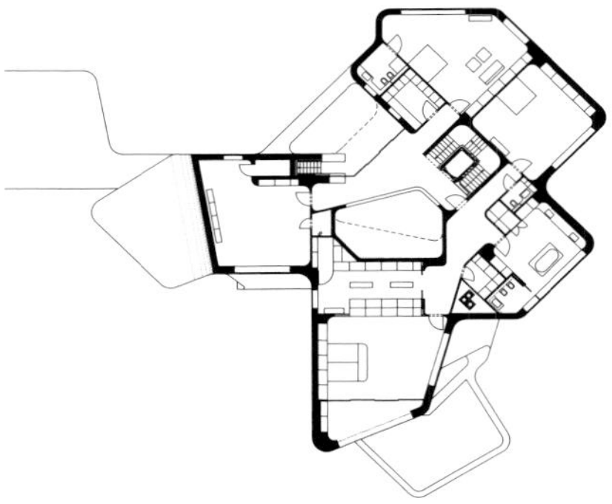

1ST FLOOR

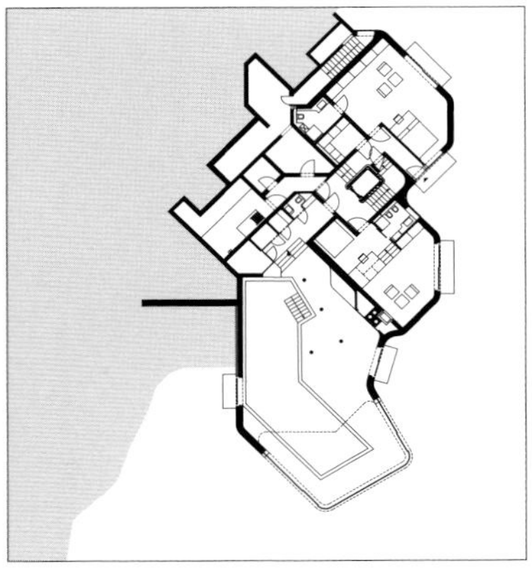

LOWER LEVEL

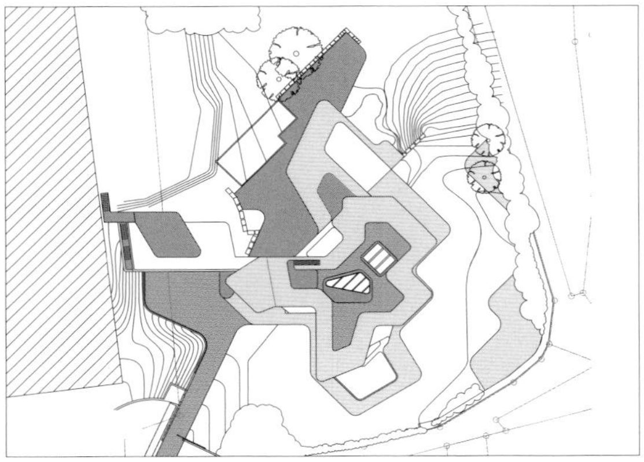

SITEPLAN

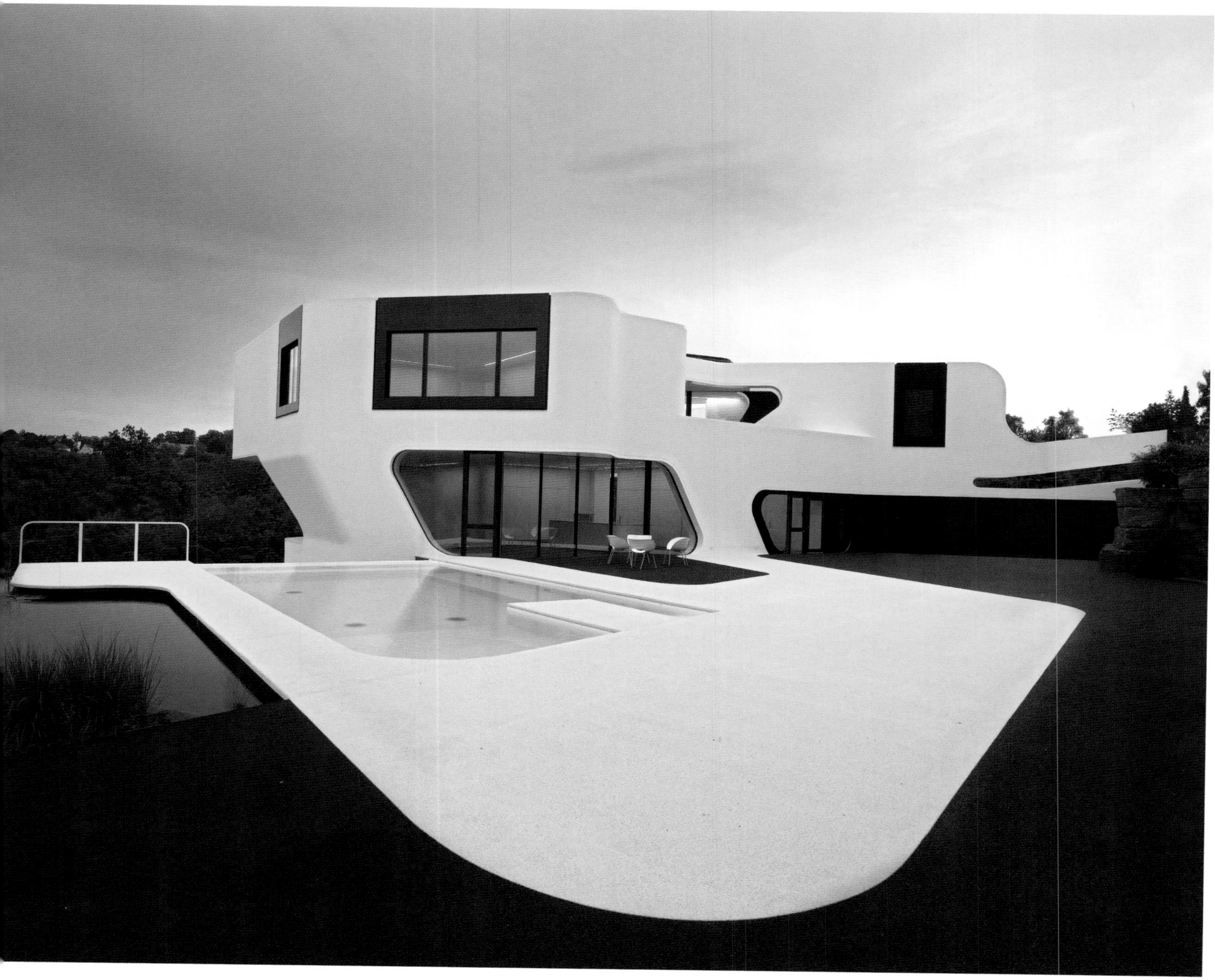

KRYSTAL HUSET

CLIENT: FORMATION A/S, DENMARK

PROJECT DATE: 2007

J. MAYER H.
JENS-MARTIN SKIBSTED
DESIGNERS: JÜRGEN MAYER H., JENS-MARTIN SKIBSTED
PROJECT TEAM: JÜRGEN MAYER H., STEPHEN MOLLOY

In recent years, the suburban house has been reinterpreted. With its new "crystal houses," the Danish company Formation is challenging the orthodoxies of the detached residence in surburban environments as well as establishing new strategies for row houses. The octagonal shape offers us various possible combinations of larger and smaller units in order to allow for public, semi-public, and private zones within a diverse community.

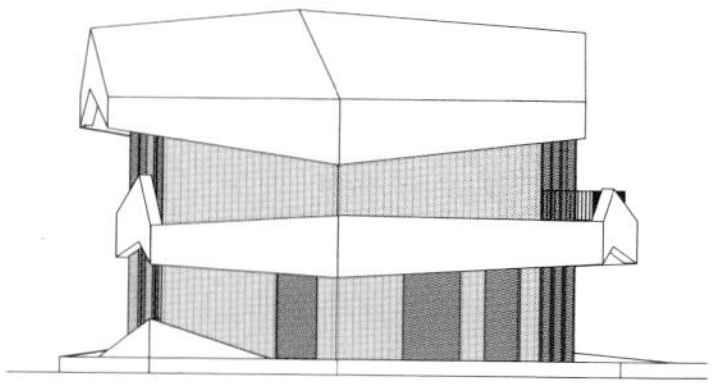

LEFT ELEVATION

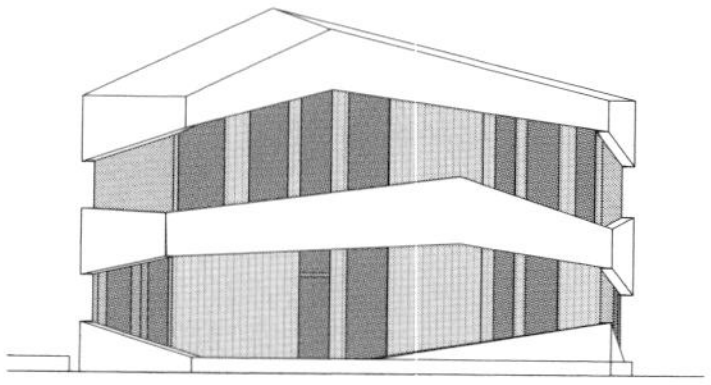

FRONT ELEVATION

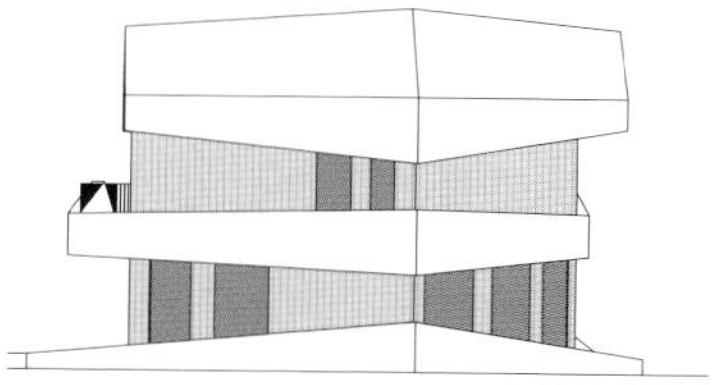

RIGHT ELEVATION

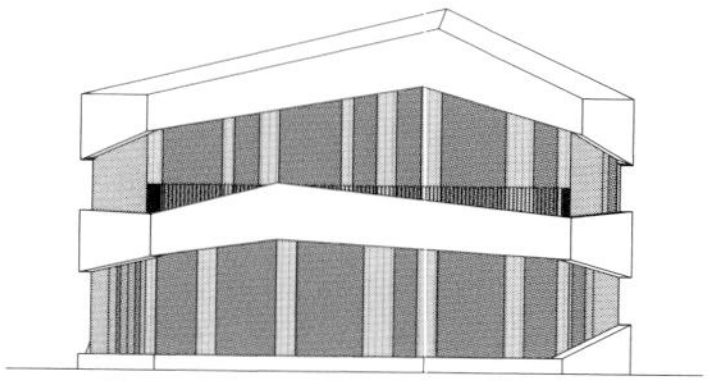

REAR ELEVATION

HEADQUARTERS EDC

CLIENT: EDC/ESPRIT, RATINGEN, GERMANY

INVITED COMPETITION: 2007, 3RD PRIZE

J. MAYER H.
COMPETITION TEAM: JÜRGEN MAYER H., JAN-CHRISTOPH STOCKEBRAND, PAUL ANGELIER, MARCUS BLUM, ALEXANDER ARNOLD, JONATHAN BUSSE, ANA ALONSO DE LA VARGA

This design is characterized by openness and dynamism. The breaking up of the building produces a strikingly sculptural silhouette with a transparent, open spatial configuration. Facing the street is a lucid main façade, which serves as the formal entrance. To the sides, where private zones are located, the building volumes spread, fingerlike, to form courtyards, which serve as recreation and communication spaces. Through the integration of the existing topography, the new building is meaningfully linked with the surrounding landscape.

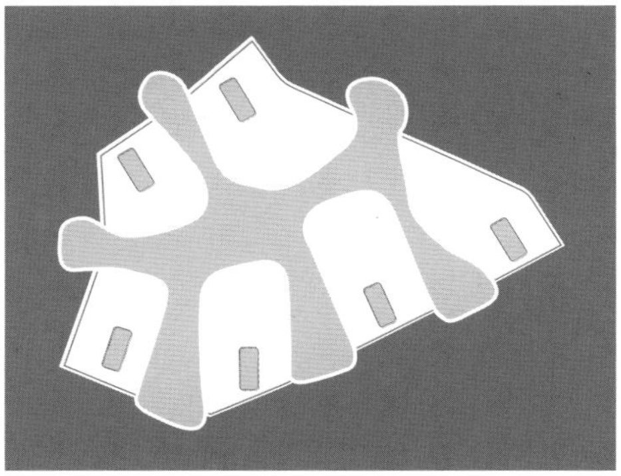

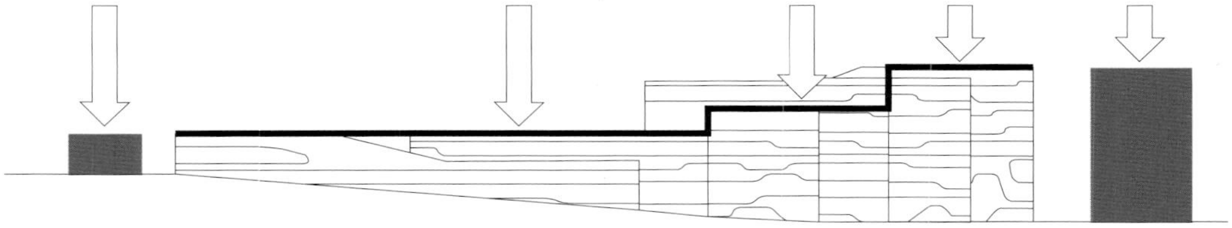

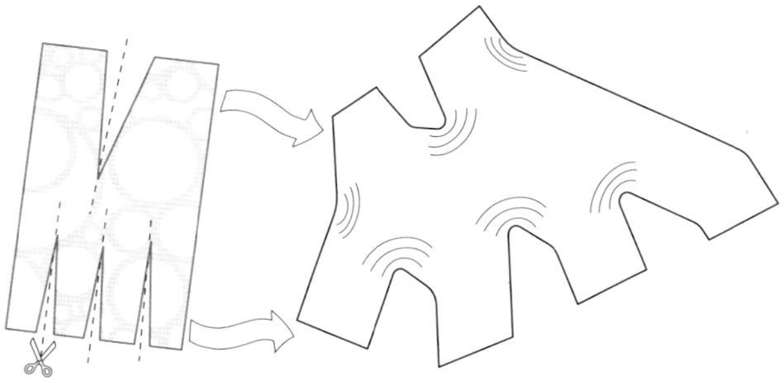

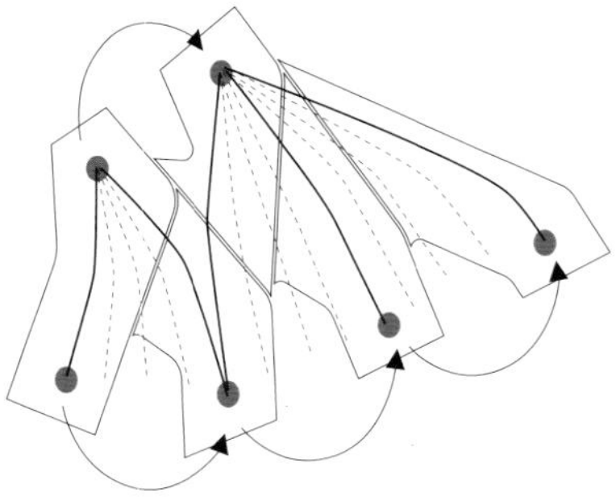

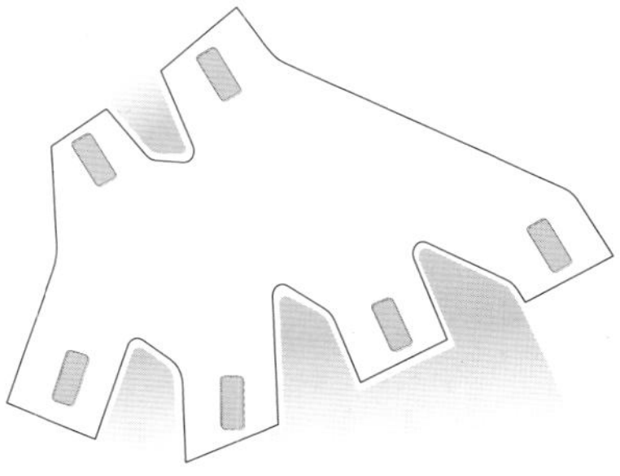

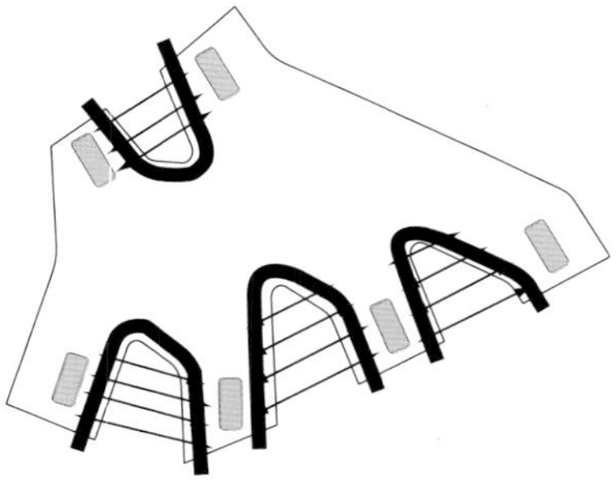

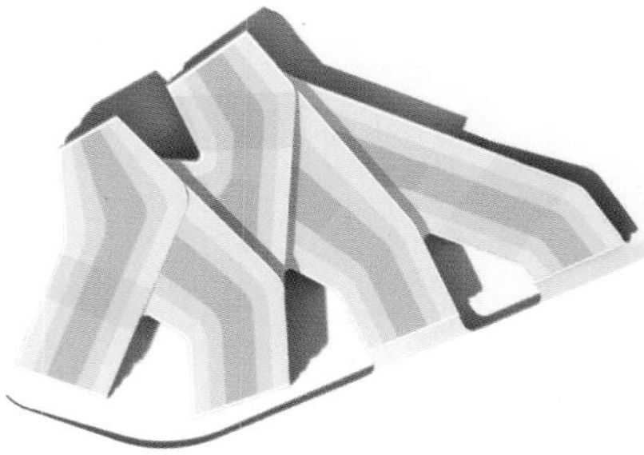

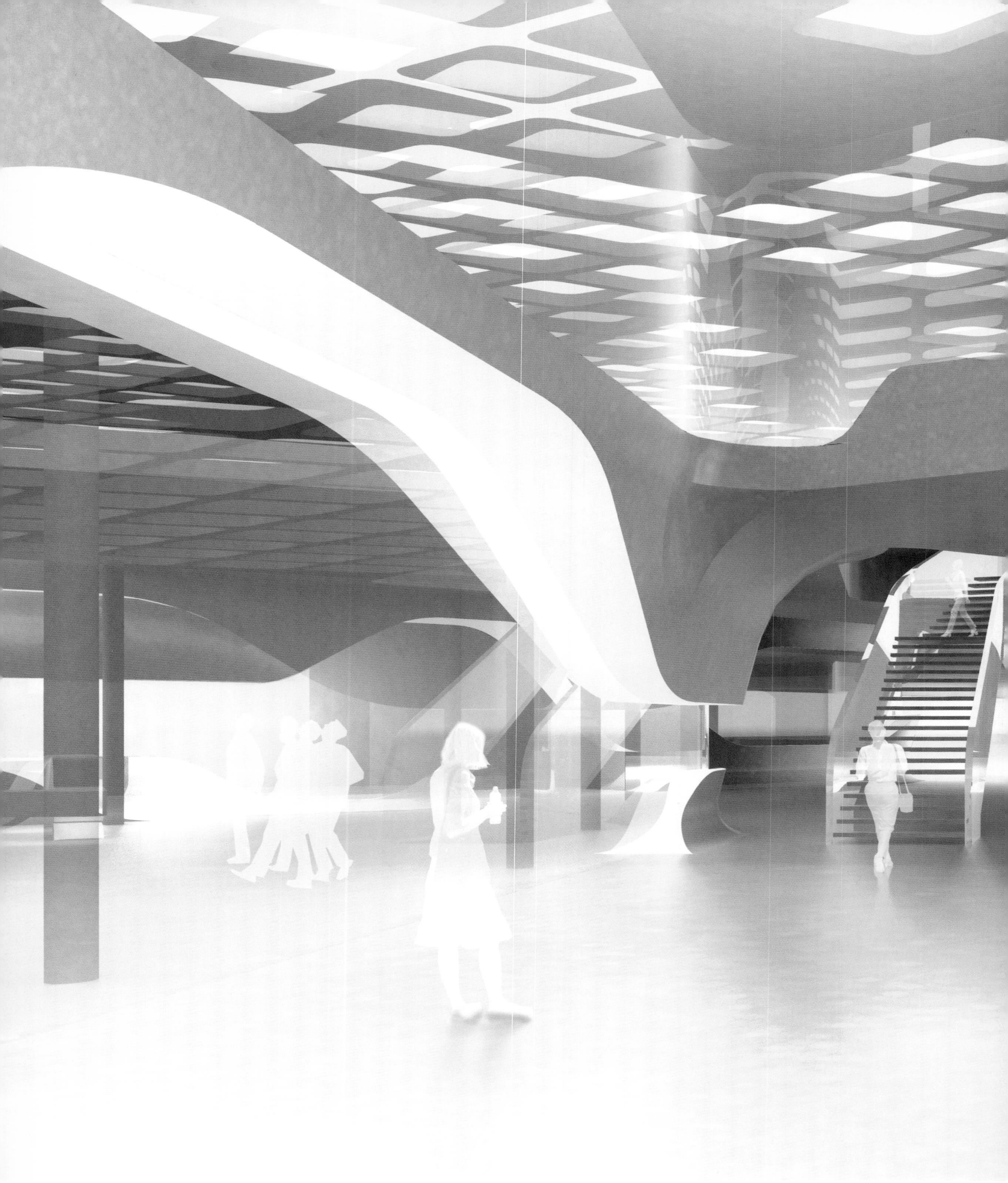

NATIONAL LIBRARY PRAGUE

CLIENT: NATIONAL LIBRARY OF THE CZECH REPUBLIC

INTERNATIONAL COMPETITION: 2006

J. MAYER H.
COMPETITION TEAM: JÜRGEN MAYER H., JONATHAN BUSSE, CHRISTOPH EMENLAUER, HANS-JÖRGEN WETLESEN, PAUL ANGELIER, MARCUS BLUM, ALESSANDRA RAPONI

MULTIDISCIPLINARY ENGINEERS: KREBS UND KIEFER, KARLSRUHE

The new national library building is regarded as a node in the worldwide network of information and communication of the twenty-first century. The Library functions as a built manifesto, connecting artifacts and virtual libraries on site as well as through the Internet. Branches of the building reach out into the surrounding urban context in order to meld building, landscape, and public space. One branch moves up to overlook this "city of a thousand towers," and, in so doing, adds one more to this ensemble, proudly proclaiming the precious collection of the Czech National Archive.

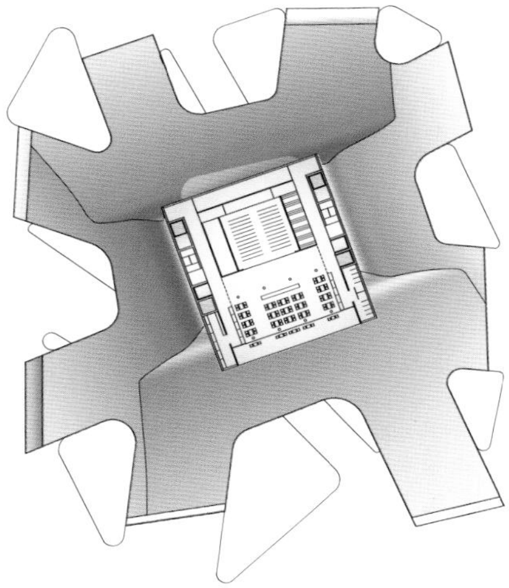

12TH FLOOR

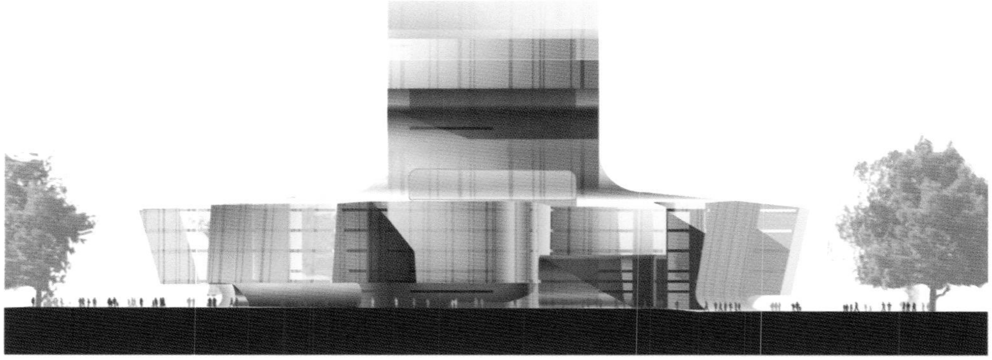

SOUTH ELEVATION

EAST ELEVATION

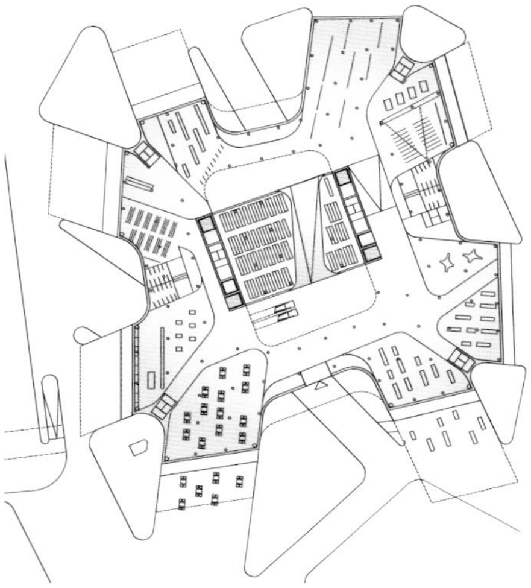

1ST FLOOR

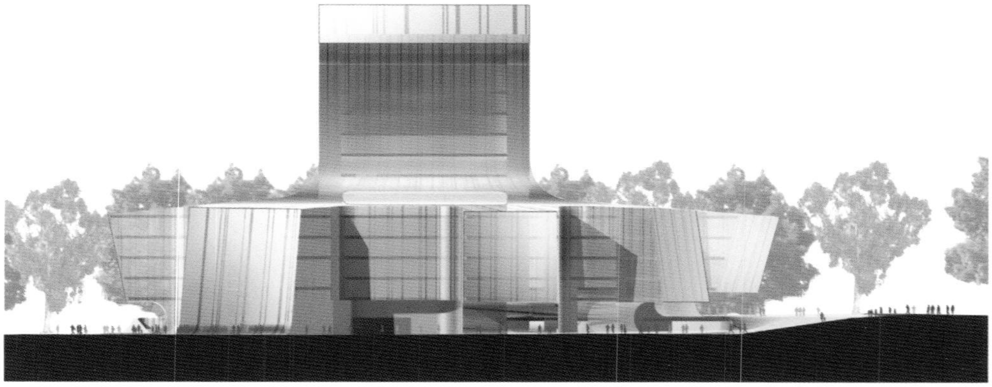

NORTH ELEVATION

POTSDAM DOCKLANDS

CLIENT: EGS—ENTWICKLUNGSGEMEINSCHAFT SPEICHERSTADT, POTSDAM, GERMANY

INVITED INTERNATIONAL COMPETITION: 2002, 1ST PRIZE

J. MAYER H.
COMPETITION TEAM: JÜRGEN MAYER H., DOMINIK SCHWARZER, MARIO ABEL, ALEXANDER ZUR BRÜGGE, SASCHA NIKOLAUSCHKE, KARLA PILZ

MULTIDISCIPLINARY ENGINEERS: ARUP GMBH, BERLIN

The historic harbor and warehousing district of Potsdam will be developed into a high-class mixed-use area. Located directly on the shore of the Havel River, the industrial nature of its historic buildings will serve as the main element in defining the location's new character. In addition to a culture and convention center, hotels, and offices, a number of spacious loft apartments will be offered to the city. The masterplan will define rules for the overall design, which will be interpreted by a number of different architects.

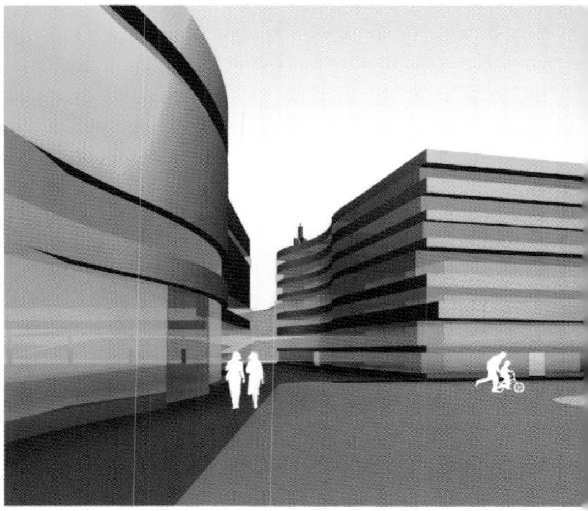

CORRIDOR

ROOFTOP APARTMENT, STYLEPARK CASE-STUDY PROJECT, BERLIN, GERMANY

CLIENT: PRIVATE

INVITED COMPETITION: 2000, 1ST PRIZE
PROJECT DATE: 2001–2008

J. MAYER H.
PROJEKT TEAM: JÜRGEN MAYER H., SEBASTIAN FINCKH, GABRIELE ROY, HANS WEIBEL, PETER MARTIN, SASCHA NIKOLAUSCHKE

ARCHITECTS ON SITE: ELWARDT UND LATTERMANN, BERLIN

Corridor is a rooftop apartment in the central Berlin district of Mitte. A stretched and winding space runs through the entire apartment. However, it is not simply a connecting space for circulation or to give orientation by the separation of individual rooms; instead, it becomes the main space for this dwelling. Independent from any formal references to its context and from any conventional floor plan, the corridor allows for further abstraction of the apartment's spatial qualities. All rooms adjacent to it function supplementarily as spaces for retreat.

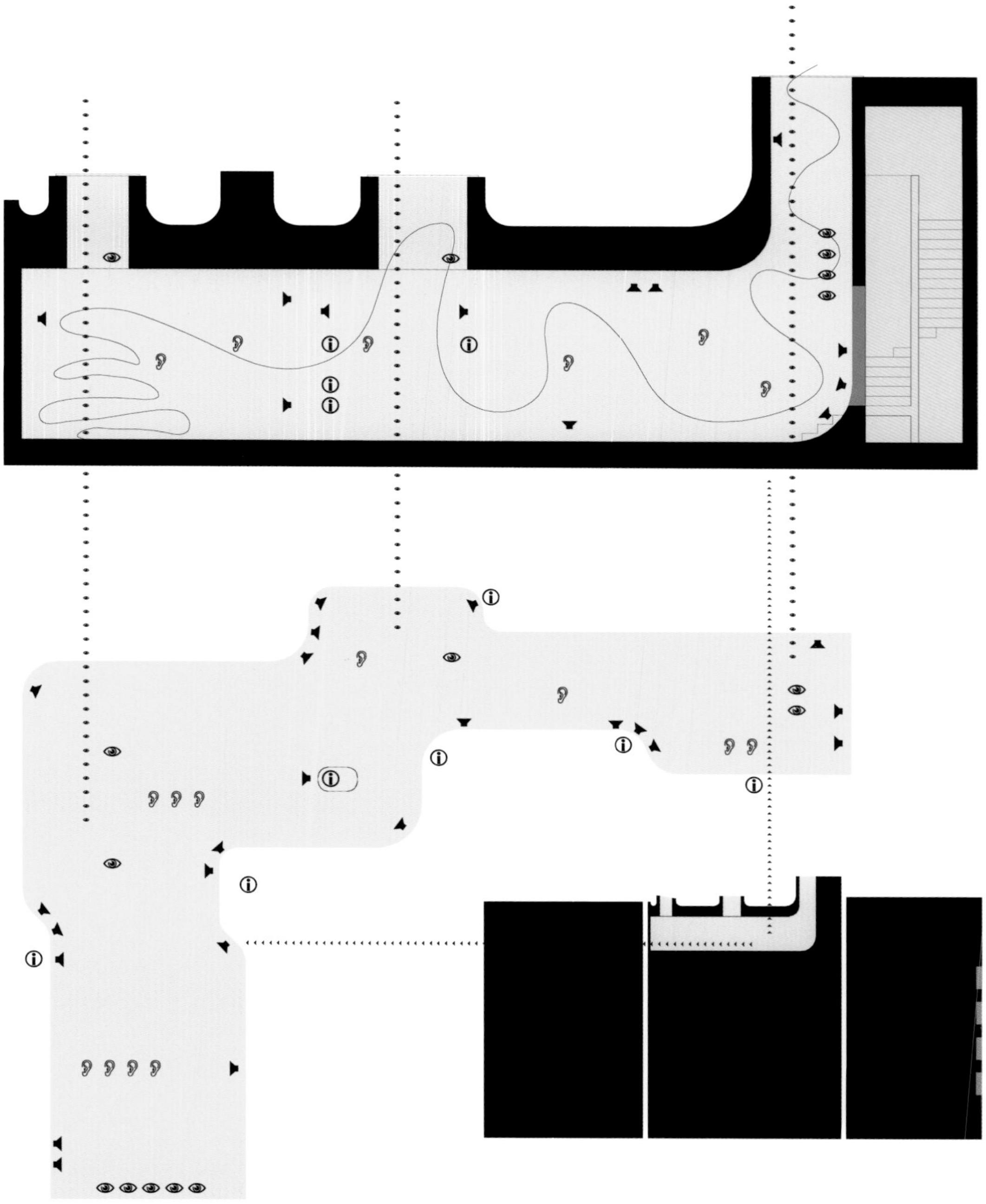

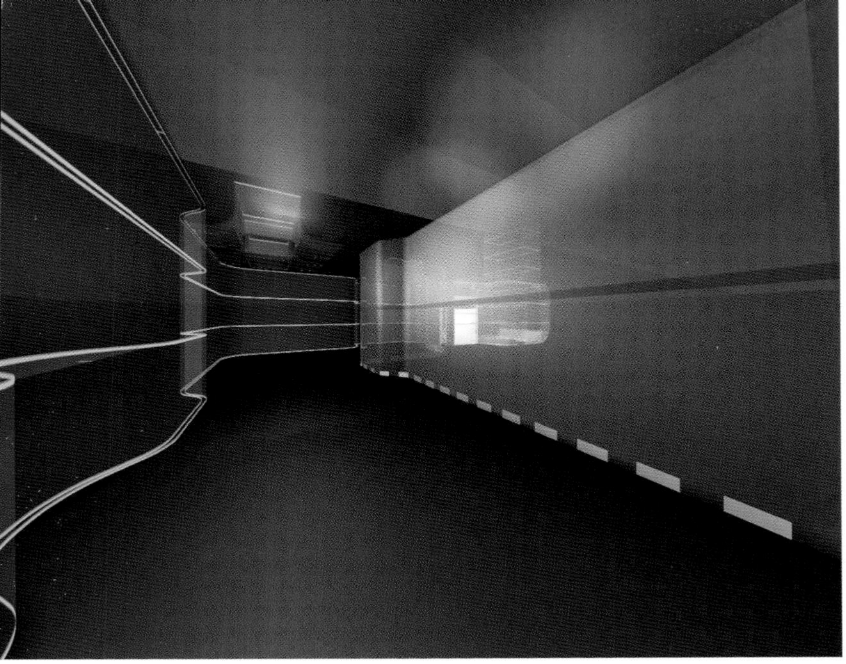

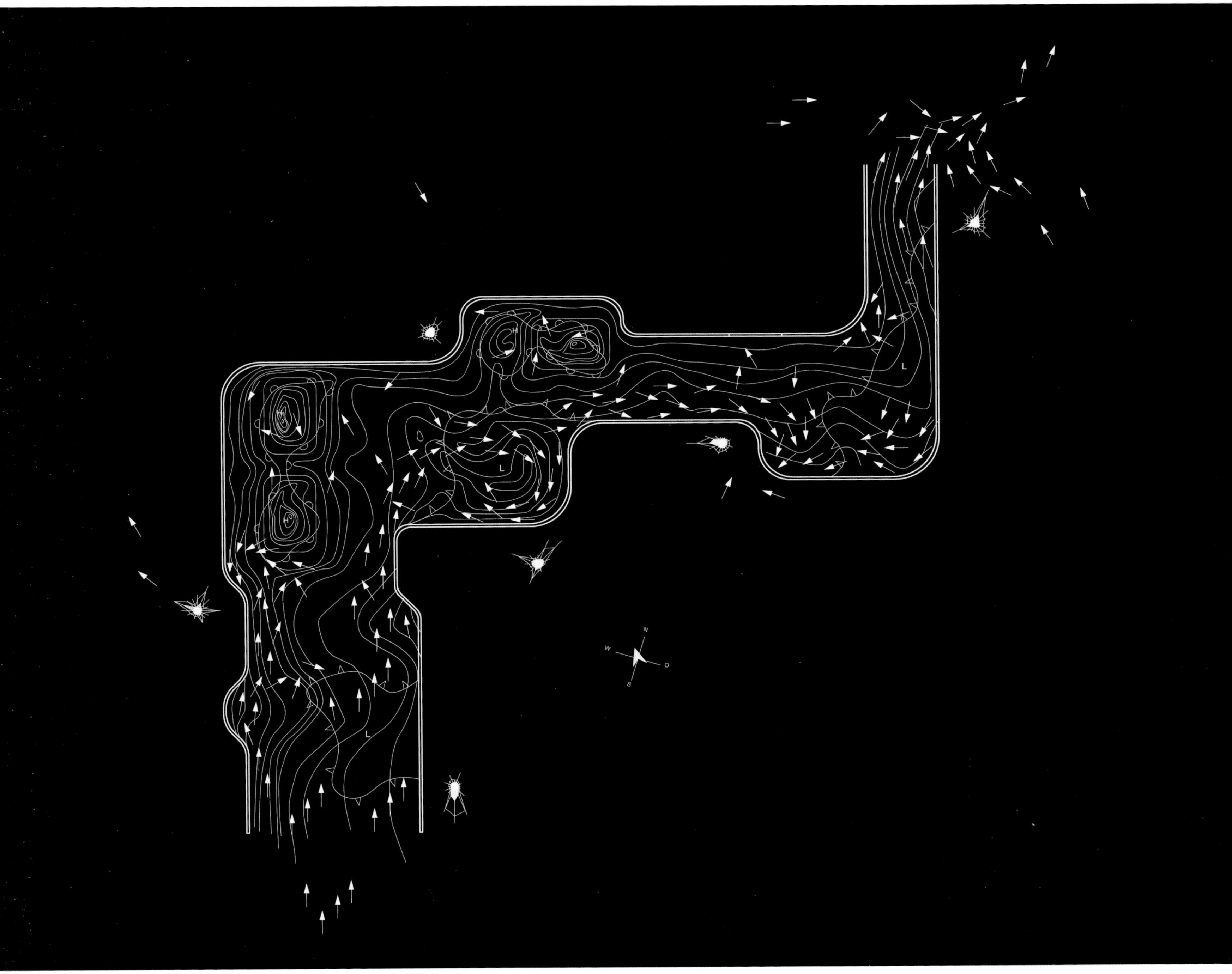
N
W
O
S
L
L
L

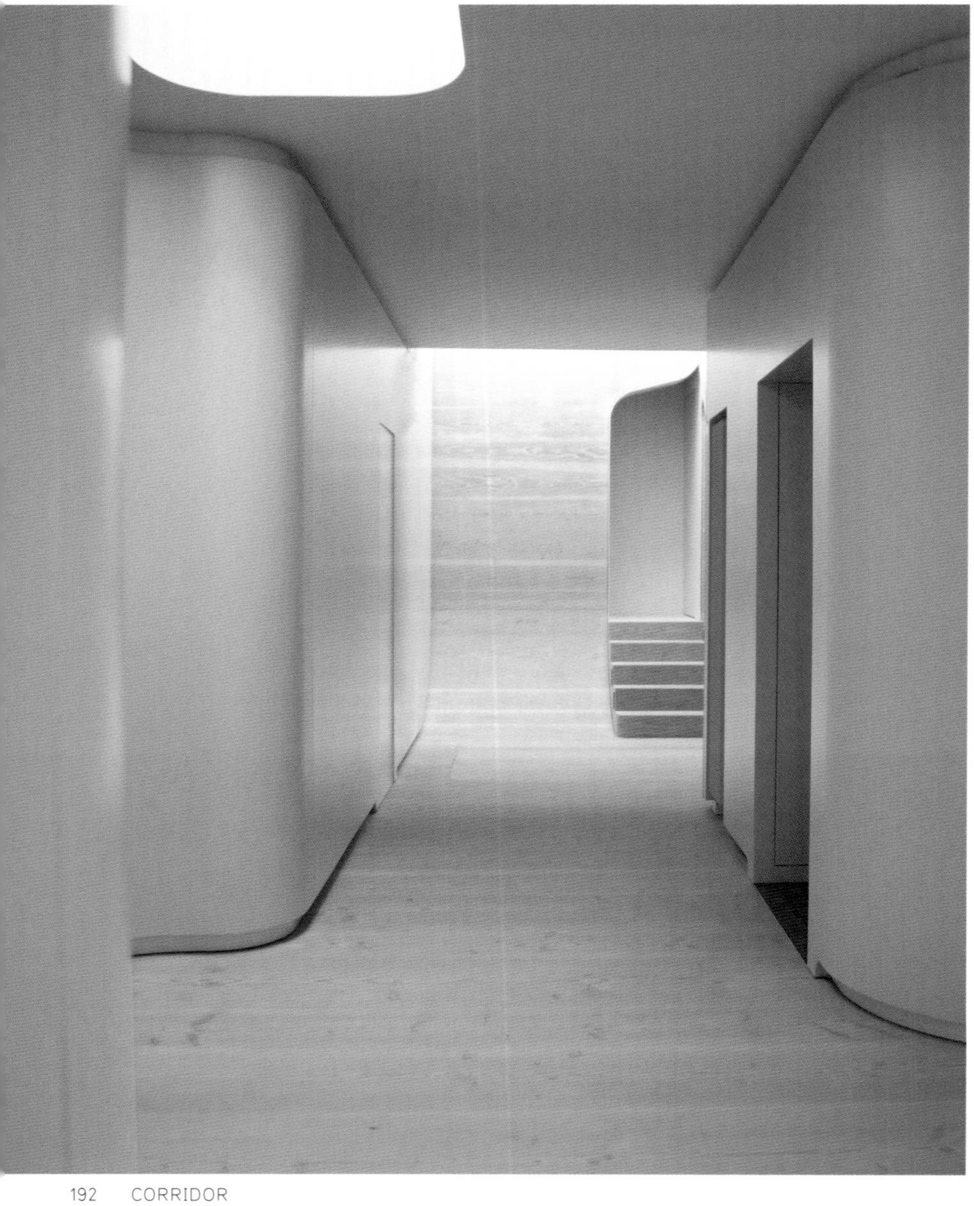

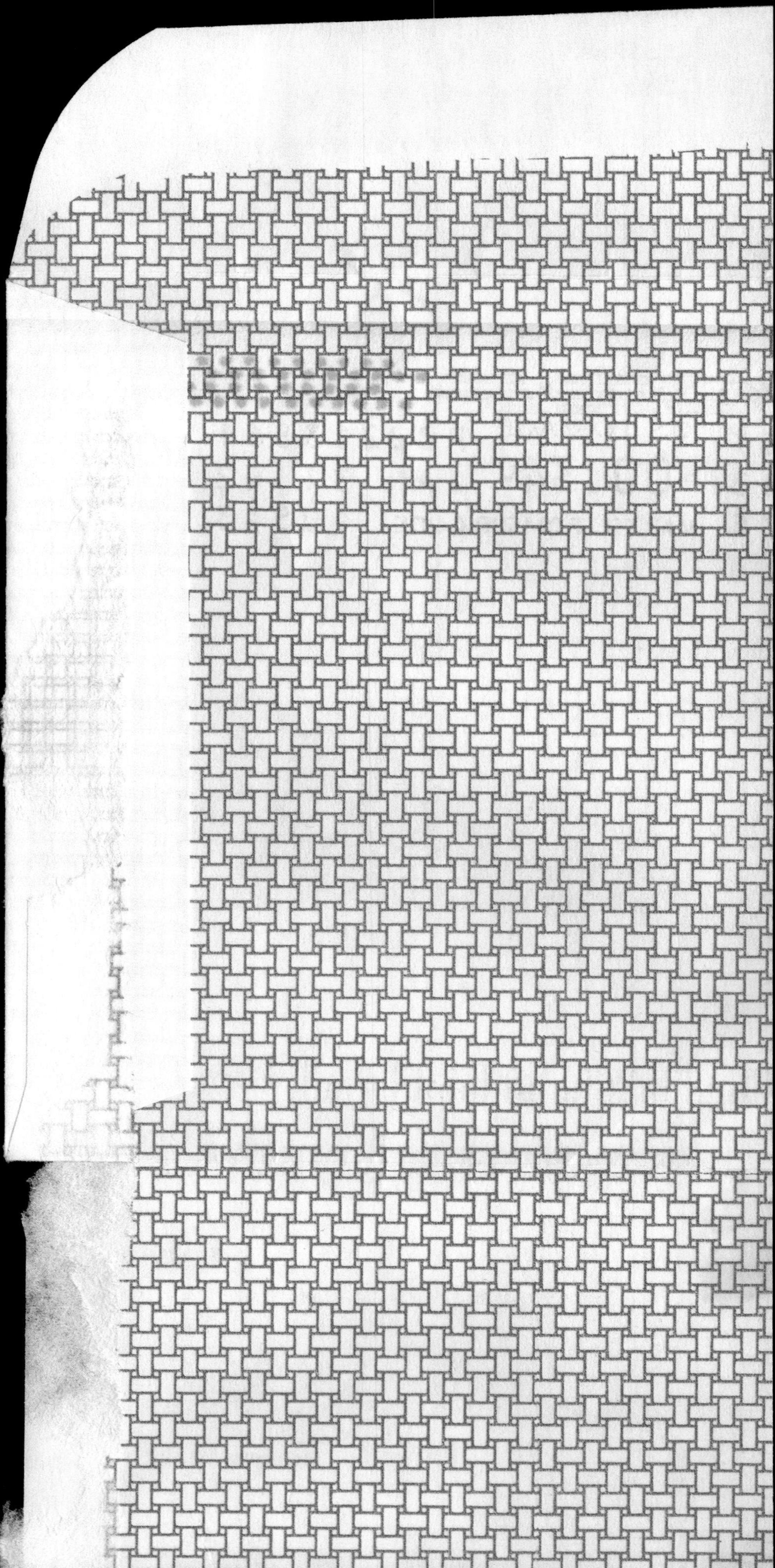

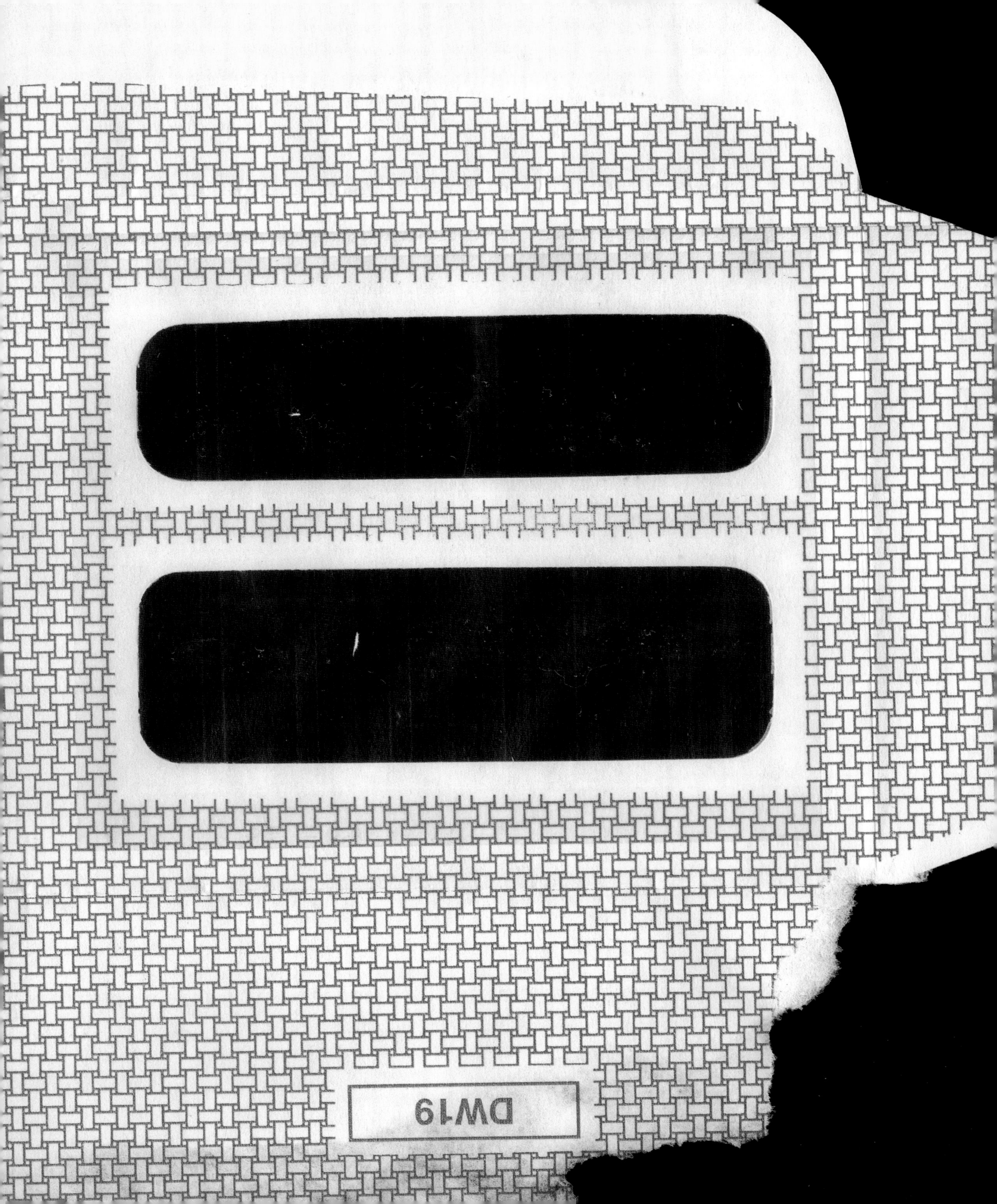
DW19

RE-ENCOUNTERING DATA

FELICITY D. SCOTT

Among its many provocations, the work of J. MAYER H. Architects suggests that we might interrogate the legacy and contemporary relevance of the architectural production of the nineteen-seventies differently, self-consciously, to other ends. In a recent conversation with Bostjan Vuga, Jürgen Mayer H. noted of that period: "there was serious excitement about technology and culture. There was hope about the future. Yet it was not uncritical. We questioned hierarchies of power, information and control." If architects in the seventies had attempted to engage potentials inherent within technology—the utopian aspects of which, as Jürgen Mayer H. noted, were often inextricable from their dystopian counterparts—it is important to recall that the technologies capturing architects' imaginations at the time were quite distinct from those that had informed high modernism. Under the impact of cybernetics, computerization, and the "third machine age," modes of production and their material substrates were no longer, strictly speaking, industrial: if not fully eclipsed by postindustrial counterparts, they had nonetheless become a complex mélange. As evidenced in the work of experimental architects—from Archigram and Cedric Price to Hans Hollein, Haus Rucker Co., Arata Isozaki, Ant Farm, and others—this historical transformation in the technological environment posed not only material and formal challenges to architects but also, and importantly, conceptual, programmatic, and organizational ones. By the early seventies, if not before, many had begun to recognize the discipline's role in giving material and spatial form to, even institutionalizing the apparatuses of, emergent techniques of power and control.[1] Jürgen Mayer H. perhaps pointed to a contemporary version of this implicit shift away from formal and semantic concerns and towards questioning "hierarchies of power, information and control" when he added to the previously cited remark: "I think the same happens today. Today we look into fluid conditions, flexibilities and horizontal organizational structures."[2]

Vuga returned later in the interview to the question of J. MAYER H.'s invocation of the seventies, referring to the office's "retro reference." To Vuga, those references risked falling into the trap of a stylistic, even fashionable, retrieval of seventies aesthetics. "Today," he remarked, "round corners, floor-wall-ceiling, continuous surfaces, soft edges, etc., are already the safe, approved and likely to be accepted derivatives of those years," to which he added that "of course, one can argue that there are still some gaps in the architectural language of the seventies to be discovered … ." Jürgen Mayer H. had earlier mentioned chamfered corners and other forms of surface continuity, and we can certainly identify such formal operations in many of his recent built works—for example, in Corridor; Mensa Moltke, and Dupli.Casa—as well as in his revisiting of Supergraphics—for instance, in In Heat and again in Housewarming MyHome. Yet, I want to suggest that this is perhaps not the register in which the office's work most evidently delaminates the dreams and nightmares of the seventies, particularly the period's anxieties regarding architecture's fate within ever-expanding information ecologies.

Vuga was, of course, entirely warranted in raising the problematic nature of a "retro-reference" methodology. Such an approach would indeed suffer from a real inefficacy in any attempt to engage historical contingencies or specificities, which would form the very matrix of a possible social and politi-

1 See Felicity D. Scott, **Architecture or Techno-Utopia: Politics After Modernism** (Cambridge, Mass., 2007); and **Living Archive 7: Ant Farm** (Barcelona, 2008).

2 Jürgen Mayer H. "In Anticipation," in **Activators, J. Mayer H.**, Design Document Series, 19 (Seoul, 2006) p. 13.

cal response. I want to ask, then, if we can read such aesthetic traces in a more symptomatic manner: not simply as stylistic or formal references, but rather as allegorical appropriations which set out to raise the very question of how to render legible both historical and contemporary anxieties about the impact upon the architectural object of new processes of data control (i.e., the loss of transparency) and their relationship with emerging techniques of power. Jürgen Mayer H. initially responded to the invocation of the term "retro reference" by suggesting that "seventies architectural language is not really revived yet. There is still something left behind, not tested. There is still a potential that I want to explore, take on and rethink for the future." If he was pointing in this context to the heaviness, even clumsiness or ugliness, of certain work from the seventies, I want to reiterate that it was perhaps not style—or even architectural language in the traditional sense—that was at stake. It was, rather, something like the manner in which bodies—both architectural and human—continued to impinge upon the apparent seamlessness of that information milieu, and the way in which that materiality could traffic in questions beyond those proper to form and aesthetics. "The materiality of architecture about thirty years ago still carries a potential to work on form and program," Jürgen Mayer H. added, offering a clue.[3]

It is important to note that in recalling such concerns we find ourselves at quite a distance from the Neo-Modernism which so captivated American architectural discourse during the seventies—as exemplified in the debate of the Grays versus the Whites, or Neo-Rationalism versus Neo-Realism—and equally distant from those more strictly European formulations of urban morphology and typology that were simultaneously offered as another starting point for a Postmodern architecture. Experimental engagement with information technology sought not to return to problems of form as the domain of architecture's contribution to the urban and social milieu, or to reassuring paradigms of representation and semantic legibility, so much as to mapping the contours of and forces driving the dissolution of both form and semantic legibility. At stake was the issue of how the discipline of architecture might operate within an electronic environment, how it could define space or territories within the streaming of data and through recursive structures of feedback, how it might negotiate to critical ends the forces that seemed to be driving that transformation. If the impact of those forces upon architecture was, in some sense, just becoming legible as critical concerns in the early seventies, then by 1996, when J. Mayer H. Architects was founded, the discipline was experiencing a new fascination with the digital. If many architects of Mayer H.'s generation sought to naturalize the discipline's relation to information technology, to render it outside the scope of critical architectural interrogation, this practice would, importantly, refuse that trend—and in so doing, it has offered some of the most compelling reconsiderations of architecture's imbrications within a contemporary technological milieu.

To understand J. MAYER H. Architects's conception of that environment, which pressures it suggests might be at work on the bodies (including architectural bodies) that inhabit it, and how the work speaks to the fate or condition of materiality under the impact of informatization, we might turn to the office's ongoing research with one of its key components: data. From early Data Protection Pattern (DPP) projects such as Gästebuch (Visitors' book) and Lie, we find Jürgen Mayer H. musing on technologies and material substrates (in this case, print) that are designed to control the flow of data. These projects retrieved an early-twentieth-century technology, DPP, that was developed to veil information in print media by producing an information overload. An excess of information (print characters) serves to camouflage or render illegible a particular message, allowing, as Jürgen Mayer H. explains, private information to be transmitted through the public realm (whether the mail system or simply the hands of others) in order to be received elsewhere. In Full.House, we find an installation in which the DPP has spread from the pages of visitors' books and the surfaces of bed linen, as mentioned above, to wallpaper, pictures, and updated versions of the office's earlier designs for tile-covered or pixelated soft furniture. Describing the project, Jürgen Mayer H. points to the archaeological nature of the work, suggesting: "these patterns can be interpreted as a contemporary ornamental byproduct of the process of data control. They are prototypical for the information transactions of the twentieth century and invoke the current debate around personal privacy and the public domain."[4] These artifacts, however, now figure as components in something like a *Gesamtkunstwerk* (total work of art), suggesting an environment in which every artifact comes saturated with the specter of information transactions, literally surfaced with "ornamental byproduct[s] of the process of data control." Here is a new type of "writing on the walls," a new type of communication or media environment.

To reiterate, and as Jürgen Mayer H. reminds us, DPP is an early-twentieth-century technology. It is the product (or by-product) of an era of analog media, in which the imprint or registration of a numeral or alphabetical character—whether in print, on printing plates, or on carbon paper—took on a recognizable physical form (just as with the trace of sound on a record or of an image in a print or photograph, or even, as was assumed, an architectural function in a building), even if those forms are here rendered so dense and impacted as to occlude that very legibility. The obsolescence of this analog form

3 Jürgen Mayer H. "In Anticipation," p. 19.

4 http://www.jmayerh.de/home.htm, accessed May 14, 2008.

of data protection in a digital age suggests, to stress the point, that its deployment here is allegorical. Its digital counterpart (whether thought of as encryption or noise) would have to operate in a condition where information had not only been reduced to streams of zeroes and ones, but in which such data could modulate from text to sound to image without recourse to a particular material form. Jürgen Mayer H.'s use of DPP perhaps also serves to remind us that the imprints or impressions of industrial technology find a certain updating in electronic and digital media. That is to say, the human body and psyche experience something like electronic imprinting in the very altered modes of reception sponsored by these new forms of transmission, in the subject's learned habituation to the vicissitudes and transmutability of post-industrial technologies. (We might additionally recall here the presence of Pitter.Patterns on the Stadthaus Scharnhauser Park, which implies not only the doubling of the material façade but which performs multiple possible transmutations through feedback systems and electronic control.)

But it is not, of course, DPP alone that establishes the performative character of these projects, for the DPP on their surfaces is printed using temperature-sensitive paint or ink, a sensing technology derived from NASA in order to render structural failures visible. Here, thermosensitivity is deployed to render the human body itself a programmatic element: at once a carrier of data in the form of the traces it leaves behind, and the vehicle for a passage towards forms of transparency. Touching, holding, sitting, lying, or pressing against these surfaces, the body interferes with the interruption of communication to facilitate data exchange, often of the most private nature. By its very presence the body serves as one more piece of communication equipment, but in so doing it also speaks to certain vulnerabilities in its activities that are a by-product of the information environment. As Jürgen Mayer H. acknowledged in the interview with Vuga, "The consciousness of leaving traces in our risk control society turns every surface into something that suspiciously captures personal information. Architecture is not innocent anymore, maybe never was."[5]

Architecture's lack of innocence regarding the body's modes of inscription within the built environment was perhaps best recalled by Path.Logic, a monitoring system which tracked visitors' pathways through the exhibition CTRL.Space at the ZKM (Center for Art and Media) Karlsruhe, presenting them with a souvenir printout of their individual trajectory upon departure. If reminding us of the early-twentieth-century time-space studies of Frank and Lilian Gilbreth—which tracked movements undertaken during simple labor tasks in order to evaluate their functional efficiency, and hence their profitability within industrial modes of capitalism—we also find here a certain epistemological distance. Path.Logic diagrams were not produced from the visual traces emitted by a light attached to a laboring body, but rather offered a data-image or data-shadow derived from an electronic monitoring system in which the body's actions were tracked not for their efficiency but for their patterns and habits, even during leisure. In this, Path.Logic recalls contemporary practices of extracting surplus information from our spending patterns (think of credit-card or Internet purchases), which is recuperated as saleable marketing data for contemporary forms of capitalist profitability.

Perhaps the most ironic troping, or most discomforting reading of the contemporary body's precarious state of suspension within this information milieu, is offered by Body.Guards. Body.Guards is a proposal for an invisible, adaptive "smart dust," a swarming nano-device that operates as a "new kind of outfit" in order to provide both a form of detection and a defense mechanism within an increasingly hostile, even militarized, environment. "Nearly invisible airborne particles," we are told, "build up a dynamic intelligent cocoon for testing, warning, spying, scouting, communicating, guarding and protection," scouring the environment for "physical, biological, chemical or radioactive hazards." Paranoid in the literal sense of the term, the project speaks not only to our suspension within interconnected information systems too complex to decode, but also to our condition as relay points within ubiquitous computing systems, mapping our capacity (or lack thereof) to launch strategies of defense (whether psychological or physiological) within it. This prosthetic device, which also updates long-standing architectural fantasies of reducing the built environment to a wearable technology, purports to offer something like an illusion of immunity or even agency within that milieu. However, it is self-consciously cast as external to the body—literally, in the architect's words, "an artificial, external immune system."[6] In this potential occlusion of our receptiveness to the environment as such, we find the appearance of a new form of blasé attitude, an updating of that which was theorized by Georg Simmel in order to account for the psychological profile of the metropolitan dweller of the early twentieth century. A new set of prosthetics are needed for this state of suspension, those which no longer simply supplement our eyes, ears, and hands, but also our very psychological makeup.

The idea that the flexible and systematic logics of postindustrial technologies might give rise to new, even liberating, modes of participation within the built environment has long fueled experimental architectural fantasies. In the work of J. MAYER H., we can begin to trace a distinct set of responses to the condition of the subject suspended within a now evidently pervasive information milieu. If, on the

5 Jürgen Mayer H. "In Anticipation," p. 23.

6 **Activators, J. Mayer H.**, p. 213.

one hand, the use of thermosensitive coatings serves to "confuse" or "merge" the viewer with the art and environment—their bodily traces literally inscribed, at least for a moment, on the surface of the objects and spaces through touch, "creating a temperature shadow"—then, on the other hand, the ghostly presence of the human and the evident disappearance of this "temperature shadow" in time seem to recall Foucault's remarks about the disappearance of "man." The very notion of humanity, he suggested in the final pages of *The Order of Things,* might prove to be an antiquated epistemological construct, the product of certain "arrangements of knowledge," which could "be erased, like a face drawn in the sand at the edge of the sea."[7] If the humanist subject can be recognized as a discursively constructed mirage, this does not imply that the human as such disappears. The work of J. MAYER H. calls upon us to ask how our understanding of subjectivity, and of the modes of inscription of a subject within both an architectural environment and a socio-political framework, might be radically rethought; how, with the historical emergence and now contemporary ubiquity of control technologies, the very figure of the human seems not simply to dissolve without a trace but to have become disseminated within those "fluid conditions, flexibilities, and horizontal organizational structures." What appears to be at stake, then, in this return of a body suspended in time or duration, suspended within an information environment, is the question of how it might appear not only as a data shadow but also be situated as something like a self-conscious and material interruption.

What I am suggesting here is that the problem of how to engage with new and emergent territories of data, or how to enlist them for new and alternative ends, might be taken as a challenge to the discipline of architecture, a challenge to continuously formulate new ethical responses to the environment, new modes of being and belonging, new forms of life. In the wake of revelations emerging from the social and technological experimentation of the seventies, and faced with ever more precise and expansive forms of regulation and control, we can read the work of J. MAYER H. as suggesting that architecture can still articulate a response to these forms, operating not only in the formal register but also to incite a set of ethical reflections. The work prompts us to ask how architecture can take into account those "hierarchies of power, information and control" even if they remain radically unstable, only partially knowable; how, as a discipline, it might continuously and without apology speak to broader pressures impacting its conceptualization and production. One testing ground for articulating responses to this uncertain and non-transparent condition is what J. MAYER H. has designated an "activator," an architectural object which sponsors a mode of interaction with the environment in which both the designer and the user emerge as co-authors of an indeterminate outcome—that is, in which they are situated in relation to a material interface that is never entirely what it seems, but in respect to which we must each take responsibility for our actions. Architecture here has become precisely that interface or activator.

7 Michel Foucault, **The Order of Things** (New York, 1970) p. 387.

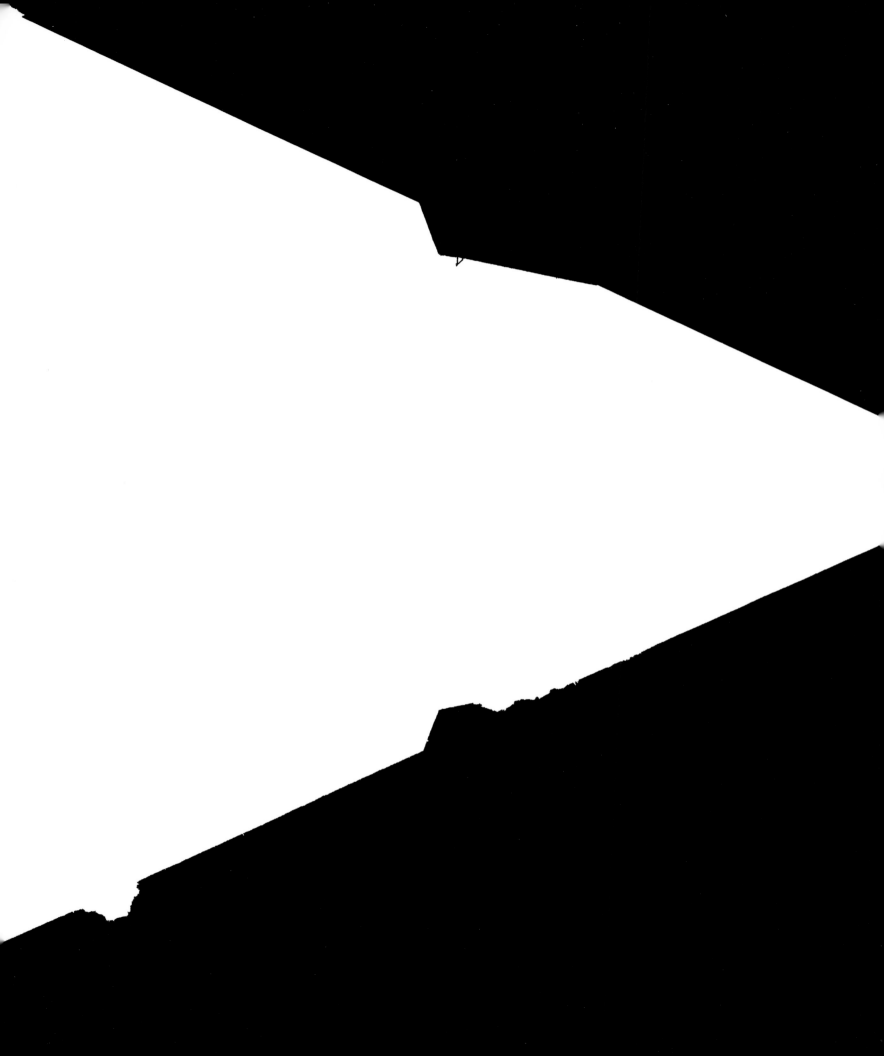

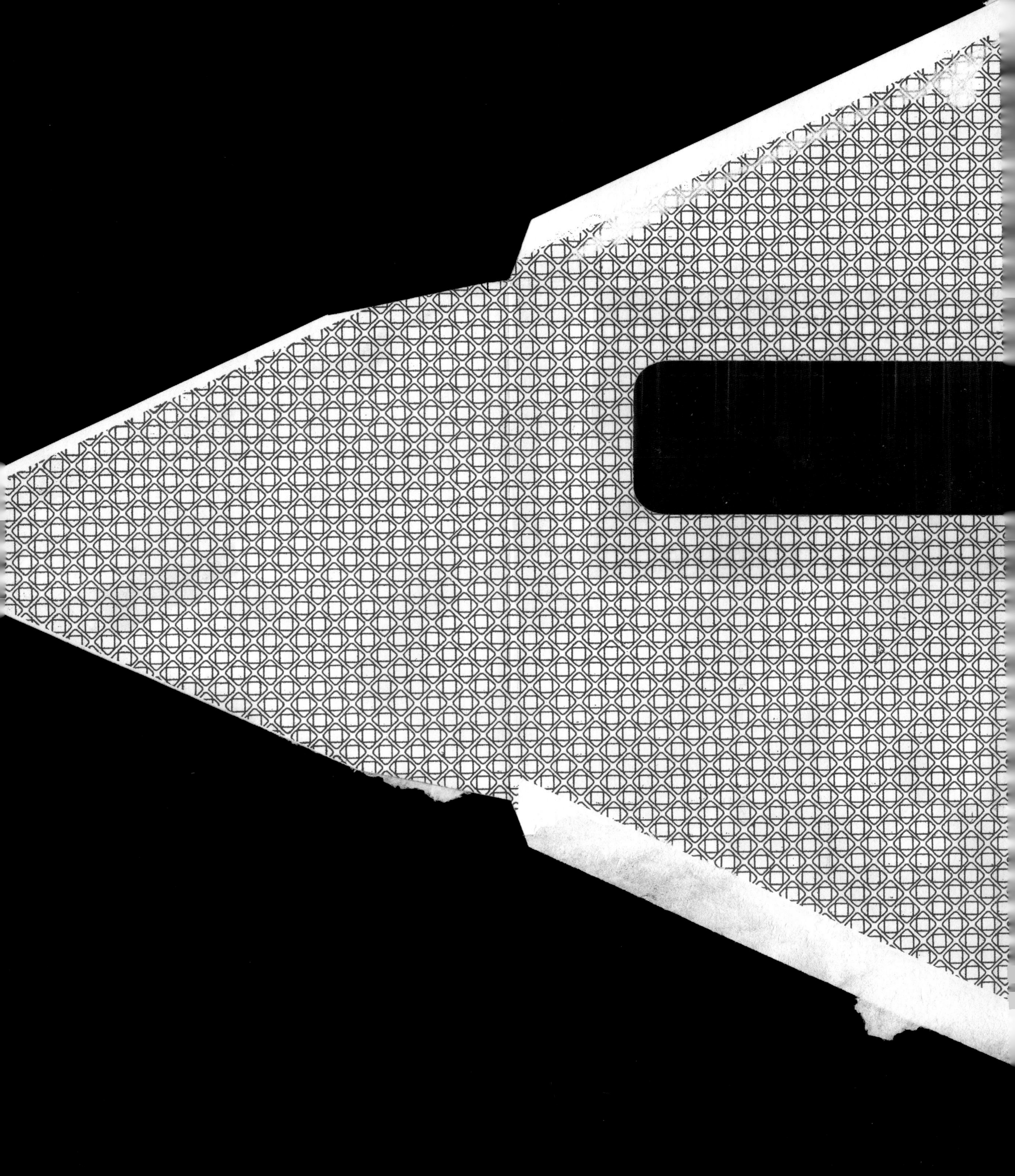

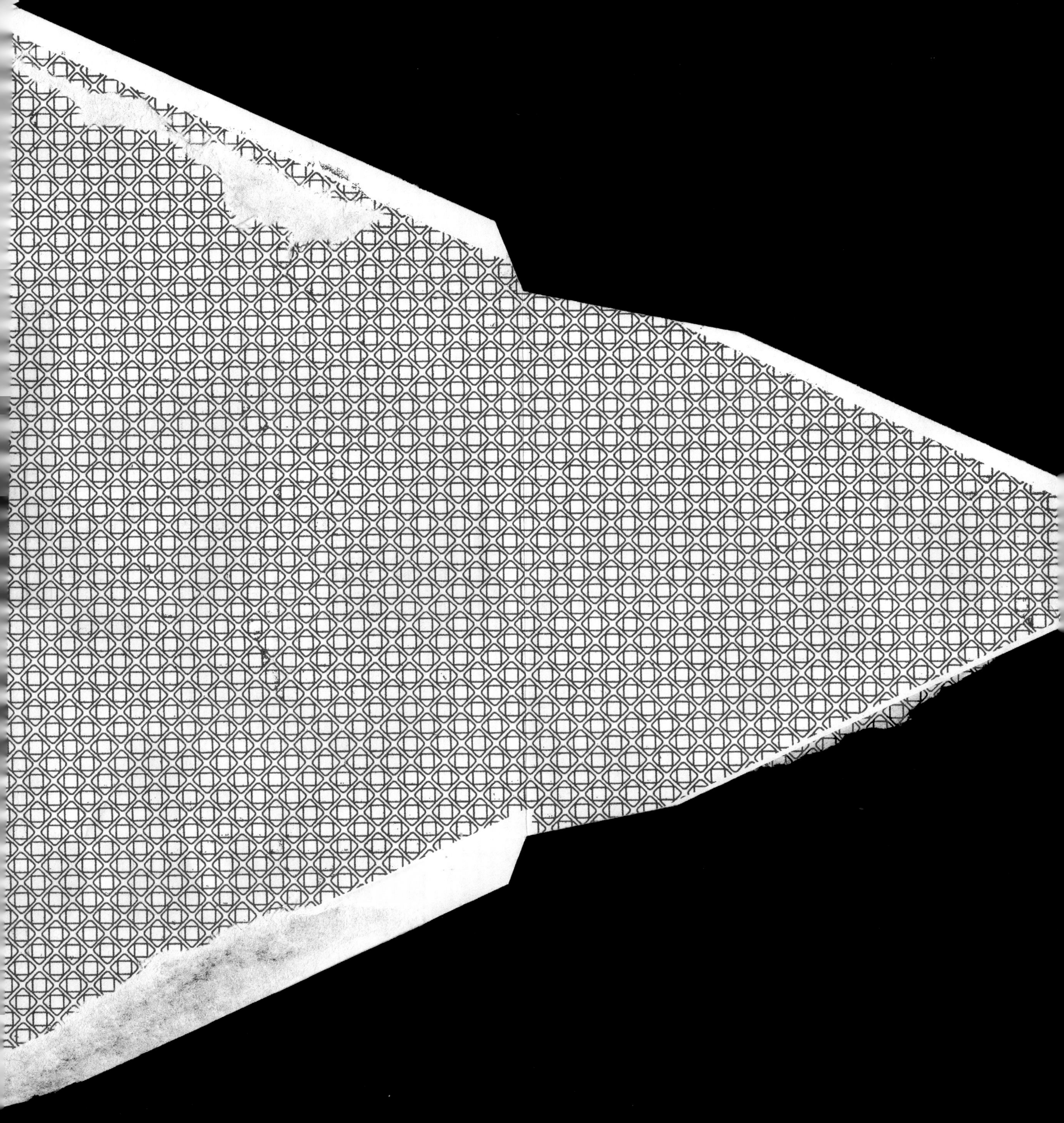

ATTRAKTION NACHHALTIGKEIT

ATTRACTION SUSTAINABILITY
CLIENT: AUTOSTADT IN WOLFSBURG, GERMANY

INVITED COMPETITION: 2007, 1ST PRIZE

PROJECT DATE: 2007–09

J. MAYER. H.
PROJECT TEAM: JÜRGEN MAYER H., JAN-CHRISTOPH STOCKEBRAND, PAUL ANGELIER, MEHRDAD MASHAIE, JONATHAN BUSSE, DANIEL MOCK, STEFAN HENTRICH

COOPERATION: ART&COM, BERLIN
ARCHITECTS ON SITE: JABLONKA SIEBER ARCHITEKTEN, BERLIN

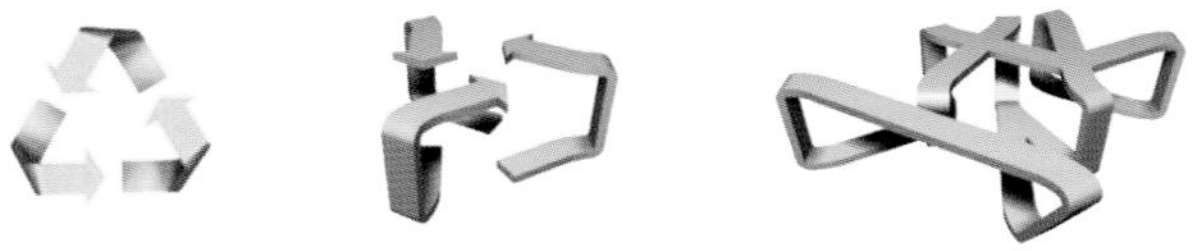

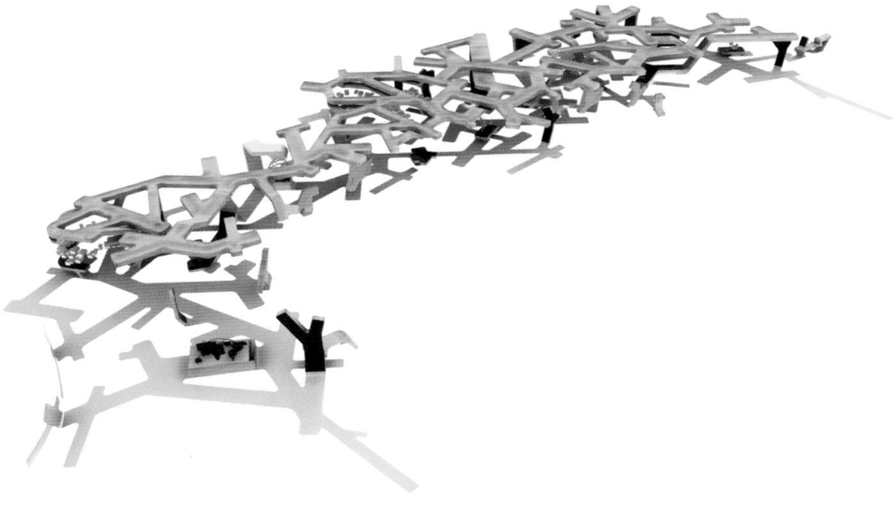

BEAT.WAVE

A SITE-SPECIFIC ENTRANCE
PULSE CONTEMPORARY ART FAIR, MIAMI, US

PROJECT DATE: 2007

J. MAYER H.
PROJECT TEAM: JÜRGEN MAYER H., JONATHAN BUSSE

COURTESY OF PULSE AND MAGNUS MÜLLER GALLERY, BERLIN, GERMANY

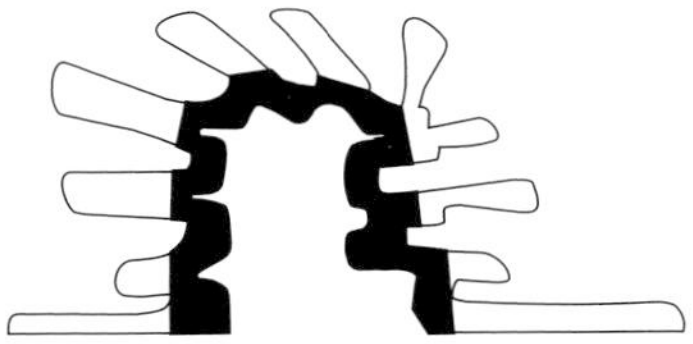

CHIT.CHAT

SEATING SCULPTURE
MAGNUS MÜLLER GALLERY, ART FORUM BERLIN, GERMANY

PROJECT DATE: AUGUST–OCTOBER 2007

J. MAYER H.
PROJECT TEAM: JÜRGEN MAYER H., MEHRDAD MASHAIE, PAUL ANGELIER

PRIVATE COLLECTION, BERLIN

CICHA.STREET

OFFICE BUILDING, WARSAW, POLAND

CLIENT: GD & K CONSULTING SP. Z.O.O., KRAKOW

PROJECT DATE: 2007–11

J. MAYER H.
GD & K CONSILTING SP. Z.O.O.
OVOTZ DESIGN LAB
PROJECT TEAM: JÜRGEN MAYER H., MARCUS BLUM, PAUL ANGELIER, MEHRDAD MASHAIE

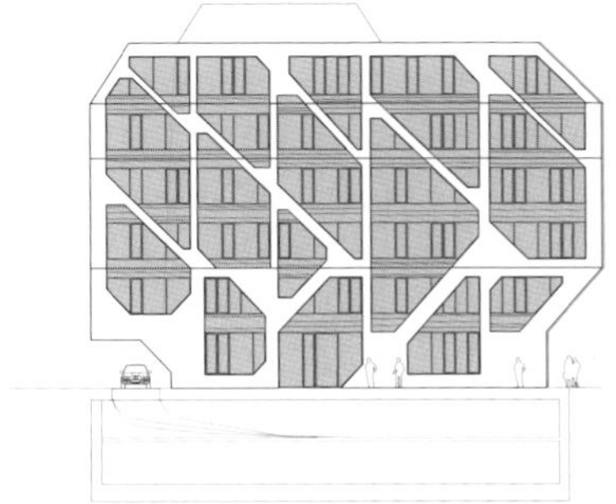

GATEWAY.GARDENS

INFOCENTER, FRANKFURT, GERMANY

CLIENT: INFOCENTER GATEWAY GARDENS, FRANKFURT

INVITED COMPETITION: 2008

J. MAYER H.
COMPETITION TEAM: JÜRGEN MAYER H., DANIEL MOCK, PAUL ANGELIER

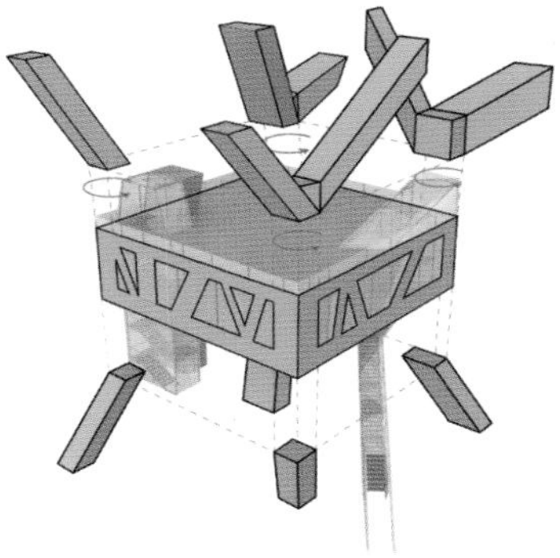

OZEANEUM DEUTSCHES MEERESMUSEUM, STRALSUND, GERMANY

INTERNATIONAL COMPETITION: 2001

J. MAYER H.

COMPETITION TEAM: JÜRGEN MAYER H., SASCHA NIKOLAUSCHKE, PETER MARTIN

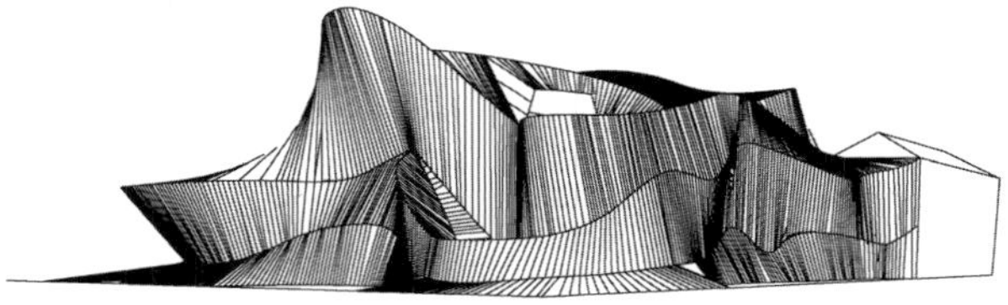

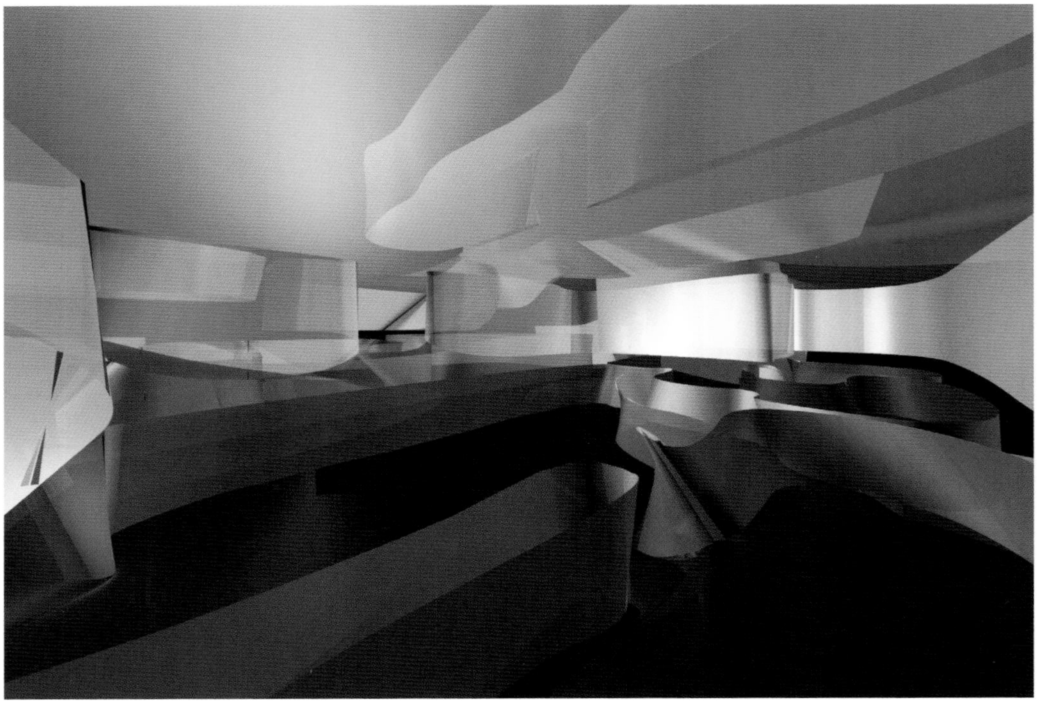

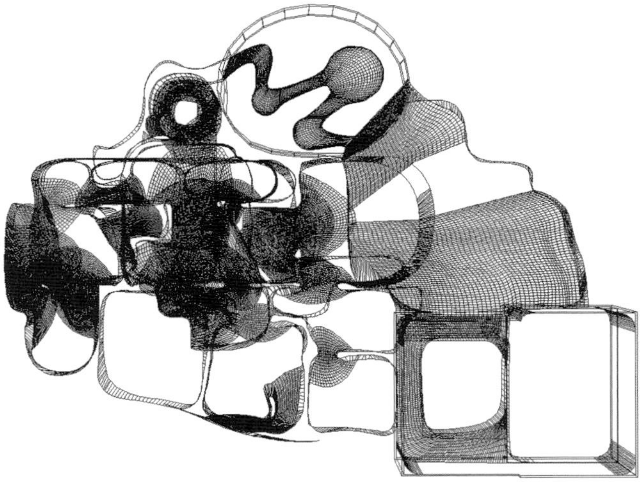

PLAYA.LAVA

REMODELING OF THE COAST AND ITS ENVIRONMENT AT PUERTA DE LA ESTACA, EL HIERRO ISLAND, SPAIN

CLIENT: CITY OF EL HIERRO, SPAIN

INTERNATIONAL COMPETITION: 2007

J. MAYER H.
COMPETITION TEAM: JÜRGEN MAYER H., PAUL ANGELIER, CHRISTOPH EMENLAUER, ALESSANDRA RAPONI, STEPHEN MALLOY, JAN-CHRISTOPH STOCKEBRAND, ANA I. ALONSO DE LA VARGA

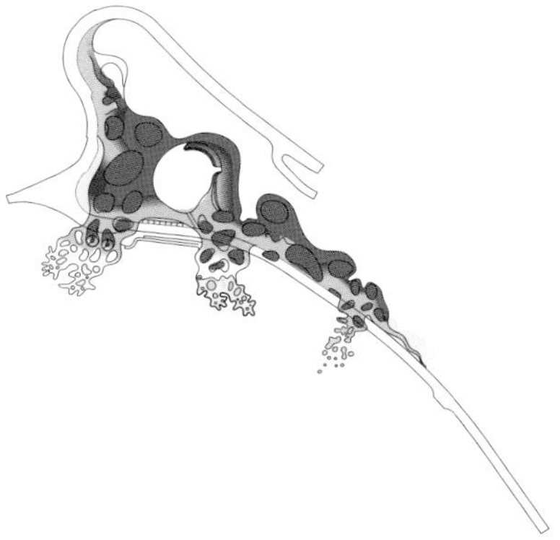

SOF HOTEL COMPLEX, KRAKOW, POLAND

CLIENT: GD&K CONSULTING SP. Z.O.O.

PROJECT DATE: 2005–09

J. MAYER H.
GD & K CONSULTING SP. Z O.O.
OVOTZ DESIGN LAB
PROJECT TEAM: JÜRGEN MAYER H., MARCUS BLUM,
JAN-CHRISTOPH STOCKEBRAND

TURKISH EMBASSY BERLIN

CLIENT: THE EMBASSY OF TURKEY, BERLIN, GERMANY

INTERNATIONAL COMPETITION: 2007

J. MAYER H.
PROJECT TEAM: JÜRGEN MAYER H., ANDRE SANTER, ALEXANDER ARNOLD, STEPHEN MOLLOY, SEBASTIAN FINCKH

LEE OFFICE BUILDING, ZURICH, SWITZERLAND

CLIENT: SWISS FEDERAL INSTITUTE OF TECHNOLOGY ZURICH

INTERNATIONAL COMPETITION: 2007

J. MAYER H.
COMPETITION TEAM: JÜRGEN MAYER H, PAUL ANGELIER, ALEXANDER ARNOLD

MENSA WESTERBERG

NEW STUDENT-CANTEEN SITE WESTERBERG, OSNABRÜCK, GERMANY

CLIENT: UNIVERSITIY OF OSNABRÜCK

INTERNATIONAL COMPETITION: 2008

J. MAYER H.
COMPETITION TEAM: JÜRGEN MAYER H., PAUL ANGELIER, MARCUS BLUM, MEHRDAD MASHAIE

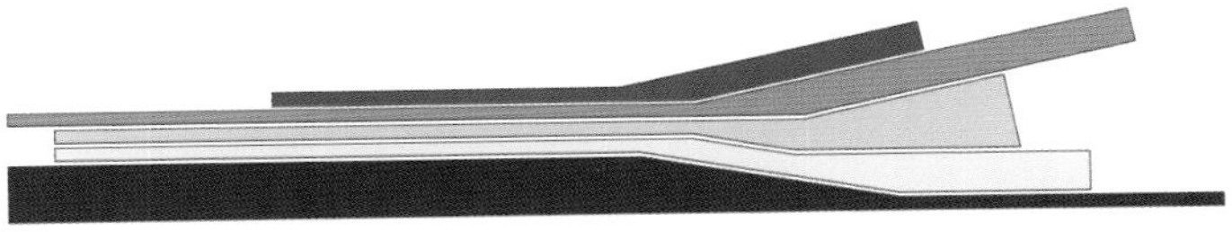

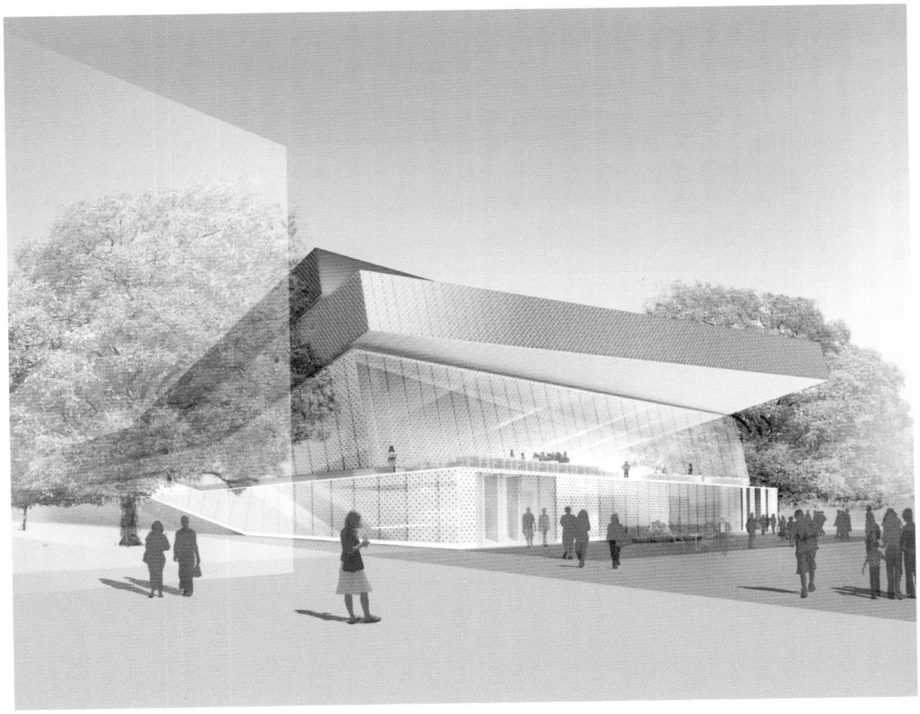

HOME.HAUS

HOME FOR CHILDREN AND ADOLESCENTS, HAMBURG-BERGEDORF, GERMANY

CLIENT: STIFTUNG UNTERNEHMER HELFEN KINDERN, HAMBURG-BERGEDORF

PROJECT DATE: 2007–08

J. MAYER H. WITH SEBASTIAN FINCKH
PROJECT TEAM: JÜRGEN MAYER H., SEBASTIAN FINCKH, MARCUS BLUM

ARCHITECTS ON SITE: IMHOTEP, DONACHIE UND BLOMEYER, BERLIN;
DIRK REINISCH, BERLIN

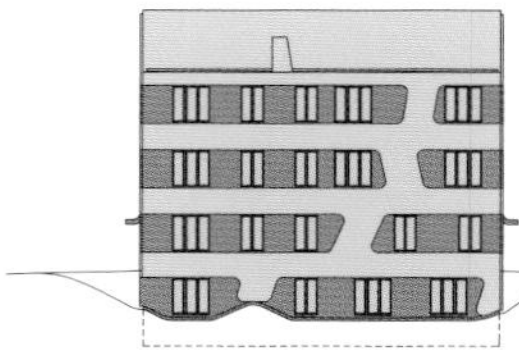

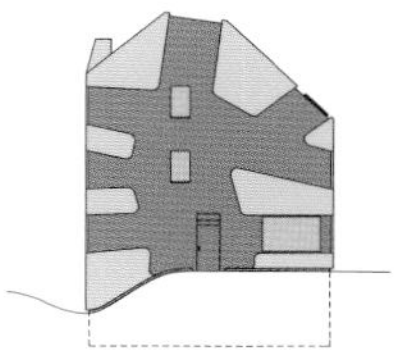

CLOUD.CATCHER

DOWLAIS TOP, MERTHYR TYDFIL, WALES, UK

CLIENT: LANDMARK WALES TRUST, UK

INTERNATIONAL COMPETITION: 2007

J. MAYER H.

COMPETITION TEAM: JÜRGEN MAYER H., STEPHEN MOLLOY, ALEXANDER ARNOLD

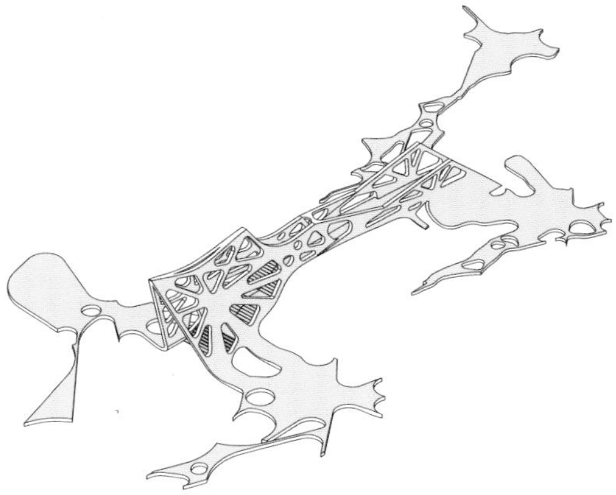

GARMENT.GARDEN

DESIGN ANNUAL, INSIDE:URBAN, MESSE FRANKFURT

CLIENT: NYA NORDISKA, DANNENBERG
LOCATION: MESSE FRANKFURT, INSIDE:URBAN

PROJECT DATE: 2006

J. MAYER H.
PROJECT TEAM: JÜRGEN MAYER H., ALESSANDRA RAPONI, SIMON TAKASAKI

NYA NORDISKA

HEADQUARTERS DANNENBERG

CLIENT: NYA NORDISKA

INVITED COMPETITION: 2008

J. MAYER H.
COMPETITION TEAM: JÜRGEN MAYER H., PAUL ANGELIER, MEHRDAD MASHAIE

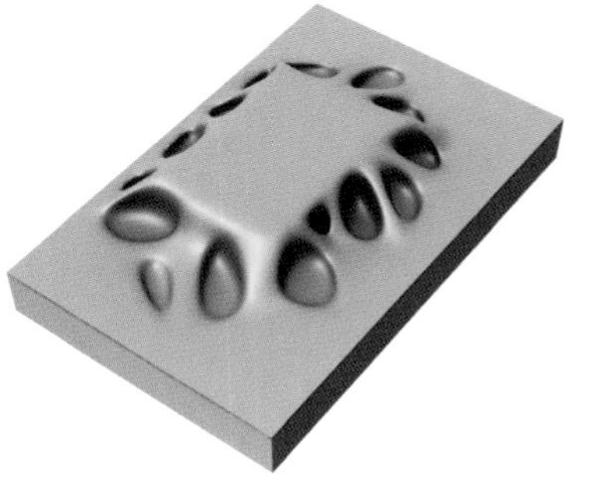

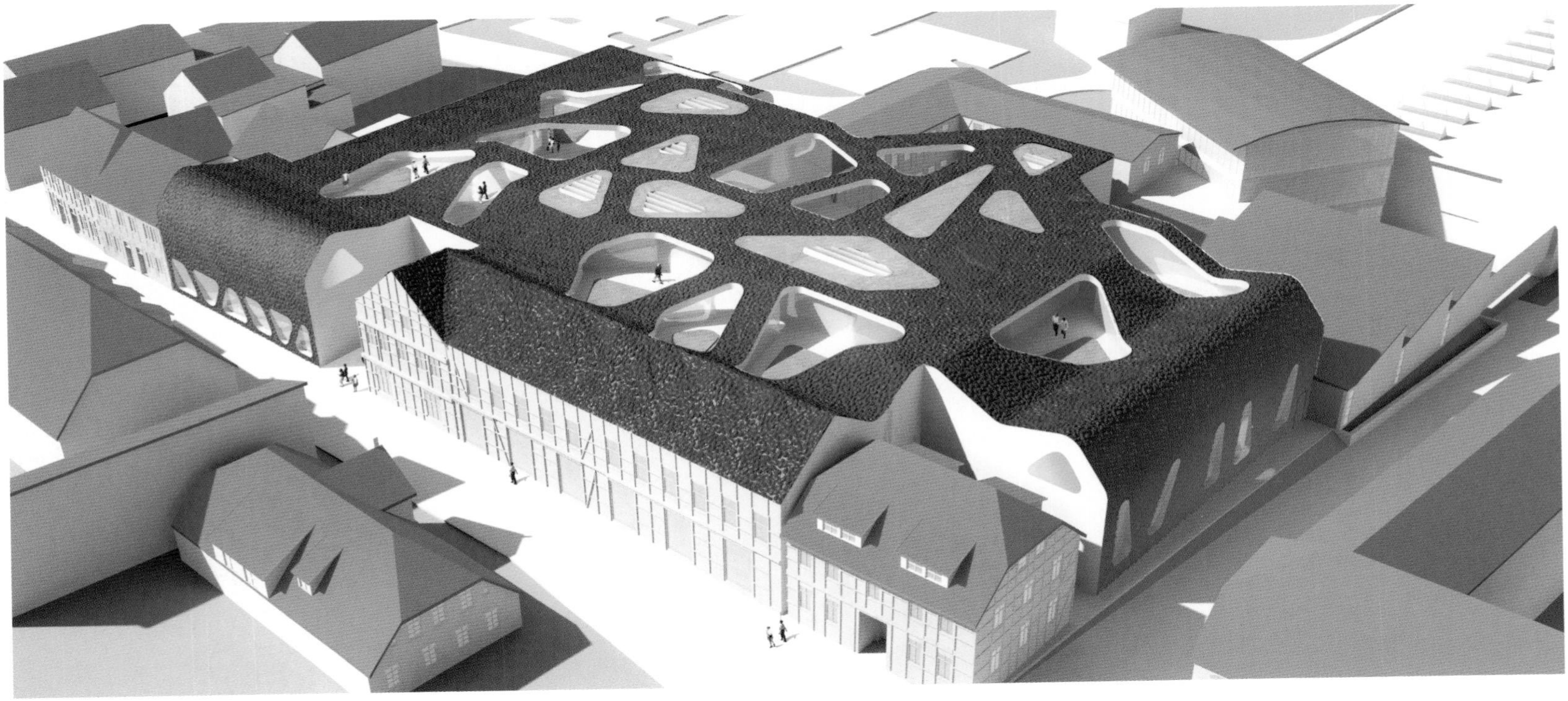

KNOT.SPOT PROPOSAL PLACE STATIONS, JERUSALEM, ISRAEL

CLIENT: CITY OF JERUSALEM

PROJECT DATE: 2007

J. MAYER H.
PROJECT TEAM: JÜRGEN MAYER H., AARON JEZZI

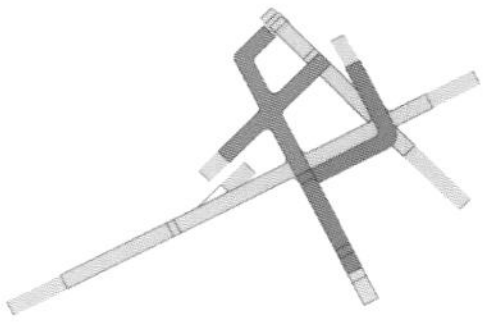

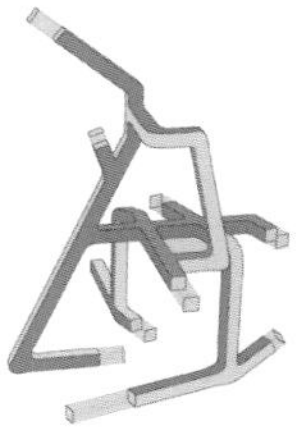

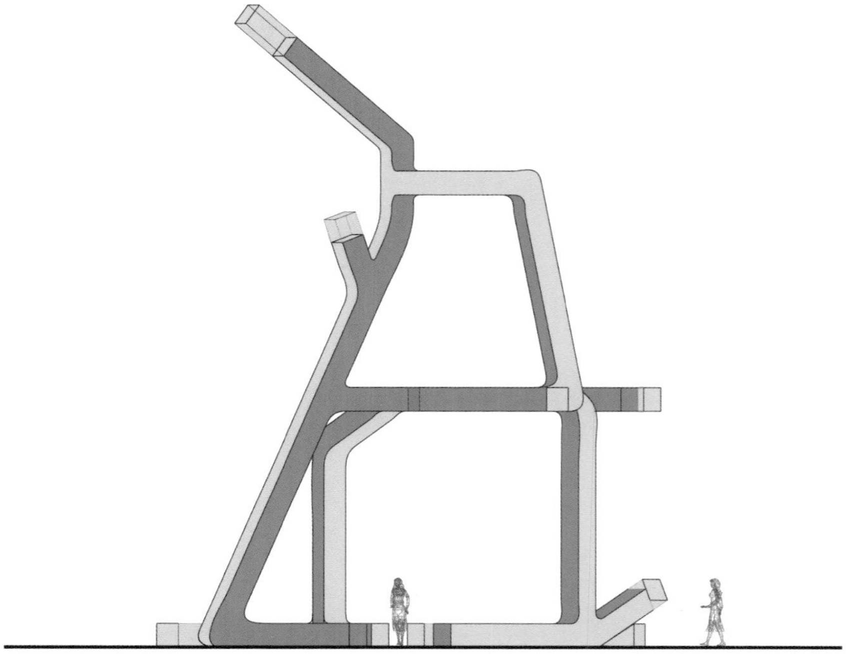

GUBEN.GUBIN CULTURE PAVILION, GUBIN, POLAND

CLIENT: IBA FUERST-PUECKLERLAND, GUBEN

INTERNATIONAL COMPETITION: 2003, 1ST PRIZE

J. MAYER H.
COMPETITION TEAM: JÜRGEN MAYER H., WILKO HOFFMANN, MARC KUSHNER, DOMINIK SCHWARZER, MACIEJ WORONIECKI

COLLABORATION: COQUI-MALACHOWSKA-COQUI

GREY.GRID TOWNHOUSE-CONCEPT, BERLIN, GERMANY

CLIENT: IMOVATE GMBH, BERLIN

PROJECT DATE: 2001–04

J. MAYER. H.
PROJECT TEAM: JÜRGEN MAYER H., SEBASTIAN FINCKH, WILKO HOFFMANN, KARLA PILZ, GABRIELE ROY, GEORG SCHMIDTHALS, DOMINIK SCHWARZER

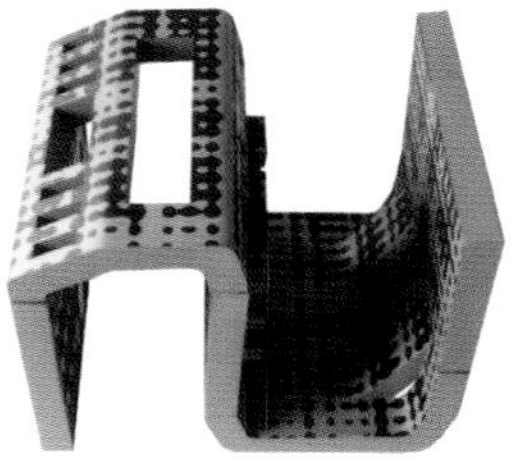

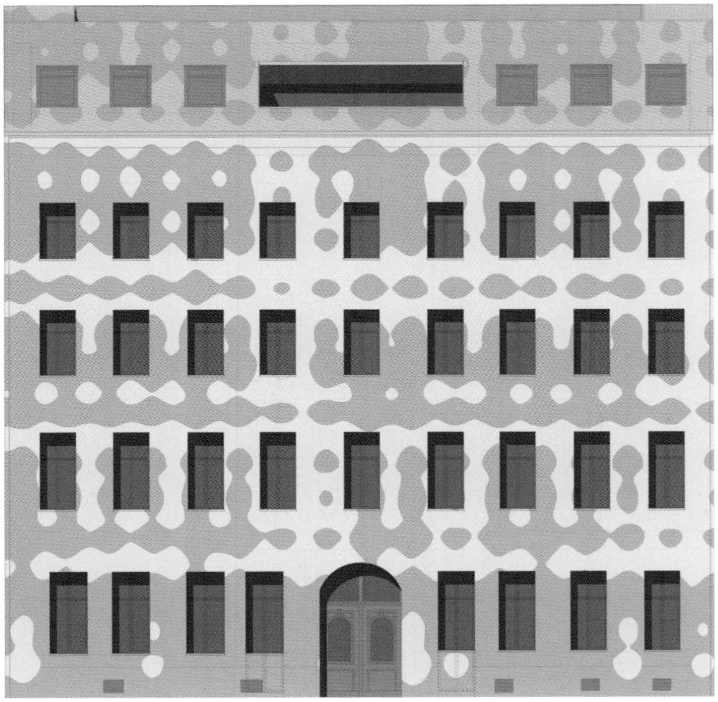

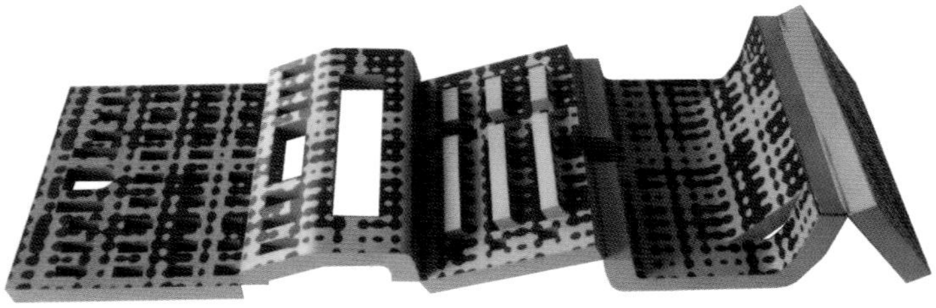

SONNENHOF JENA

CLIENT: WOHNUNGSGENOSSENSCHAFT CARL ZEISS EG

LOCATION: JENA, GERMANY

PROJECT DATE: 2008–2011

J. MAYER H.
PROJECT TEAM: JÜRGEN MAYER H., JAN-CHRISTOPH STOCKEBRAND, CHRISTOPH EMENLAUER, CHRISTOPH EPPACHER, MEHRDAD MASHAIE, CHRISTIAN PÄLMKE

ARCHITECTS ON SITE: KAPPES UND PARTNER, BERLIN

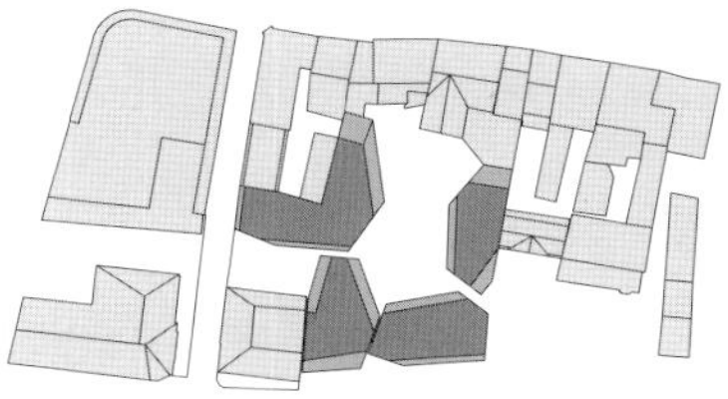

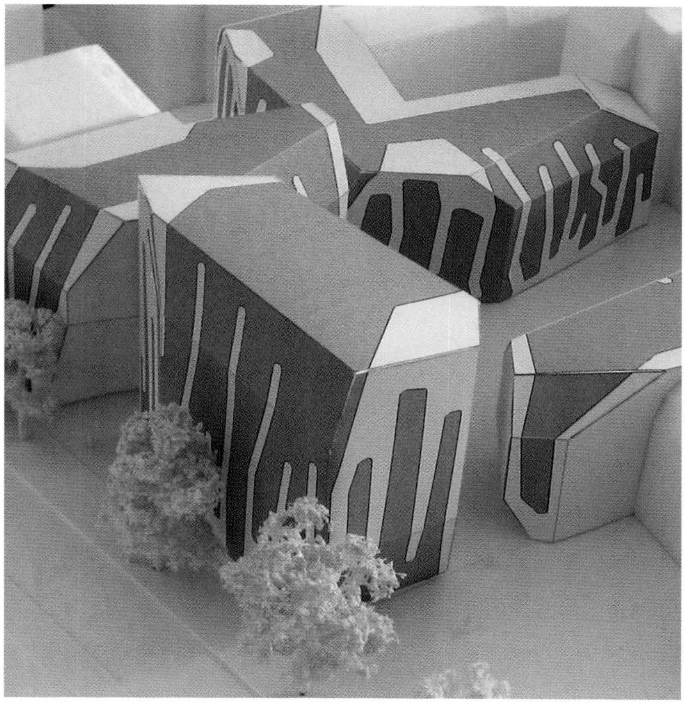

OBER.WALL PENTHOUSE APARTMENT, BERLIN, GERMANY

CLIENTS: PRIVATE

PROJECT DATE: 2008

J. MAYER H.
PROJECT TEAM: JÜRGEN MAYER H., SEBASTIAN FINCKH, STEPHANIE KALLÄNE

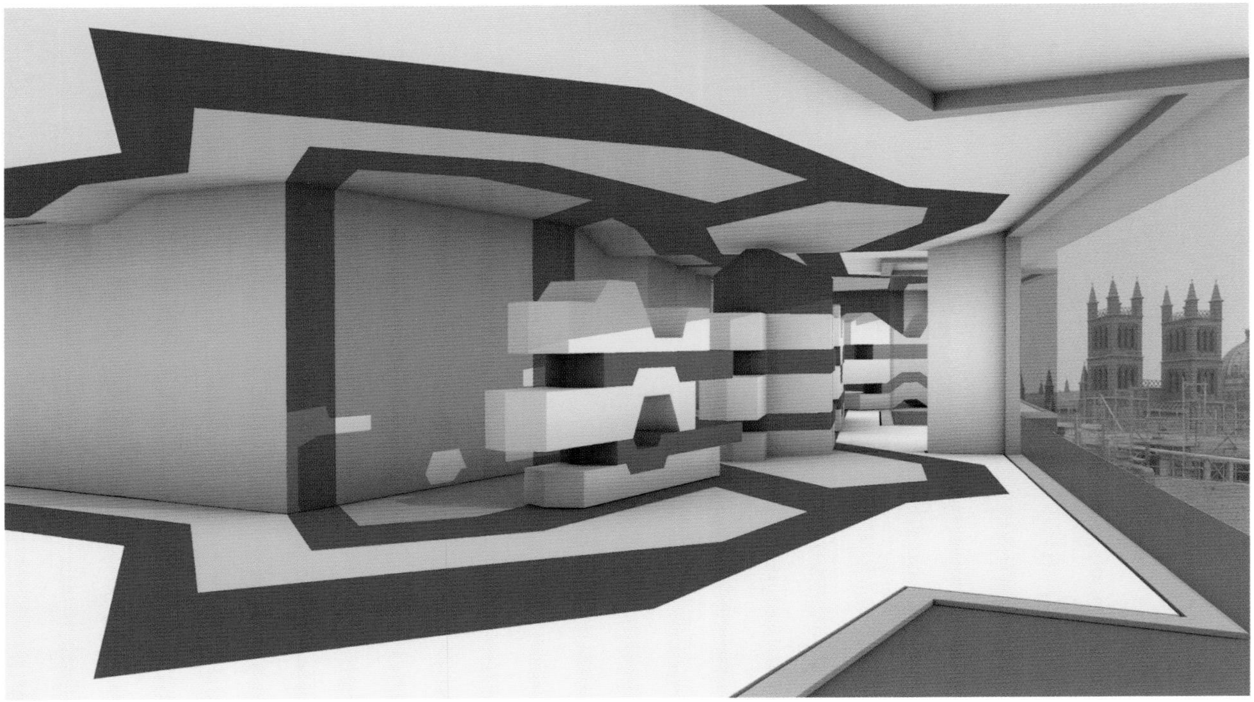

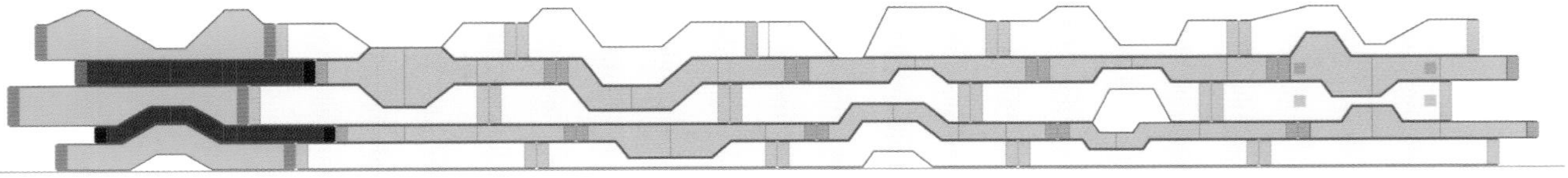

comdirect Bank
0180 / 333 63 63

In dem verschlossenen Umschlag befinden sich Ihre persönlichen TAN. Hiermit können Sie Transaktionen im Homebanking der comdirect bank freigeben. Jede Tan ist nur einmal verwendbar. Wenn Ihnen dieser TAN-Brief nicht verschlossen zugeht, rufen Sie unverzüglich bei der comdirect bank an und lassen Sie Ihre TAN-Liste sperren. Sie können auch Ihre TAN-Liste direkt in Comhome im Menüpunkt Stammdaten sperren. Sie erhalten dann umgehend eine neue TAN-Liste.

Bitte hier aufschneiden und die inliegende Mitteilung entnehmen!

OPAQUE MEETINGS, MELTING ENCOUNTERS

STEPHEN HARTMAN

Stamped on façades, rolled out on carpets, memories evaporating from gallery walls and oozing from oblong apertures: the data-protection patterns placed by J. MAYER H. in built landscapes and urban passageways cradle the excitement of the opaque much as the psychoanalyst holds the density of the patient's unhomed wish.

It is a Freudian cliché that the analyst perceives the patient's true wish more clearly than the patient does. And, by extension, a similarly self-serving truism that the architect builds what the client would want if only he or she knew better. These constructions nevertheless clue us into the politics of longing that attend any creative process. Ultimately, it takes great sensitivity to the other's erasure by one's own insight to allow dreams to be interpreted.

Holding an other's intention in concert with one's own, as the British analyst D. W. Winnicott taught us, is an intersubjective process that is filled with longing. There is no baby without a mother. No history without encounter. No containment without building. The only way to intuit an intention is to trace its history as a relation.[1]

By savoring the skin of layered surfaces to an almost fetishistic degree, J. MAYER H. draws us into the multiple strokes that gave a sensate pattern its texture. He attenuates this encounter by rendering it opaque. Since we can only imagine the others' brush against the surface, J. MAYER H. invites us to activate the façade and so plumb it for the melancholic residue of human erosion that is vested in a contoured image, a dented surface, a formed self. J. MAYER H.'s subject pines for a body obscured by a protective pattern, and elicits its mnemonic embrace as the press of his touch fades. Not a mirror self, this evaporating reflection, but a hybrid relation.

J. MAYER H.'s work shares the emphasis that contemporary Relational Psychoanalysis places on potential space. This multi-layered space of unconscious encounter is where an omnipotent *all-me* wrangles with *not-me* until, in fits and starts, my need to understand the other through control yields to empathy. It is a messy business, a nimble communication between subjects coursing through that which unfolds rather than that which is made clear. Play becomes the medium for getting to know the self in the other. City fathers route historic streets through a whimsical Parasol that flaunts memories of *ramblas* past, passing on a tension between the private and the public demand, the lonely and the related shape of encounter. That which is taken away is given back on a dense analytic field: which walk did I take, or might I have were I to? And, with whom in order to be whom? In whose presence, given whose past? The slippy interaction between architect and "architectee," analyst and analysand, parent and child, requires lucid planning—but its logic is not hidden, repressed, simply to be rehearsed by docile generations. Rather, in its dissociated opacity, its melting recovery, it awaits dialogic formulation. The transformation from object to subject ambles along in a manner that is dense yet spry, saturated with history and emergent from encounter.

J. MAYER H. brings the elusive object of encounter, Jean Laplanche's enigmatic signifier, into play slowly and subtly. For Laplanche, all that begot us awaits recovery in our moments of strangeness to ourselves.

The unconscious is thus in no sense another "myself" in me, possibly more authentic than me, a Mr Hyde alternating with a Dr Jekyll, the one with his hatred,

1 D. W. Winnicott, **Psychoanalytic Explorations** (Cambridge, Mass., 1989).

the other with his love ... It is an other thing (das Andere) *in me, the repressed residue of the other person* (der Andere). *It affects me as the other person affected me long ago ...* — Jean Laplanche[2]

Jürgen Mayer H. explains: "technology is more convincing to me if it doesn't show too much in the foreground but as something that looks normal and hidden, to be dis-covered."[3] Rocking to and fro, heat-sensitive and weather-soluble, J. MAYER H.'s technology begets emotional resonance that—here and gone—is never mine, never yours, never lost. Its discovery is the sense of the other in *my* fading touch. So much that would seem foiled is contained, so that it bounces back unaware of its depletion. So much that would seem lapsed leaps into fantasy. The primal scene lost in oedipal battle reemerges in a heated trace: the presence of the mother's first kiss revived in the son's first touch. A quotidian surface—the anti-graffiti screen of an *S-Bahn* (subway) car—a page in a guest book, a chaise, becomes a surface of longing vexed by a condition of permanent temporaneity. Where was I once loved? Whose love am I made of? Where is my love now? Whom will I love next? If J. MAYER H. means to join Winnicott in tracing how long the creativity of an illusion can be sustained given the limitations of history and difference, he draws out the quest. He celebrates the lusciousness of lurking after the fact of eventual encounter.

Dense with hope and yet only surface, J. MAYER H.'s foils alert us that the holding environment cannot always hold. Failure is implicit in architecture, just as it is necessary in human development. Entropy, difficult to anticipate, gives us difference and time. In defiance of this, J. MAYER H.'s Pixy. Pieces recalls the bad breast of Kleinian psychoanalysis: an empty feed that leaves us swooning for connection and yet terrified to risk it. Beautiful to the eye yet cold and sleek to the touch, its promise is reliable only as a fetish. These surfaces that efface depth and promise rapture: are they a projection of my longing for the softness below the skin? What erasure of the other do they carry in order that I may face my longing? J. MAYER H.'s patterns memorialize a space that is suspended between a public life of encounter and one built on privacy, one that can no longer contain libidinal excitement and, so, must retreat. Pattern that can be touched, licked, rubbed, admired; a fetish, then, always remembers the clear moment of connection in an atmosphere of disappearance. This is the melancholy that thrives in the opaque.

So it is that J. MAYER H.'s patterns are both perverse and playful. Refusing to be locked in by being quizzically elusive, these are militant fetishes that burst out of fetishism. Leaky enigmas. The Pitter. Patterns of the Stadthaus Scharnhauser Park are a favorite of mine. They have been described as "a computerized rain curtain"—visitors to the civic space's private quarters are forced to walk through computer-animated artificial rain dripping from the undergarment of a flat, cantilevered roof. The "ephemeral skin" fetishizes weather not so much as span: the time between the first drop and the deluge. Rain beams, sinus drops, pixel pour, falling clouds: these are the joyful sadnesses that drying off evacuates. Moments of extreme pleasure (drop to drop) that are drenched with finitude (too wet, the wettest ever) and renounced. Moments that fetishists refuse in search of ever-repeating patterns of meaning—only to become trapped in fog.

The difference between cynical elision and quixotic inclusion of the elusive signifier lies in the quality of curiosity implicit in its disavowal. J. MAYER H.'s erasure of the surface blankets the primal scene with an evanescent coat. The other is there to be stroked in the history of self as it fades away. In a Family of Data Protection, different erasures emerge from the law of censorious sameness. This is architecture terminable and interminable; in which, to update Freud's famous portrayal of melancholic longing, the shadow of the object tickles the subject.

2 Jean Laplanche, **Essays on Otherness** (New York, 1999), p. 108.

3 Jürgen Mayer H., **Activators,** J. Mayer H. (Seoul, 2006), p. 14.

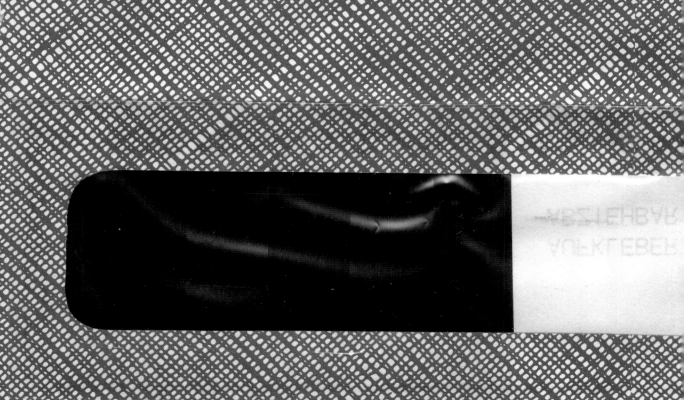

APPENDIX

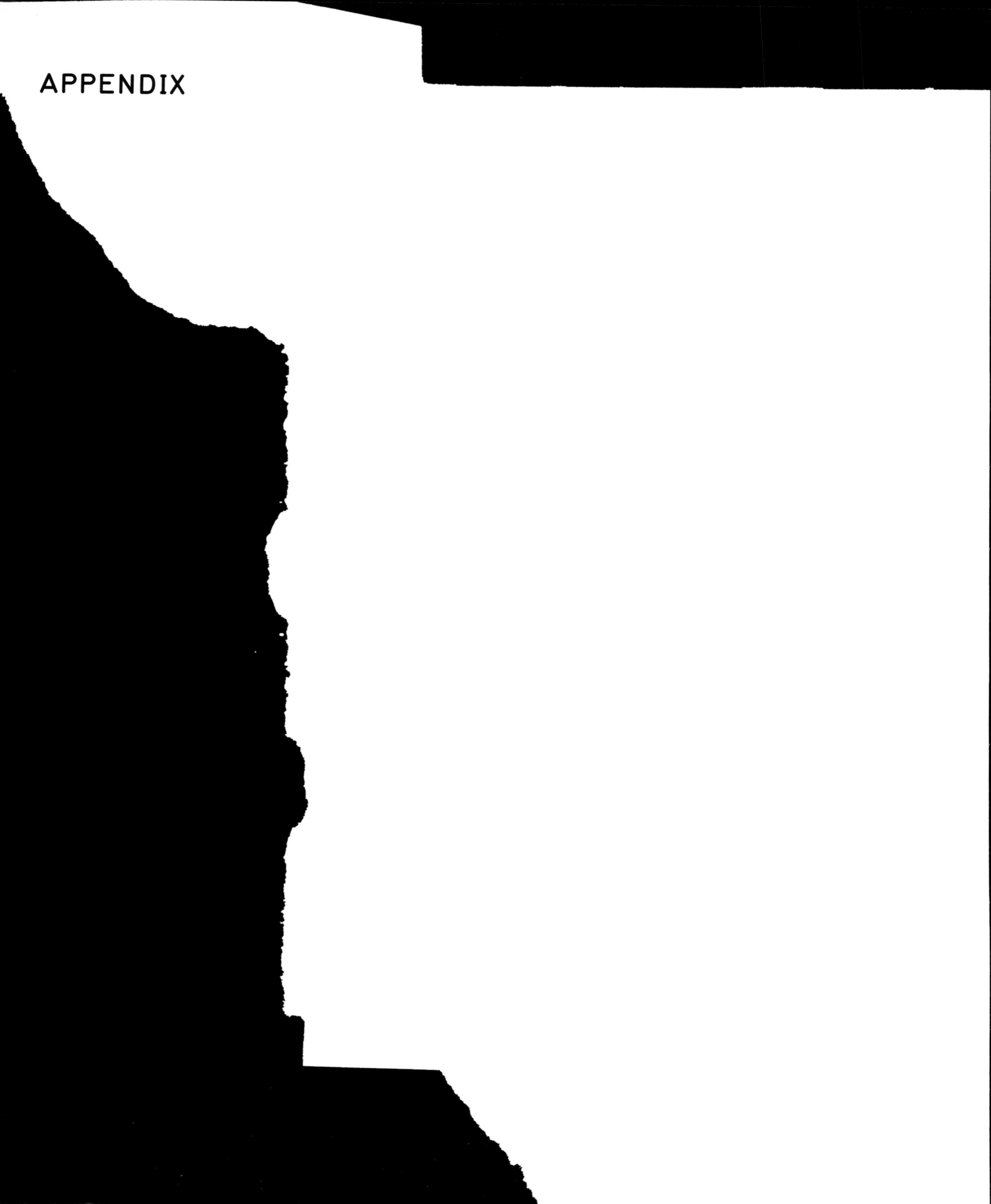

JÜRGEN MAYER H.

EDUCATION

- Princeton University, M.Arch., September 1992–February 1994, School of Architecture, Princeton, New Jersey, US
- The Irwin S. Chanin School of Architecture, Thesis Year Visiting Student, September 1990–May 1991, The Cooper Union for the Advancement of Science and Art, New York, US
- Universität Stuttgart, Dipl.Ing. Arch./Städtebau, September 1986–May 1992, Architekturfakultät, Stuttgart, Germany, Architecture and Town Planning

J. MAYER H.

PROJECTS

- Positive.Negative, Kicken Gallery, 2008, Berlin, Germany
- Attraktion Nachhaltigkeit, Autostadt, Volkswagen, 2007–09, Wolfsburg, Germany
- Cicha.Street—office building, 2007–09, Warsaw, Poland
- S11—office building, 2007–09, Hamburg, Germany
- Reggiani, Design Lighting, 2007–08
- Home.Haus—home for children and adolescents, 2007–08, Hamburg, Germany
- Krystal Huset, Formation A/S, 2007, Denmark
- Datoo—tattoo parlor, Miami Design, 2007, Miami, US
- Lo Glo—light-sensitive elastic furniture, Vitra Edition, 2007
- Knot.Spot—proposal place stations, 2007, Jerusalem, Israel
- Garment.Garden, 2006, Inside: Urban, Messe Frankfurt, Germany
- Hasselt Court of Justice, in collaboration with a2o-architecten and Lens°ass architecten, 2005–2011, Hasselt, Belgium
- SOF—hotel complex, 2005–09, Krakow, Poland
- Dupli.Casa—villa near Ludwigsburg, 2005–08, Ludwigsburg, Germany
- Danfoss Universe—food factory and curiosity center, 2005–07, Nordborg, Denmark
- AdA1—office building, 2005–07, Hamburg, Germany
- Mensa Moltke—student canteen, Universities of Karlsruhe, 2005–07, Karlsruhe, Germany
- Metropol Parasol—redevelopment of the Plaza de la Encarnacion, 2004–2010, Seville, Spain
- Rotor—penthouse in Copenhagen, 2004–06, Copenhagen, Denmark
- Body.Guards, 2004
- Menardie—concept for restaurant-club-lounge, 2004, Berlin, Germany
- Soft Mosaic—glass mosaic on polyurethane foam, 2003–08, Bisazza, Italy
- Marin BLVD—housing complex, 2003, Jersey City, New Jersey, US
- "Arium": International Designer Congress in Hanover—lounge for Nya Nordiska and Stylepark, September 2003, Hanover, Germany
- Guben.Gubin—culture pavilion, in collaboration with Coqui-Malachowska-Coqui, 2003, Guben, Poland
- Smartware—store concept, 2003
- Potsdam Docklands, Masterplan, 2002, Potsdam, Germany
- Warm-up Table—temperature-sensitive furniture, 2002, courtesy magnus müller gallery, Berlin, Germany
- UIA Stylepark Lounge, UIA Congress, July 2002, Berlin, Germany
- Corridor—rooftop apartment, 2001–2008, Berlin, Germany
- Grey.Grid—concept for an apartment building, 2001–04, Berlin, German
- Path.Logic—exhibition architecture, CTRL.Space, Zentrum für Kunst und Medientechnologie Karlsruhe, October 2001–February 2002, Karlsruhe, Germany
- Heat.Seat—temperature-sensitive furniture, 2001, courtesy magnus müller gallery, Berlin, Germany
- O-RAI GmbH—office space, May–October 2000, Berlin, Germany
- Open Spaces, 1999–2001, Vaihingen an der Enz, Germany
- Lightbulb: Myth of Everyday Life—exhibition design, 1999–2000, Berlin, Germany
- VPRO—installation, 1999, Hilversum, The Netherlands
- Hotel Scharnhauser Park, 1999, Ostfildern, Germany
- Stadthaus Scharnhauser Park—mixed-use civic center, 1998–2001, Ostfildern, Germany
- S-Bahn Berlin—anti-graffiti design, 1998, Berlin, Germany
- Hermes, in collaboration with Frisch, Summer Collection, 1998
- Cover Address—single-family house, 1997–2001, near Stuttgart, Germany
- HOM-Y Collection—installation at Gramercy International Art Fair, May 1997, New York, US
- Misskommunikation—installation at Eigen+Art, July–August 1996, Berlin, Germany
- 3 Secrets—pavilions at the F.-Möller-Foundation, 1995, near Berlin, Germany
- Future Temps Passe—concept for a house, 1994–96, near Poitiers, France
- Weather.House, Princeton University, 1994, New Jersey, US

COMPETITIONS

- Nya Nordiska—headquarter, Invited competition 2008, Dannenberg, Germany
- Gateway.Gardens—infocenter, Invited Competition 2008, Frankfurt, Germany
- Mensa Westerberg—new student canteen site Westerberg, International Competition 2008, Osnabrück, Germany
- Drents Museum, International Competition 2007, Assen, The Netherlands
- Playa.Lava—remodeling of the coast and its environment at Puerta de la Estaca, International Competition 2007, City of El Hierro, Spain
- LEE—office building, ETH Swiss Federal Institute of Technology, International Competition 2007, Zurich, Switzerland
- Turkish Embassy Berlin, International Competition 2007, Berlin, Germany
- Volantes Passantes—Portada de la Feria, International Competition 2007, Seville, Spain
- Cloud.Catcher, International Competition 2007, Landmark Wales Trust, UK
- Headquarters EDC, Invited Competition, 2007, 3rd Prize, Ratingen, Germany
- Attraktion Nachhaltigkeit, Volkswagen, Invited Competition, 2007, 1st Prize, Wolfsburg, Germany
- Culture and Congress Center Würth, International Competition 2006, Künzelsau, Germany
- National Library Prague, International Competition 2006, Prague, Czech Republic
- Octobar 2, Invited Competition 2005, Wolfsburg, Germany
- OSZ Körperpflege, International Competition 2005, Berlin, Germany
- AdA1—office building, Invited Competition 2005, 1st Prize, Hamburg, Germany
- Hasselt Court of Justice, in collaboration with a2o-architecten and Lens°ass architecten, International Competition 2005, 1st Prize, Hasselt, Belgium
- Kissing Bridges, International Competition 2004, City of Baruth, Germany
- Metropol Parasol—redevelopment of the Plaza de la Encarnacion, International Competition 2004, 1st Prize, Seville, Spain
- Mensa Moltke—student canteen, International Competition 2003–04, 1st Prize, Karlsruhe, Germany
- Bockenheim Masterplan, International Competition 2003, Frankfurt am Main, Germany
- Kulturforum Westfalen, International Competition 2003, Osnabrück, Germany
- Kerykes—activity tool for the 2004 Cultural Olympics, International Competition 2003, Honorable Mention, Athens, Greece
- Potsdam Docklands, Invited International Competition 2002, 1st Prize, Potsdam, Germany
- Ozeaneum, International Competition 2001, Stralsund, Germany
- EAZ BMW—event and delivery center, Invited International Competition 2001, Munich, Germany
- Museion, International Competition 2001, Bolzena, Italy
- Corridor—rooftop apartment, Invited Competition 2000, 1st Prize, Berlin, Germany
- Neue Bremm—Holocaust Memorial, International Competition 2000, Saarbrücken, Germany
- Casla, International Competition 2000, Almere, The Netherlands
- Central Glass, Invited International Competition 2000, 2nd Prize, Japan
- Culture and Congress Center, International Competition 1999–2000, Reutlingen, Germany
- Seasonscape—lakeshore, International Competition 1999–2000, 3rd Prize, Ascona, Switzerland
- Stadthaus Scharnhauser Park—mixed-use civic center, International Competition 1998, 1st Prize, Ostfildern, Germany
- MMKZ, Invited Competition 1998, 2nd Prize, Frankfurt am Main, Germany
- Metaplan Consulting, Invited Competition 1998, Quickborn, Germany
- Multimediakreativzentrum, Invited Competition 1998, 2nd Prize, Frankfurt am Main, Germany
- S-Bahn Berlin—anti-graffiti design, 1998, 1st Prize, Berlin, Germany
- Generaldirektion Deutsche Post AG, International Competition 1998, Bonn, Germany
- Museo Costantini, International Competition 1997, Buenos Aires, Argentina
- Shinkenchiku Residential, 1996, 2nd Prize, Japan
- Auslaufmodell, 1995
- Écoles etc et est sierre, 1993, Switzerland
- Revitalization of the Riverfront, International Competition 1990, Honorable Mention (3rd prize), Antwerp, Belgium

AWARDS

- Deutschland—Land der Ideen, 2008, Laureate, Mensa Moltke, Karlsruhe, Germany
- ADAM Award 2008, Garment.Garden for Nya Nordiska at The Design Annual, 2006, Frankfurt am Main, Germany
- The Great Indoors 2007, Nomination, Mensa Moltke, Karlsruhe, Germany
- Marcus Prize Nominee, 2007, all projects
- Deutscher Holzbaupreis 2007, Special Mention, Mensa Moltke, Karlsruhe, Germany
- Holz 21 Prize 2006, Commendation, Mensa Moltke, Karlsruhe, Germany
- Holcim Award, 2005, Winner Europe Bronze for Sustainable Construction, Metropol Parasol, Seville, Spain
- Marcus Prize Nominee, 2005, all projects
- Contractworld Award, 2004, Pixy.Pieces
- Mies van der Rohe Award, 2003, Emerging Architect Special Mention, Stadthaus Scharnhauser Park, Ostfildern, Germany
- Contractworld Award 2003, UIA Stylepark Lounge, Berlin, Germany
- Nomination for the Hugo-Häring-Prize, 2003, BDA Baden-Württemberg, Stadthaus Scharnhauser Park, Ostfildern, Germany
- "Auszeichnung Guter Bauten 2002," Stadthaus Scharnhauser Park, Ostfildern, Germany
- AR+D Award, 2002, UIA Stylepark Lounge, Berlin, Germany
- Deutscher Fassadenpreis, 2002, Honorable Mention, Stadthaus Scharnhauser Park, Ostfildern, Germany
- Glass House 3000, 2001, Nominated for the Graz Biannial for Media and Architecture, Austria
- Hans-Schäfer-Preis, 1998, BDA Berlin, all projects
- Suzanne Kolarik Underwood Prize, 1994, Princeton University Thesis Prize
- Gunton Prize 1993, Princeton University
- DAAD Scholarship 1992–94, for study at Princeton University
- Princeton University Fellowship Offer 1992–94
- Fulbright Scholarship 1990–91, for study at The Cooper Union

COLLECTIONS

- Danfoss Universe, Model, Collection of NAi, Rotterdam, The Netherlands, 2006
- Mensa Moltke, Concept model, Collection of The Museum of Modern Art, New York, US, 2006
- Metropol Parasol, Model, Permanent Collection of The Museum of Modern Art, New York, US, 2006
- Metropol Parasol, Model, Staatliche Museen zu Berlin, Preussischer Kulturbesitz, Berlin, Germany, 2006
- E.gram, Collection of The Museum of Modern Art, New York, US, 2002
- Heat.Seat, Collection of SFMOMA San Francisco, California, 2002

EXHIBITIONS / INSTALLATIONS

- BIACS, Fundación Bienal Internacional de Arte Contemporáneo de Sevilla, October 2008, Metropol Parasol, Seville, Spain
- La Biennale di Venezia, Italian Pavilion, September–October 2008, Pre.text/Vor.wand, Venice, Italy
- Ready to Take Off, Bienal Internacional de São Paulo, DAM Frankfurt, November 2007–August 2008, Mensa Moltke, Karlsruhe and Metropol Parasol, Seville, Spain, Frankfurt am Main, Germany
- Ornament Neu Aufgelegt, Schweizerisches Architekturmuseum, June–September 2008, Danfoss Universe, Basel, Switzerland
- Pulse, Art Fair, December 2007, Beat.Wave, Miami, Florida, US
- Nature Design, Museum für Gestaltung Zürich, August 2007–January 2008, Zurich, Switzerland
- Art Forum, Chit.Chat, magnus müller Gallery, September–October 2007, Berlin, Germany
- Lo Glo, Vitra Edition 2007, June–July 2007, Weil am Rhein, Germany
- Housewarming IV MyHome, Vitra Museum, June–September 2007, Weil am Rhein, Germany
- Digitally Mastered, E.gram, The Museum of Modern Art, New York, November 22nd, 2006–2007, New York, US
- LAV01: Laboratori d'arquitectures Vives, COAC, September–October 2006, Girona, Spain
- P.A.N. (Progressive Architecture Network), Frederieke Taylor Gallery, October–December 2006, New York, US
- ON SITE: Contemporary Architecture in Spain, Pabellón Villanueva, Royal Botanic Gardens, September 2006–January 2007, Madrid, Spain
- New Faces of European Architecture, Netherlands Architecture Institute, Maastricht, September 2006–January 2007, Maastricht, The Netherlands
- The Design Annual, Inside:Urban, Frankfurt Fair, May 2006, Frankfurt am Main, Germany
- On Site: Contemporary Architecture in Spain, The Museum of Modern Art, New York, February–April 2006, Metropol Parasol, New York, US
- Metropol Parasol, Stylepark in Residence, IMM, 2006, Cologne, Germany
- E.gram, Stadthaus Scharnhauser Park, Permant Collection of The Museum of Modern Art, New York, Fall 2005–Spring 2006, New York, US
- Metropol Parasol, Kulturforum, September–November 2005, Berlin, Germany
- Housewarming III, magnus müller Gallery, September–November 2005, Berlin, Germany
- In Heat, Henry Urbach Architecture Gallery, April–May 2005, New York, US
- New Trends in Architecture, Group Show, traveling exhibition, starting Fall 2004, Lille, France; Hong Kong, China; Tokyo, Japan; Cork, Ireland; Melbourne, Australia
- Glamour, San Francisco Museum of Modern Art, Group Show, Fall 2004, San Francisco, California, US
- La Biennale di Venezia, Arsenale, German Pavilion, Polish Pavilion, 2004, Venice, Italy
- W.I.P., Soft Mosaic Collection, F. Novembre Space, Salone Mobile, 2004, Milan, Italy
- Hyperlink Tower, Monitor, April 2004, Milan, Italy
- Trial and Error: Working Models, The Building Centre, May–June 2004, London, UK
- Re:Locations 6, Laznia Center for Contemporary Art, 2004, Gdansk, Poland
- Mies Award 2003, Royal Institute of British Architects, April 2004, London, UK
- Activators, Architectural Association London, October–November 2003, London, UK
- Designparcours, Bayerischer Hof, July–August 2003, Pixy.Pieces, Munich, Germany
- Ephemeral Structures, Cultural Olympiad 2003, Byzantine and Christian Museum, February 2003, Athens, Greece
- Designmay 2003, with Bisazza/Stylepark, Stilwerk, 2003, Berlin, Germany
- 1ab, Architecture Biennale 2003, May 2003, Rotterdam, The Netherlands
- Super-Ficial, dpp, New Museum of Contemporary Art, January 2003, New York, US
- Heat.Seat, San Francisco Museum of Modern Art, December 2002, San Francisco, California, US
- Twoways, with Luca Pancrazzi, müllerdechiara, July–August 2002, Berlin, Germany
- UIA, Stylepark Lounge, July 2002, Berlin, Germany
- Latent Space, Netherland Architecture Institute, July–October 2002, curated by Henry Urbach, Rotterdam, The Netherlands
- Surphase Architecture, Aedes West, May–June 2002, Berlin, Germany
- Layered Histories, 45°, (former Staatsbank), May–June 2002, curated by Uli Kremeier, Berlin, Germany
- Rotversteck, magnus müller Gallery, May–June 2002, Berlin, Germany
- The Armory Show, Henry Urbach Architecture Gallery, February 2002, New York, US
- The Berlin Files, DeChiara Gallery, February–March 2002, New York, US
- CTRL.Space, Heat.Seats -the Pad, Zentrum für Kunst und Medientechnologie, October 2001–February 2002, Karlsruhe, Germany
- Wattage and Friendship, müllerdechiara, October–November 2001, Berlin, Germany
- Archilab, May–June 2001, Orleans, France
- Wolfgang Wittrock Kunsthandel, Group Show, February 2001, Dusseldorf, Germany
- E.gram, during Ars Electronica, Art+Tek Institut Linz, September 2000, Linz, Austria
- Open Spaces, Leer/Limit/Landschaft, Galerie Alte Post, May 2000, Stuttgart, Germany
- Schwarz/Weiss/Bunt, Design Transfer Galerie, October–November 1999, Berlin, Germany
- Hands On, GSD, Harvard University, October–November 1999, Cambridge, Massachusetts, US
- 16 RÄUME, Edison Höfe, September–October 1999, Berlin, Germany
- Luster, Henry Urbach Architecture Gallery, June–August 1999, New York, US
- Space/Sight/Self, Smart Museum, November 1998–January 1999, Chicago, Illinois, US
- Danke 500, Pavilion of the Volksbühne am Rosa-Luxemburg-Platz, March–April 1998, Berlin, Germany
- HOM-Y Collection, Henry Urbach Architecture Gallery at Gramercy International Art Fair, May 1997, New York, US
- Euro, Come Visit, Galerie Eigen+Art at Chicago Art Fair, May 1997, Chicago, Illinois, US
- Housewarming II, at DISAPPEARED, Randolph Street Gallery, curated by John Paul Ricco, November–December 1996, Chicago, Illinois, US
- MissKommunikation, with Yana Milev, at Urban Twist, Galerie Eigen+Art, July–August 1996, Berlin, Germany
- Housewarming, an Installation at Storefront for Art and Architecture, June–July 1994, New York, US

J. MAYER H.
TEAM SINCE 1996

Mario Abel
Paul Angelier
Ana Alonso de la Varga
Alexander Arnold
Andreas Berzborn
Thorsten Blatter
Marcus Blum
Markus Bonauer
Sybille Bornefeld
Alexander zur Brügge
Jonathan Busse
Stefan Dambacher
Cristiane Egger
Christoph Emenlauer
Christoph Eppacher
Daniel Fielitz
Sebastian Finckh
Robert Frenzel
Balthasar Hellwig
Wilko Hoffmann
Olivier Jacques
Luis Jativa Quiroga
Aaron Jezzi
Stephanie Kalläne
Sabine Kukel
Klaus Küppers
Marc Kushner
Carlos Lara
Kate Lemmen
Kathrin Lind
David Magid
Mehrdad Mashaie
Claudia Marcinowski
Peter Martin
Marcello Mazzei
Daniel Mock
Stephen Molloy
Julia Neitzel
Sascha Nikolauschke
Julia Olsson
Güvenc Özel
Christian Pälmke
Karla Pilz
Heike Prehler
Marta Ramírez Iglesias
Alessandra Raponi
Dirk Reinisch
Gabriele Roy
Andre Santer
Erika Schaar
Ingmar Schmidt
Georg Schmidthals
Hans Schneider
Moritz Schöndorf
Gunda Schulz
Dominik Schwarzer
Jan-Christoph Stockebrand
Jörg Stollmann
Simon Takasaki
Daria Trovato
Georg Vrachliotis
Nai Huei Wang
Hans Weibel
Philip Welter
Hans-Jörgen Wetlesen
Sonja Wiese
Matthaeus Wirth
Maciej Woroniecki
Christof Zeller
Marco Zürn

Edited by Henry Urbach and Cristina Steingräber

Managing editors: Julika Zimmermann, Wilko Hoffmann, Marcus Blum

Copyediting: Ian McDonald, Carmen Miller

Translations: Ian Pepper

Graphic design: Kerstin Riedel

Production: Christine Emter

Reproductions: LVD Gesellschaft für Datenverarbeitung mbH

Typefaces: Archer, Typ 1451

Paper: Galaxi Supermat, 170 g/m^2

Binding: Conzella Verlagsbuchbinderei, Urban Meister GmbH, Aschheim Dornach

Printed by sellier druck GmBH, Freising

Published by
Hatje Cantz Verlag
Zeppelinstrasse 32
73760 Ostfildern
Germany
Tel. +49 711 4405-200
Fax +49 711 4405-220
www.hatjecantz.com

Hatje Cantz books are available internationally at selected bookstores. For more information about our distribution partners, please visit our homepage at www.hatjecantz.com.

ISBN 978-3-7757-2223-0 (English)
ISBN 978-3-7757-2222-3 (German)

Printed in Germany

Cover illustration: photo by David Franck, image programming by Thomas Thiemich

All images J. MAYER H. Architects, except: pp. 15–23: David Franck, Ostfildern; p. 27: Hiepler & Brunier, Berlin; pp. 28–29: Dirk Fellenberg, Hamburg; p. 30: fotografieSCHAULIN, Hamburg; pp. 32–37: Hiepler & Brunier, Berlin; pp. 78–79: Uwe Walter, Berlin; pp. 86–87: Uwe Walter, Berlin; pp. 90–91: Christina Dimitriadis, Berlin; p. 103: Uwe Walter, Berlin; pp. 104–06, 108–15: David Franck, Ostfildern; pp. 120–21: Thomas Dix; pp. 123–25: Mauro Restiffe, Sao Paolo; pp. 126–27: Hans-Joerg Walter; pp. 130–33: Ludger Paffrath, Berlin; pp. 138–39: Stuart McIntyre, Copenhagen; pp. 160–61: Uwe Walter, Berlin; p. 162: SACYR, Sevilla; pp. 169–79: David Franck, Ostfildern; p. 218: Constantin Meyer